Those Girls

CultureAmerica

ERIKA DOSS

PHILIP J. DELORIA

Series Editors

KARAL ANN MARLING

Editor Emerita

Those Girls

*Single Women in
Sixties and Seventies
Popular Culture*

KATHERINE J. LEHMAN

 University Press of Kansas

Published by the
University Press of Kansas
(Lawrence, Kansas 66045),
which was organized by the
Kansas Board of Regents and
is operated and funded by
Emporia State University,
Fort Hays State University,
Kansas State University,
Pittsburg State University,
the University of Kansas, and
Wichita State University

Library of Congress Cataloging-in-Publication Data

Those girls : single women in sixties and seventies
popular culture / Katherine J. Lehman.
    p.   cm. — (CultureAmerica)
    Includes bibliographical references and index.
    ISBN 978-0-7006-1808-8 (cloth : alk. paper)
    1. Single women in motion pictures. 2. Single
women on television. 3. Popular culture—United
States—History—20th century. I. Title.
    PN1995.9.S547L45 2011
    791.43'651—dc23   2011022656

British Library Cataloguing-in-Publication Data
is available.

Printed in the United States of America

10 9 8 7 6 5 4 3 2 1

The paper used in this publication is recycled and
contains 30 percent postconsumer waste. It is acid
free and meets the minimum requirements of the
American National Standard for Permanence of
Paper for Printed Library Materials Z39.48-1992.

Contents

Acknowledgments

Many people helped bring this book into being and supported my writing and research along the way. This book began at the Department of American Studies at the University of New Mexico, where I was privileged to work with amazing scholars. I am deeply grateful to Beth Bailey for her generous feedback and expert guidance at every stage of the process; her example largely inspired my interest in cultural history. Rebecca Schreiber offered continual encouragement and thoughtful questions on each chapter, and Alex Lubin and Laura Andre provided close readings and helpful suggestions for revision. Betsy Erbaugh, Brian Herrera, Melanie Cattrell, Naomi Gabriela Schwartz, and Stephanie Gustafson provided camaraderie and smart ideas.

Archival research was one of the most rewarding aspects of this project. The following archives provided much-appreciated travel grants and research support: the John W. Hartman Center and Sallie Bingham Center at Duke University, the American Heritage Center at the University of Wyoming, the Sophia Smith Collection at Smith College, and the Arts Library Special Collections at the University of California at Los Angeles. I also would like to thank the staff of the UCLA Film and Television Archive, the Margaret Herrick Library in Los Angeles, and the Paley Center for Media in New York and Los Angeles for their research assistance. The interlibrary loan staff at the University of New Mexico graciously fielded many requests, and the staff at Photofest helped me locate ideal illustrations.

Many institutions contributed to this book's development. The Albright College Professional Council provided grants that covered image and production costs, as well as summer writing support. The University of New Mexico's Graduate and Professional Student Association and American Studies Department offered funding that enabled me to visit archives and present this research at conferences. The University of Miami's American Studies and Women's and Gender Studies programs also provided essential research and travel support.

The staff at the University Press of Kansas have been unwavering in their enthusiasm and support for this book, and it has been a joy to work with them. I especially would like to thank Acquisitions Editors Ranjit Arab and Kalyani Fernando, Production Editor Jennifer Dropkin, and Assistant Director Susan Schott for their collaboration and guidance.

Many other scholars contributed valuable ideas and historical frameworks for my research. Elana Levine and Bonnie J. Dow offered close readings and constructive suggestions on initial drafts. I also benefited from conference dialogues with Kirsten Pike, Miriam Forman-Brunell, Jennifer Scanlon, Carrie Pitzulo, and Leslie Fishbein, among others. My colleagues in the Albright College English Department have provided a supportive community and a schedule conducive to writing.

My family and friends have always supported my writing ambitions and eagerly anticipated this book release. I would like to thank my parents, Charles Lehman and Jan Williams, who taught me to appreciate writing and media—and modeled how to talk back to the television set. Barbara Lehman provided lodging for my Los Angeles journeys. Nicole Cajori, Kelly Davis, Estelle and Irwin Matus, Pete and JoAnn Byers, Art and Nancy Liberatore, and Risha and Stephan Falke offered their ideas and interest. My grandmother Joyce Barnes taught me much about women's history, and I like to think she lives on in these pages. Above all, Rachel Liberatore assisted my writing process with her humor, enthusiasm, skilled editing, and shared interest in feminism and media criticism. She is my partner in the truest sense of the word, and it is to her that I dedicate this book.

Screening the "Single Girl"

The young woman steps out onto a bustling city street, her slim body adorned in the latest fashions. She gawks at skyscrapers and gazes in shop windows, her eyes gleaming with fascination and desire. Perhaps she twirls her parasol or tosses her hat heavenward in a moment of unrestrained glee. The fact that she negotiates the city alone, reveling in her independence, marks her as a distinct character type: the single woman.

Contemporary audiences often take single heroines for granted, given the recent popularity of characters like Carrie Bradshaw and Bridget Jones across media forms. For media audiences of the 1960s and 1970s, however, the single woman was a compelling and often controversial figure. Viewers watched these fictional women leave their hometowns, pursue careers, find dating partners, and, in some cases, engage in premarital sex. Many single characters—such as the virtuous Merritt Andrews in the 1960 film *Where the Boys Are*—were intended to serve as role models for young women facing sexual temptation. Others, such as the troubled heroines of 1967's *Valley of the Dolls*, provided cautionary tales about female ambition and urban living. Regardless of the moral, the "single girl's" glamour and allure resonated with audiences and provided a welcome alternative to traditional media representations of women as wives and mothers. At the same time, singles' independence, sexuality, and career ambition posed a potential threat to viewers, one that had to be carefully managed through characterization, plot devices, and strategic endings.

This book takes a critical look at the "single girl" in American media of the 1960s and 1970s, focusing strategically on television shows and movies featuring young, never-married women. I argue that the single woman was a pivotal figure in postwar popular culture who helped viewers negotiate sweeping changes in gender roles and sexual mores. She posed a direct affront to the sexual double standard and defied the dominant trend toward early marriage in the 1960s. Her attitude and ambition marked her as a liberated woman, although her actions and dialogue sometimes contradicted feminist ideals. She opened new avenues for female representation in media, particularly as she moved into male-dominated action and dramatic genres. However, producers and censors often tamed the single woman's sexuality and strength to meet industry standards and appeal to diverse audiences.

In many films and television programs, single characters minimized threats posed by feminism and the sexual revolution. The virginal heroine of ABC's sitcom *That Girl*, for example, contradicted media accounts of sexually licentious singles scenes; the stars of the action drama *Charlie's Angels*, which aired in the aftermath of Equal Rights Amendment debates, suggested that women could be empowered professionals without sacrificing their femininity and sexual appeal. However, other representations positioned the aggressive, autonomous woman as a danger to herself and others. In films as different as *Valley of the Dolls* (1967) and *Looking for Mr. Goodbar* (1977), single characters suffered heartbreak, addictions, and violence when they carried their newfound sexual freedoms too far.

These characters and plotlines illustrate how media trends often coincided with cultural values. Accordingly, this book analyzes individual films and programs against broader conceptions of women's sexual and societal roles. For instance, sex comedies of the early 1960s reveal Americans' high estimation of female virginity, while action dramas of the mid-1970s reflect widespread ambivalence about feminism in the workplace. However, the cultural history contained in these pages extends far beyond static screen images of single women, as it draws from published accounts of real-life women's ambitions, desires, and struggles. As my research addresses activists as well as women who did not consider themselves feminists, it acknowledges how individuals outside organized social movements have contributed to processes of social change.

Of course, popular-culture texts did not passively reflect society; rather, they were shaped by commercial considerations and censorship standards within media industries. Throughout the 1960s and 1970s, critics and consumers complained about the increasing prevalence of sex and violence in TV and film as censorship standards weakened and producers endeavored to reach youthful audiences. Yet scripts and production correspondence reveal that producers often minimized sexual content and violence in narratives featuring single women. Repeatedly, scripts were changed to prevent heroines from having affairs or even voicing desires, and moments of female heroism were rescripted to emphasize characters' dependence on men. These behind-the-scenes negotiations remind us that, even as media industries evolved with the times, images of female sexuality and power were still carefully controlled and shaped for mass consumption.

Commercial Media and Cultural Change

Historically, single characters arose in media in response to both commercial and ideological trends. This book focuses primarily on the "single girl," the most commercially viable character type—that is, a woman generally in her twenties or thirties, never married, heterosexual, and without children. The term "single girl" emerged in the 1960s as an appealing alternative to "spinster," and it characterized the unmarried woman as youthful and playful well into her thirties. By calling themselves "girls," single women treated the period between schooling and marriage as an extended adolescence and resisted the adult pressures to marry and have children.[1] However, as many second-wave feminists point out, referring to grown women as "girls" reinforced their dependence and lack of power. Of course, other groups such as unwed mothers, divorcées, and lesbians have been classified as single in American culture, and they occasionally surface in this book. However, I believe the "single girl" is distinct from these groups, given her lack of familial responsibilities and absence of a clearly defined sexual past.

In the early 1960s, unmarried women were a small, marginalized demographic group, and their appearance in popular culture primarily reflected women's wider frustrations with domesticity. By the mid-1960s, single working women had become an economic force in their own right—according to *Time*, urban singles were a $60 billion market by 1967.[2] By representing single women, popular media tapped into this attractive demographic group but also appealed to youth audiences and working women more broadly. By the early 1970s, these representations assumed a more feminist tone, as networks and advertisers leveraged images of single working women to appease feminist critics and address independent, upwardly mobile, politically conscious consumers.

The independence and ambition of single characters like Mary

3

Richards (of *The Mary Tyler Moore Show*) and Jaime Sommers (of *The Bionic Woman*) often make them seem, in retrospect, ideal symbols for second-wave feminism. However, media producers' need to create narratives that were both profitable and politically relevant often resulted in mixed messages about politics and women's roles. While many seventies feminists criticized TV and film for ambivalent and often distorted views of women's liberation, more recent scholarship has reclaimed popular culture as a source of pleasure and insight for female viewers.[3] Susan Douglas and Bonnie Dow, among many others, have conceptualized media as a powerful force that inspires activism and helps viewers interpret feminist politics. Yet the inherent contradictions of pop culture can make it difficult to define any one media text as entirely feminist or antifeminist.[4] This book draws from both historical and contemporary criticism, acknowledging both the pleasures and politics of popular media. While I critically analyze how television and film have interpreted movements for social change, I tend to avoid labeling individual media texts as profeminist or antifeminist. Instead, I argue that these stories and characters helped viewers come to terms with single women's changing roles and reflected broader ambivalence about the meanings and effects of feminism and the sexual revolution.

In addition to analyzing media productions, I also provide a cultural history of the women who inspired and consumed popular media. Television and film narratives were hardly created in a cultural vacuum; they were shaped by the same issues and events that animated newspaper articles, advertisements, magazines, activist pamphlets, and popular novels. By examining these print sources, I demonstrate how electronic media responded to and amplified existing political discourses. I also use print and archival sources to counter the exclusions and omissions in electronic media. While mainstream television and cinema tended to feature white, middle-class urban dwellers, print media addressed women across lines of race, class, and region, and often expressed cultural tensions that were not represented onscreen.

Women and Media in the Sixties and Seventies

The sixties and seventies provide the historical framework for this book—and rightly so, as dramatic changes in women's work roles, marriage trends, and sexual behavior happened during these decades. Consider for a moment how dramatically single women's lives changed between 1960 and 1980. In the early 1960s, the average American woman married at age twenty, and single women comprised a small percentage of the population.[5] The limited career fields open to these women tended to be tedious and low paying, as employers assumed that single women were only biding their time before marriage. In relationships, single women were expected to fiercely guard their virginity — or at least remain monogamous with the men they planned to marry — and were warned that premarital affairs could hinder their hopes to find a husband.[6]

By the late 1970s, the percentage of single women in their late twenties and thirties had grown dramatically, as more American women chose to delay marriage or pursue divorce.[7] Women worked in larger numbers and entered new career fields; these trends were spurred not only by feminist reforms but also by the growth of white-collar jobs in the 1960s and high inflation in the 1970s. Single women also benefited from greater sexual freedoms during the seventies, as popular advice literature, novels, and films acknowledged the prevalence of casual and promiscuous sex among this group. These trends transformed single working women from a small percentage of the population to a sizable demographic that was central to economic and consumer life.

However, cultural change happens incrementally, and it is rarely neatly confined within decades. For example, singles subcultures of the late 1960s may have promoted popular notions of "free love," but women still faced a strong sexual double standard as they pursued affairs and even monogamous relationships. Also, while the rise of second-wave feminism helped propel single women into professional careers in the early 1970s, once inside the workplace women confronted a wage gap and gender-specific expectations. Additionally, the cultural gains of the 1960s strongly influenced the 1970s as Americans grappled with the meanings of feminism, civil rights, and gay and lesbian liberation. Thus, this book documents patterns of change within decades rather than treating the 1960s and 1970s as distinct and self-contained time periods.[8]

These decades were also a time of significant change in media industries. Middle-class youth by the mid-1950s had become a consumer group in their own right, and Hollywood catered to their tastes.[9] Films such as *Where the Boys Are* (1960), a moralistic melodrama about adventurous female college students, both addressed this youthful demographic and managed broader anxieties about single women's sexual behavior. Like most sixties films featuring single women, *Where the Boys Are* inspired close scrutiny from the Motion Picture Association of America's Production Code Administration, which regulated sexual content in popular film prior to the rise of a formal film ratings system in 1968. While the gradual loosening of Production Code restraints enabled filmmakers to raise the possibility of premarital sex, the single woman's sexuality still was cause for concern. The fact that this popular movie both punished its most promiscuous character with sexual assault and placed her marriage prospects in doubt not only appeased the censors, but also supported a wider cultural insistence on virginity for white, middle-class women.[10]

The rise of single women in television occurred more slowly, partly because producers feared that a single woman—or any female character, for that matter—would fail to carry a series and capture viewers' loyalty.[11] As marketing models changed in the late 1960s and early 1970s, networks saw the growing demographic of young, working women as a more attractive advertising audience and used the single working woman to prove their relevance to these consumers. Popular TV series placed tight constraints on the single woman's independence and sexuality. Sitcoms, in particular, commonly situated single characters within a workplace "family," tempered their professional ambitions, and failed to represent their sex lives onscreen.[12] These trends reflected not only the limitations of network television but also cultural anxieties about single women's changing identities. However, as television brought the "single girl" into viewers' living rooms, it helped to normalize new roles for women.

Throughout this period, young single women appeared most often in situation comedies and melodramas, which have conventionally been considered "feminine" genres. While these genres do offer progressive possibilities, they tended to treat the single woman as a comical character or to emphasize moral rewards and punishments. When single characters did appear in atypical action and dramatic roles, producers went to great lengths to emphasize characters' femininity and sexuality.[13] As this book explores a diversity of narrative forms, it also considers how genre conventions affected the portrayal of women's lives and politics.

Intersections of Gender, Race, and Class

Mainstream electronic media of this time period tended to be regionally and racially exclusive, usually portraying single women as white, middle class, and living in a large coastal city. These biases were partly due to industry constraints, as producers and advertisers feared that minority characters would not be appealing to white consumers. New marketing research in the 1970s, as well as pressures to be socially relevant, enabled broader representations of women of color, but they most often functioned in stereotyped or supporting roles when they appeared in single-woman narratives.[14]

Thus, in addition to analyzing limited representations of diversity in TV and film, this book turns to print media to highlight regional, racial, and class-based differences in single women's experiences. The lives and work of African American singles in particular were chronicled in *Essence* and *Ebony*, as well as in newspapers and mainstream magazines. These print sources remind us that, much like their white counterparts, minority women moved to large cities in search of greater work opportunities and independence. While civil rights gains enabled African American women to move into white-collar careers starting in the mid-1960s, their lives and work were shaped by legacies of racial segregation. As I explore in this book, black single women in cities like Washington, D.C., complained of segregated housing and limited dating prospects, and their wages lagged behind those of white women. Black women also felt the pressure to serve as a credit to their communities. Magazine articles urged African American singles to dress conservatively and act like strong, capable women rather than frivolous girls.[15]

Significant media shifts happened in the late 1960s and 1970s, as television and film tried to capture new demographic groups. The NBC series *Julia* offered a portrayal of a widowed African American working mother, and late 1960s *Star Trek* featured Uhura, both a model of black professionalism and the source of TV's first interracial kiss. Particularly in the case of *Julia*, however, these texts were judged less as representations of single working women than as barometers for race relations

7

in America.[16] In popular film, the mid-1970s blaxploitation genre provided new representations of African American women as autonomous, powerful, and highly sexualized. This genre was tamed for television in the short-lived series *Get Christie Love*, which offered a similarly strong and sexual lead.[17]

However, Kimberly Springer reminds us that "race is *always* present" in media narratives. "Even when they are not on the screen, women of color are present as the counterpart against which white women's ways of being . . . are defined and *re*defined."[18] While this book addresses absences and stereotypes of women of color, it also considers how mainstream images of single women reflected a white racial identity. For example, the cultural emphasis on female chastity and early marriage in the 1950s and early 1960s was aimed most strongly at white women.[19] Thus, the sex comedies and moralistic melodramas of the era reflect race as well as gender norms.

As young white women moved en masse to large cities starting in the late sixties, popular narratives often positioned people of color as a threat to white women's safety. The rising crime rate in New York and other large cities was often blamed on racial tensions, despite the "lily white" profile of predators and victims.[20] When single New Yorker Roseann Quinn was brutally murdered in 1973 — at the hands of a white man — early news reports emphasized the dangers posed by Quinn's West Side interracial neighborhood.[21] Accordingly, popular media narratives often positioned people of color in threatening roles, as kidnappers, drug dealers, and stalkers.

In other media, minority women played sidekicks to white heroines. The TV film *Gidget Grows Up* (1969) and sitcom *Karen* (1975) featured actress Karen Valentine rooming with Asian American and African American women (played by Helen Funai and Aldine King, respectively) and occasionally engaging in banter about racial politics. White ethnic women also assumed distinct roles. *The Mary Tyler Moore Show* featured a friendship between Mary and Rhoda (Valerie Harper), a brash Jewish woman from the Bronx who contrasted with Mary's more wholesome midwestern whiteness. In late 1970s movies, Jewish and white ethnic characters are associated with promiscuous sexuality, drawing from older tendencies in film to cast ethnic women as sexually available and expendable.[22]

As single-girl narratives emphasized glamour and consumerism, they

8

also conveyed messages about class. Characters usually lived in material comfort, with wardrobes and apartments that belied their meager salaries as working women in entry-level positions. The single life was presented as a route to class mobility, as both advice books and popular media suggested that a woman from a humble background could rise to wealth and fame with talent, a little luck, or the right husband.[23] In contrast, women's magazines more often acknowledged singles' economic realities, offering readers tips on budgeting and advocating equal pay for women.

Chapter Structure and Common Themes

Whether she was affluent or struggling to get by, the "single girl" appeared in a range of narratives and genres. This book does not attempt to provide a comprehensive survey of single women in media. Instead, I analyze prominent, mainstream narratives that illustrate important historical trends and shifts in representation. However, as many of these television shows and films are rarely accessible outside of media archives, this study extends beyond the most familiar representations to consider the messages and influence of B-grade movies and short-lived sitcoms. The chapters advance chronologically through the 1960s and 1970s, but also emphasize themes that are common to stories about single women.

"This is what happens to the women who *didn't* marry at 20," intones the male announcer in advertisements for the 1959 film *The Best of Everything*. The voiceover adds to the allure of a melodrama in which women pursue romance and publishing careers in the big city, often meeting with ruinous consequences.[24] However, the ad also reminds us that the single woman was once remarkable and rebellious by her very existence. The very title of the film *Sex and the Single Girl*, which dared to place the words "single girl" and "sex" in the same phrase, sparked protests in 1964.[25]

In chapter 1, I analyze how the single girl challenged convention both in society and on the silver screen. When watching films of the very late 1950s and early 1960s, we tend to see women who are headstrong, confident, and polished on the surface. The youthful Natalie Wood, for example, portrayed a suave psychologist and author named Helen Gurley Brown in *Sex and the Single Girl,* and the more mature Doris Day played an interior designer and advertising executive in her films. These women openly challenged sexual double standards but were revealed in the end to be insecure and inexperienced. Conniving men in these screwball comedies typically tricked the women into revealing their secrets and falling in love. While these romantic endings met audience expectations, they were also a response to the stringent Production Code Administration censorship process that existed prior to the rise of a film ratings system. Chapter 1 affords the closest attention to production processes, given the unusually rich and comprehensive archival material from this time period. However, I trace patterns of explicit and implicit censorship throughout this book. Often, movie and television scripts were edited for sexual suggestiveness and violence, and wayward characters were punished to reinforce moral consequences.

Single-women narratives of the 1960s and 1970s often highlight the moment when a young woman leaves home to create a new life for herself in the city. Consider Marlo Thomas's exuberant train ride in *That Girl*—or, for that matter, Diane Keaton's stormy departure in *Looking for Mr. Goodbar*. This journey was dramatized in the opening credits of key television programs and propelled the plots of many popular narratives. However, as I explore in chapter 2, the theme of leaving home coincided with the lived realities of many viewers who had begun to pursue alternatives to early marriage and conventional family life. Both electronic media and advice literature urged young women to move to large cities, which were increasingly becoming home to singles bars, singles-only apartment complexes, and white-collar careers that enabled women's financial independence.

In popular media narratives, leaving home enabled the single woman to evade the watchful eyes of her parents and community and pursue a dream career as an actress or model. While these stories presented a glamorized picture of the singles life, they also warned of the risks that urban living posed to women's safety and morality. Both lighthearted comedies and moralistic melodramas emphasized women's vulnerability to crime and predatory men, and they sometimes suggested that people of color posed a particular threat to white women's sense of safety. Aware of the threats that urban living posed, parents in these narratives sometimes followed their offspring to the city and urged them to return home.

Narratives such as *That Girl* and *Thoroughly Modern Millie*, which were released prior to the rise of second-wave feminism, tended to feature women who were freelance workers, tethered to home or hoping for marriage. Early 1970s media inaugurated the new working woman, who was more independent and pursuing a professional career path, and I explore the meanings of these texts for the emergent women's liberation movement in chapter 3. In addition to the memorable Mary Tyler Moore, who played a news producer on her self-titled sitcom, women in primetime television took on a range of professional roles—designer, political activist, globe-trotting photographer—and clearly enjoyed their independence. However, the rise of the "new woman" on television reflected the insights of popular feminism and marketing research, presenting liberation as a lifestyle option more than a political stance. These affable sitcom characters also broached feminist issues like equal pay and hiring discrimination through the medium of comedy. While single characters sometimes stood by their principles, they usually yielded to the authority of their male bosses. Additionally, their independence was curbed by the constant presence of coworkers and neighbors, who served as symbolic family members.[26]

With the rise of dramatic heroines in the mid-1970s, women in media moved from supportive and secretarial roles to tackling traditionally male professions. At the same time in American culture, discussions of the pending Equal Rights Amendment and sexual harassment laws centered on the necessity of preserving differences between men and women in the workplace. Series such as *Police Woman* and *Wonder Woman* proved that heroines could solve cases and wield strength while still maintaining a feminine appearance and demeanor. Rather than aim for a sexless equality, these characters often relied on their sexual appeal as a source of power and leverage. Chapter 4 analyzes key narratives and common critiques of these programs, as well as demonstrating how fears of female strength and sexuality factored into production. While action series like *Wonder Woman* clearly focused on characters' physical attractiveness, they also emphasized characters' cleverness and professional competence. Despite offering mixed messages about feminism and sexual harassment, these series helped diversify a decidedly masculine genre of prime-time programming.

Female sexuality may have spiced up television action dramas in the seventies, but in real life women's increasing sex drives had begun to pose a problem in the bedroom. In contrast to the "safe" heroine of seventies television, films of the mid- to late 1970s such as *Looking for Mr. Goodbar* presented single women as desperate and dangerous, corresponding with alarmist reports about relationships. As I observe in chapter 5, popular media insisted that single women's increasing sexual demands were causing male impotence and gender-role confusion. In addition, when journalists reported on murders and assaults of young women, they insinuated that sexually aggressive singles courted danger by pursuing flings with strangers. In fictional narratives such as Jacqueline Susann's *Once Is Not Enough,* single women surfaced as sexually aggressive, self-destructive figures who spurred cruel and often violent retaliation from their male partners. While these stories blamed singles—and the feminist movement, by extension—for taking sexual freedom too far, they also resonated with female viewers by providing sexually forthright characters.

My epilogue addresses the pervasive influence that past television and film texts continue to have on more contemporary representations and understandings of the single woman. While this book is specific to the 1960s and 1970s, I believe it provides the historical lineage and critical tools essential to understanding subsequent representations of femininity and illuminates the media's broader role in interpreting and inspiring social change.

Defining Singleness

What makes a woman "single"? Does the term refer to her legal marital status or whether or not she happens to be romantically partnered? In this book, I use the term "single" to refer to women who were legally unmarried, even if they were actively dating. Popular media of the 1960s and 1970s catered to "singles" as a defined cultural group, and unmarried women frequently used the term to describe themselves.

Given this book's strategic focus on the "single girl," I do not provide an exhaustive account of other groups commonly categorized as single. This study addresses never-married women more often than divorcées, partly due to the rarity of such representations in media until the mid-1970s. Case in point: When Mary Tyler Moore took the helm of her own sitcom in the 1970s, she was originally scripted to be a divorcée. The network warned producers that "the public would never accept a divorced heroine," and so Mary became a woman who had merely left a long-term dating relationship.[27] This change reminds us that divorcees historically represented a greater threat to the sexual and social order than did never-married women. By the mid-1970s, divorced women added to the growing numbers of women living single, and they were featured prominently in media narratives. For example, the television series *Police Woman* starred Angie Dickinson as a divorcée gaining new experience on the force, and *One Day at a Time* addressed feminist themes in its portrayal of a mid-thirties divorcée with two teenage daughters. Once a taboo topic, divorce conferred on characters greater sexual and life experience than the never-married woman possessed, and it resonated with feminists' critique of marriage.

The single mother has been a more prominent and complicated figure in popular culture. On one level, she supports traditional femininity, as she fulfills her maternal role and is usually less sexualized than the childless "single girl." In some media representations, notably the popular sitcom *One Day at a Time*, motherhood serves as a source of authority and responsibility for single women.[28] However, single motherhood has historically carried strong racial meanings. Historian Rickie Solinger has argued that in the postwar decades prior to legalized abortion, unwed pregnancies were perceived and managed very differently according to race. While many unwed white women opted for adoption, black women more often bore the visible stigma of single motherhood, and "public discussion of unwed mothers at this time routinely conflated race and class."[29] Whereas childless single women possessed consumer clout, single mothers were stereotyped as a financial burden on society. Given these pervasive stereotypes—and the distinct discourses shaping single motherhood—I do not attempt to address single mothers or motherhood as a category in this book.

Lesbians also numbered among the singles who congregated in cities in the late 1960s, though they were rarely represented in mainstream media. While predatory gay and lesbian characters surface in the movies *Sheila Levine Is Dead and Living in New York* (1975) and *Looking for Mr. Goodbar* (1977), they are largely absent from the narratives covered in this study. On a broader level, however, the "single girl" blurs the lines between gay and straight, "functioning within heterosexuality but nonetheless opening other avenues that lead to other feminine identities outside marriage," as Hilary Radner puts it.[30] In addition, single women narratives often emphasized the importance of female friendship, a theme that appealed to straight and lesbian women alike.

The characters and narratives addressed in this book do not represent single women's lives in all their diversity and complexity. Still, it is my hope that this study contributes to a greater valuation of the unmarried, independent woman in American history and popular culture, and to the feminine genres and female audiences that are often marginalized in media scholarship. Given that the single woman was often associated with movements for gender equality and sexual freedom, the movies and series that I address in this book were always, on some level, political. Even before the rise of second-wave feminism, single characters represented women's desires to live independent, fulfilled lives and pursue their dreams without shame or judgment. From *Sex and the Single Girl* to *Looking for Mr. Goodbar*, these stories often conveyed harmful stereotypes and constricting moral messages. However, they also inspired generations of consumers—including many working women, cultural rebels, and emerging feminists—who sought some reflection of their pleasures and struggles in mass media.

Challenging Convention

Single Women, Sex, and Censorship in
Early 1960s Cinema

With her best-selling 1962 book, *Sex and the Single Girl,* author Helen Gurley Brown cleverly challenged the primacy of marriage and perceptions of singleness itself. At a time when the average American woman married at twenty, and women routinely sacrificed educational and career ambitions for familial ones, Brown proposed a life of work, leisure, and sexual pleasure for the unmarried woman nearing thirty. Her personal, chatty advice was bolstered by her public image—that of a married, forty-year-old advertising executive whose life had been enriched rather than ruined by sexual assertion and career ambition.[1]

Within a year Warner Brothers bought the film rights to Brown's best seller for $200,000, the highest sum paid to date for the rights to a nonfiction book. More accurately, since screenwriters transformed Brown's fragmentary advice tome into a screwball comedy, Warner Brothers merely bought the rights to the title—at a rate of $40,000 per word.[2] The 1964 film *Sex and the Single Girl* starred Natalie Wood as an unmarried, much younger, and more tentative Helen Brown. Like her real-life counterpart, Wood's character verbally challenged the double standard and wrote advice books advocating premarital affairs. However, the brazen tone of her advice broke sharply with her own prudish, insecure personality and cautious approach to dating.[3]

By portraying Brown as a twenty-three-year-old ingenue, the film comedically cut Brown's strength down to size and quelled censors' stated fears that the film would "advocate sexual freedom for unmarried girls."[4] However, the film *Sex and the Single Girl* also advanced stereotypes of single career women that circulated in the popular press and sexological studies of the late 1950s and early 1960s. In scripts, advertisements, and the final picture itself, Natalie Wood's character surfaced alternately as the aggressor who sought to dominate men, the pitiable neurotic who used sex to compensate for inner insecurities, and the innocent who ultimately desired marriage above all else.

The film adaptation of *Sex and the Single Girl* was one of many attempts by Hollywood to capitalize on and contain the figure of the single woman in the late 1950s and early 1960s. In these films the unmarried woman assumed an air of sexual knowledge and experience, mirroring the perceived trend toward sexual liberalism among young women, and she often prioritized her career above romantic prospects. Yet conservative plotlines undermined her knowledge, revealed her inexperience, and ultimately contained her desire and independence within marriage. By humbling the single woman and restoring her to a proper feminine role, these often-comedic narratives served serious purposes: They countered the threat that the single woman posed to traditional gender roles and sexual mores, and they warned impressionable viewers about the dangers of promiscuity and unbridled ambition.

In this chapter, I draw from popular press accounts, novels, and sexological studies to illustrate the anxieties that surrounded single women in the early 1960s. I then examine how filmmakers and censors collaborated to bring acceptable images of the "single girl" to the silver screen. Movie plots, dialogue, and characters often changed markedly from the initial proposal to the final script, and I analyze these changes as evidence of both industry and societal attitudes.

Mixed Messages: The "Single Girl" and Marital Imperatives

Scholars writing on women in the 1950s and early 1960s emphasize the contradictory messages presented to young women in popular culture and public life. In *Where the Girls Are,* Susan Douglas notes that the political climate of the early 1960s urged white teenage girls to excel academically and become involved in social causes, if only to prove the exceptional potential of American youth. However, this emphasis on ambition and achievement in public life was undermined by the lack of career opportunities for girls to grow into and by "retrograde messages about traditional femininity" in popular culture.[5] Simultaneously encouraged to achieve and acquiesce, Douglas's generation sensed that "being a real American and a real girl at the same time required the skills of a top-notch contortionist."[6] Wini Brienes notes

A woman's words: Natalie Wood, as Helen Gurley Brown, entices Tony Curtis in this promotional shot for Sex and the Single Girl. *Courtesy of Warner Brothers/Photofest.*

a similar contradiction in the "sexual puzzles" presented to teens and young women in the fifties and early sixties: At a time when popular media and consumer imperatives idealized sexiness and glamour, teens were "encouraged to pursue the sexual cues that assailed them but were threatened with the loss of respectability (and acceptable futures) if they did so."[7]

Historian Joanne Meyerowitz finds more positive meaning in the contradictory messages conveyed through postwar women's magazines. In her analysis, which extends through the late 1950s, Meyerowitz argues that the predominant emphasis on domestic identities for young women was countered by magazine profiles on career women and articles that emphasized the importance of paid work for wives. According to Meyerowitz, acknowledging these multiple messages provides a necessary corrective to Betty Friedan's *The Feminine Mystique* and its pervasive influence on histories of postwar women. Meyerowitz writes: "For the past few years, historians have questioned the stereotype of postwar women as quiescent, docile and domestic. . . . [Postwar] married women, black and white, joined the labor force in increasing numbers, and both married and unmarried women participated actively in politics and reform. Just as women's activities were more varied and more complex than is often acknowledged, so, I argue, was the postwar popular ideology."[8] Thus, the contradictory nature of mass media posed possibilities as well as "puzzles" for young women. These postwar media texts provide important historical insight, as they suggest women's ambitions were not wholly constrained to domestic spheres.

Images of the "single girl" in the late 1950s and early 1960s, however limited and compromised, offered an alternative to domesticity that had resonance for women who delayed marriage, as well as for wives who worked outside the home. These representations of single women, like much of popular media, were fraught with contradictions. They served to both challenge and reinforce conventional feminine roles and aptly illustrated the internal conflicts that many young women felt during this time.

Sex and the Single Girl embodied the contradictions of the early sixties, as it seemed to challenge societal insistence on early marriage yet encouraged women to lead a "man-centered life."[9] While Brown's book is commonly read as stemming from and contributing to the sexual revolution, recent scholarship has positioned it alongside Betty Friedan's

The Feminine Mystique as a formative work that proposed nondomestic identities for women.[10] Jennifer Scanlon positions Brown as a pioneering "founder of the second wave," a writer whose distinctive vision of female empowerment resonated with working-class women and appealed to readers outside organized feminist movements.[11] Reviewers in the 1960s drew clear connections between *Sex and the Single Girl* and *The Feminine Mystique*, recognizing both books as "woman's rights" texts that documented how "women are discriminated against, underpaid and otherwise abused." According to a 1965 review, both Brown and Friedan posed the question, "Are women people?" and answered it affirmatively by advocating the pursuit of personal pleasure and fulfillment.[12] (For her part, Brown openly expressed admiration for Friedan's writings and publicly promoted *The Feminine Mystique*.)[13]

Brown wrote that the "single girl"—financially independent and freed from the drudgeries of housework—was "emerging as the newest glamour girl of our times."[14] In glorifying the working girl, she pitied the housewife, whom she saw occupying a separate sphere. "I don't understand her," Brown said in a 1962 interview. "She lives in a different world so occupied with housework, the jammed clothes dryer, repairs to the TV. It is a shame the typical married woman has no men to talk to."[15] Brown's premise was echoed in a lesser-known 1962 book, *The Lonely Sex*, which sought to establish a more positive identity for the unmarried woman. "Today it is rather the wife who is the household slave while the bachelor girl keeps one step ahead . . . in the larger world outside the home," wrote author Estelle Ries.[16]

Brown ostensibly addressed her advice to the single woman nearing thirty, urging her to pursue her own livelihood, acquire her own apartment, and surround herself with wealthy men. Her glorified vision of the singles life, of course, contrasted sharply with the limited lifestyle and career options available to young white women in the early 1960s. As Elaine Tyler May argues, prescriptive literature of the 1950s had "advocate[d] early marriage as the prerequisite for a healthy family and sexual life," and it cast as suspect women who remained unmarried past their early twenties. "Most guidelines gave 21 as a healthy age for marriage, and public opinion polls indicated that most Americans agreed," May writes. "Moreover, it was the woman's responsibility to achieve it" through "good looks, personality and cheerful subservience."[17] Accordingly, the average age of first marriage for women in the early 1960s hovered around 20.5 years for women (23 for men).[18] *Redbook* lamented as late as 1969 that "more and more pressure has been brought to bear on American women not only to marry, but to marry young," noting that in 1960, only 7 percent of 30-year-old women were unmarried, compared to 14 percent in 1940.[19] The *New York Times* similarly observed "the case of the vanishing spinster," observing that the unlucky minority of women who remained single into their late twenties soon developed into "champion husband-hunters."[20] *Look* warned in 1960 that women who fail to reach the altar at an early age "are likely to get stranded," as "it's a downhill slide" for women seeking marriage after 24.[21]

At the same time that popular culture and advice literature emphasized the virtues of early marriage, the numbers of women in the paid labor force rose dramatically. As historian Ruth Rosen notes, the percentage of American women who worked doubled from 15 to 30 percent between 1940 and 1960, and by 1955 more women worked in the labor force than had during World War II.[22] While the growth of white-collar jobs attracted increasing numbers of "educated, middle-class mothers" into the workforce, the very conditions of women's work made it difficult for single women to pursue the independent lifestyle that Brown had envisioned.[23] *Time* reported that employers in this era preferred to hire married women for fear that young single women "would marry, become pregnant and quit."[24] The assumption that working women were seeking supplementary income, or "pin money," kept women's wages low. On average, a full-time female employee in 1961 made sixty cents for every dollar earned by her male counterpart.[25]

Furthermore, *Time* reported that because "women perform[ed] best in jobs that require stoic patience, an eye for detail and nimble fingers," they were often channeled into "tedious, routine jobs that would drive men up the walls."[26] The few service professions that did cater to single women, such as airline stewardessing, hired women fresh out of high school or college on the expectation that they would leave to get married within a few years. Such assumptions, reinforced by discriminatory employment policies that fired stewardesses when they married or turned thirty-two or thirty-five, increased profits for the airlines by bolstering the idea that the single career woman was merely biding her time between schooling and marriage.[27]

Attitudes toward and experiences of work also differed by race.

Although *Ebony* reported in 1963 that "few Negro women believe that a woman's place is [solely] in the home," African American women workers endured greater limits and lower wages than white workers. *Ebony* reported that black women workers in the early 1960s were largely concentrated in service and domestic fields; in 1962 only 21 percent worked in professional careers, compared to 61 percent of white women. Furthermore, their wages lagged behind those of white women and black men. Full-time African American women workers earned on average $2,372 in 1960, compared to $3,410 for their white counterparts and $3,789 for African American men.[28]

Given the social and financial pressures *against* remaining single, many young women conceded that "the best guide to the single life is one that leads to its happy termination in matrimony."[29] Accordingly, Brown's dating tips and frequent boasts about her own successful marriage were seen as reinforcing the husband hunt. As one British reviewer summed up *Sex and the Single Girl*'s central point: "Let's all have a whee of a time for as long as possible, girls . . . but let's never forget that the object of it all is to land the biggest fish in the pond."[30] *The Nation* joked that, given Brown's focus on meeting men, a better title for the book would be *Sex and the Single-Minded Girl*.[31] Even the reviewer who placed Brown's book in the same league as Betty Friedan's perceived the authors working at cross-purposes: "Mrs. Brown urges the single girl to be independent enough and attractive enough to marry and to get out of the office and into the home, while Mrs. Friedan urges the married woman to be independent enough to flee her home and return to the office."[32]

Despite Brown's claim that her book gave some married women "the absolute shudders," her message appealed to a broad audience.[33] Her emphasis on careers as lifelong pursuits appealed to married working women, who, as Ruth Rosen notes, were often encouraged to downplay their work ambition.[34] Her acknowledgment of female sexual desire supported the trend toward companionate marriage in which both partners sought sexual and emotional fulfillment. Accordingly, Brown included married women among her target readership for the revamped *Cosmopolitan* magazine, which covered "the wide, wonderful woman's world outside PTA, laundromats and school lunches."[35] As Brown described the magazine's ideal reader in a 1965 proposal:

[She is] chic . . . has class . . . and money to spend . . . (either her own or her husband's money). . . .

Probably has a job. If not, she's hip, lively, and interested in a lot of things.

Not primarily house and home-oriented. . . .

May or may not have children. If she does, she loves them and is a good mother but doesn't live *through* the children. She doesn't live through her husband either. SHE LIKES TO DO IT HERSELF.[36]

Brown's figure of the single woman ostensibly challenged the traditional emphasis on domesticity, providing a refreshing alternative to Friedan's "domestic drudge." Yet, for both demographic and marketing reasons, even Brown sought to reconcile the "single girl" with a societal emphasis on early marriage. *Sex and the Single Girl* suggested that the single woman's ambition and allure—when properly channeled into marriage—could make her both an enchanting wife and a fulfilled person. Brown's message had resonance in an era when, as *Time* put it, "the American woman increasingly tries to combine the roles of wife and mistress—with the same man, that is."[37]

Alarmist Reports and Changing Attitudes

However, Brown also insisted that marriage need not be a prerequisite for engaging in sex. "Theoretically a 'nice' single woman has no sex life. What nonsense!" Brown exclaimed.[38] Her challenge to the sexual double standard came at a time when young, single women were perceived to be a driving force behind changes in sexual mores yet were still limited and stigmatized by traditional attitudes toward sex. According to historian David Allyn, Brown merely put a marketable spin on the behaviors and attitudes that were becoming public knowledge.[39] Alfred Kinsey's *Sexual Behavior in the Human Female*, published a decade earlier, had "pointed to a vast hidden world of sexual experience sharply at odds with public espoused norms," with the finding that 50 percent of white female respondents admitted to having sex before marriage.[40] Magazine surveys and sexological studies of the early to mid-sixties documented single women's willingness to more publicly challenge the sexual double standard.[41] "Many girls of this generation have completely discarded the moral standards of their elders," reported the author of a 1964 study.

"As Kinsey and others have shown in their surveys, moral codes have been eroding steadily for many years."[42]

Some observers, such as rising journalist Gloria Steinem, credited the Pill for changes in young women's attitudes and behaviors. In a 1962 article she penned for *Esquire*, Steinem credited contraception for inspiring new attitudes among privileged college women. "There is evidence . . . that removal of pregnancy fears increases sex drive," she wrote. "Removing the last remnants of fear of social consequences seems sure to speed American women, especially single women, toward the view that their sex practices are none of society's business." Changing mores and widespread use of contraception, Steinem argued, signaled the rise of an "autonomous woman" who no longer defined her identity solely through men, and who had the freedom to indulge in affairs and marry later in life.[43] Although single women were legally barred from obtaining contraception in the early 1960s, many women did obtain it by donning a fake wedding ring or complaining of gynecological health problems. Contrary to the impression that Steinem's article gives, however, most college women were much more secretive about their use of birth control.[44]

While Steinem's tone is forthright and almost celebratory, most authors were more alarmist about young women's changing attitudes and dating patterns. A female judge's report in the more conservative *Ladies' Home Journal,* titled "Too Much Sex on Campus," decried the "depersonalized, meaningless, degrading pattern of courtship" among college women that too often led to "ruinous promiscuity."[45] In contrast to Steinem's autonomous women who were freed from fears of pregnancy, the naive girls in the judge's anecdotal report typically ended up pregnant and at the mercy of a back-alley abortionist.

In several reports on college mores, previously pure girls were led astray by a peer culture that disdained virginity and mocked traditional morality. "It isn't just the boys who pressure you into bed, it's the girls," one student informed Steinem.[46] Because their peer groups considered a virgin to be "downright square," college and professional women alike were embarrassed to admit to sexual inexperience.[47] Researchers studying the sex habits of single women reported in 1964 that "the woman without sex experience hedges, makes excuses and even lies, pretending she has had affairs when she has not. . . . Few women willingly admit that they have never been to bed with a man."[48] While some women simply lied about their status, others reportedly indulged in ill-fated affairs to prove their sophistication.[49]

College women were central to reports on changing sexual mores partly because they provided evidence that educated, once-respectable women were succumbing to promiscuity. Experts warned that the women who became promiscuous and pregnant were not "the tough skid-row girls of former days" but rather "the cream of the crop, girls from comfortable backgrounds."[50] Their status as students, newly freed from parental and community oversight, made them seem particularly vulnerable. One study noted, "Most people are inclined to shrug when they hear that a twenty-one year old secretary is in liaison with a man, but eyebrows fly high when a twenty-one year old college junior does the same."[51]

However, sexologists took a similar approach and tone in reporting on the increasingly licentious nature of the urban workplace. A 1960 study on secretaries fretted over how many office workers doubled as "courtesans, call girls and semi-professional tarts" and estimated that 10.9 percent of secretarial workers bedded their employers before their twenty-second birthday.[52] In a 1964 study, 40 percent of the single white-collar workers under thirty-five admitted to engaging in office affairs.[53] While these studies acknowledged that workplace affairs were nothing new, they fretted over the increasingly public nature of the single woman's liaisons and her insistence on her right to sexual pleasure.

While the statistics charting sexual behavior were cause for alarm, so were the bold attitudes voiced by many young women. A repeated refrain in these studies of college and career women was interviewees' insistence that individuals should define sexual morality for themselves, rather than having it dictated to them. "The emphasis is now on the individual," Steinem concluded, "and group reactions to individual actions are out-of-date."[54] A woman in one sexological study justified her affairs with a "set of self-made rules": "As long as she does not violate them, [she] is strong in her belief that she is neither promiscuous nor a tramp," the study observed.[55]

However, historians writing on the early 1960s have argued that promiscuity among women was not as widespread as popularly reported, nor did young women wholly reject the social conventions of their elders. Susan Douglas argues that the sensationalized media reports of the early and mid-1960s "greatly exaggerated the speed and scope of the Sexual Revolution" by falsely claiming that young women "were shedding their virginity en masse": "The truth was that while some college women, especially those pinned and engaged, were violating the taboos against premarital sex, most young women in and out of college in the early and mid-1960s still kept their undies on until they were married. . . . Several researchers in the mid-1960s documented that sexual permissiveness had not yet overtaken the youth of America."[56]

Douglas's recollection is supported by a 1964 Harvard report that concluded "three-fourths or more of unmarried college women are virgins," and "promiscuity probably is confined to a very small percentage of college women," despite students' bold attitudes toward sex.[57] Gael Greene prefaced her nationwide survey *Sex and the College Girl* (1964) by noting that attitudes toward sex differed by region: "Candor itself is going to vary sharply from one campus to the next and within various crowds on one campus," she cautioned. "Girls do not necessarily speak the same language."[58] A sexologist quoted in a 1964 study of single women conceded that only a small percentage—urban libertines—were overtly breaking from traditional mores. "The ancient standards and taboos still survive, and are being observed everywhere," he warned. "So a girl thinks twice before she has an affair. It very well might ruin her chances of making a good marriage. She may say she approves of the new approach, but she doesn't live accordingly. And in time she will become one of the staunchest defenders of the old order."[59]

Because women's worth was still largely tied to sexual status, a woman with a reputation for promiscuity risked ruining her chances for marriage or being disrespected by dates. "Whether a woman has had one affair or 20, it is the same promiscuity. She has shown herself available," warned Pearl S. Buck in a 1964 *Ladies' Home Journal* article.[60] *Time* posed the idea more bluntly: "Campus sex is not casual. Boys look down on a 'community chest,' meaning a promiscuous girl."[61] Given that a woman who engaged in premarital sex still risked gaining a bad reputation or diminishing her chances for marriage, most young women confined their affairs to the men they planned to marry.[62] These realities belied media reports of sexual revolution and indicated that some young women were more daring in their talk than in their behavior.

Sexual Frustrations and Unfeminine Aggressions

Single women who chose to be sexually active not only risked ruining their reputations, but also being labeled as psychologically unstable and emasculating. Despite Helen Gurley Brown's attempt to reframe the single career woman as a "glamour girl," the unmarried woman who demonstrated sex drive and career ambition remained an object of pity and fear in many writings of the early 1960s. According to these psychologists and sexologists, the single woman rarely pursued sex for its own sake, but rather used it to misguided or manipulative ends. Secretaries who remain unmarried past twenty-five, one sexological study reported, were well aware that "their chances of getting a husband diminish with each passing year of their lives," and thus they indiscriminately "fling themselves at men in the hopes of luring them into marriage." The author warned that an aging single woman who was "too blatantly willing to let a dinner-and-movie date develop into a sex bout" risked "overplaying her hand" and remaining unhappily unwed.[63] Another 1964 study on the promiscuous woman argued that the woman who is "sufficiently bitter about her failure to marry . . . indulges in sex with a vengeance to prove, to herself and to the world, that she can do as well singly in this regard as other women can do in the married state."[64]

Whether chaste or promiscuous, the single woman was also thought to suffer from frigidity, a malady that was reported to plague maladjusted single girls and dissatisfied housewives alike. Frigidity was defined as a major national health concern in the 1950s and early 1960s, encompassing a wide range of women, from those who completely lacked sexual response to those who failed to recognize orgasm. "In some the loss of capacity was partial and sporadic, in others complete. In all to whom it happened it was profoundly disturbing," wrote the authors of *Modern Woman: The Lost Sex*, an influential 1947 study of women's psychological disorders. *Modern Woman* cited sexological and psychological studies that found 50 percent or more of American women suffered from frigidity.[65] *The Mark of Oppression*, a 1951 study on African American psychology, also claimed that "sexual disturbance" and frigidity were common among middle-class African American women.[66]

In many experts' writings, the sexually unresponsive woman posed a threat to normative gender roles. Her refusal to assume a properly passive role during intercourse contributed to her frigidity, and her failure to achieve satisfaction put greater pressure on men to perform sexually.[67] The authors of *Modern Woman* explained the dynamic collectively: "Challenging men on every hand, refusing any longer to play even a relatively submissive role, multitudes of women found their capacity for sexual gratification dwindling as their feelings of love gave way to hostility."[68] Frigidity was often framed as a marital problem that hindered a wife's ability to achieve sexual partnership with her husband; according to Betty Friedan, the housewife directed an inordinate amount of her energy toward sex out of fear of being labeled frigid. However, in several early 1960s studies, frigidity was also blamed for single women's failure to marry and was viewed as one factor that fueled their promiscuity.[69]

As the author of the 1964 book *The Sexually Promiscuous Female* explained:

> If . . . [a single woman] has not married due to an inability to relate to men, the same inability will mark her sex life. The result will be frigidity of one sort or another. . . . Each failure to achieve the full release of orgasm makes her more thoroughly frustrated and dissatisfied with her unmarried state, and spurs her on to greater reaction against it through the medium of promiscuity.[70]

Experts warned that using promiscuity to compensate for sexual and emotional shortcomings could lead to psychosis. *The Sexually Promiscuous Female* told the story of a single woman who was found "cavorting hysterically in the nude . . . exposing herself and shrieking obscenities" at the termination of another unfulfilling affair.[71]

While a lone shrieking woman humiliated only herself, the prospect of growing numbers of single women that demonstrated sexual assertion and career ambition posed a threat to men's increasingly fragile grasp on masculinity. In postwar writings on a supposed masculinity "crisis," sociologists and psychologists claimed that men's innate masculine drive was undermined by the communal nature of the white-collar workplace and the demands of domineering wives. These experts feared gender roles were converging, as increasing numbers of working women challenged the traditional male role of wage-earner and provider.[72] Although the playful term "single *girl*" diminished the threat that a mature, actualized woman might pose to men, she too was perceived as challenging masculine prerogatives. This challenge even surfaced in an early 1960s ad for ballpoint pens. "The man-sized ballpoint: Should girls be allowed to borrow it?" asked the ad, under the headline "Sex and the Single Jotter." Parker Pen Company resolved the conflict by offering single female jotters a new "smaller, daintier" pen that "writes as long as the man-sized one." The ad's subtext relies on the common idea that the sexually active single girl seeks to appropriate (or "borrow," if you will) masculine modes. By providing her a "smaller, daintier" implement with a duration that matches the "man-sized" pen, the advertiser both accentuates gender difference and acknowledges the single woman's sex drive.[73]

On a more serious note, the pages of *Playboy* abounded with ruminations on the "womanization of America," arguing that women were usurping masculine prerogative in the bedroom and boardroom in misguided attempts at equality. In a 1962 panel discussion on the topic, male experts characterized the dedicated career woman as an insecure "misfit" rebelling against biological imperatives and argued that single women's assumption of "active roles" in sex fostered resentment in men who were denied their "masculine capacity" to "conquer" their dates.[74] Author Philip Wylie, who had earlier popularized the term "momism" to describe the threat posed by overbearing, domineering mothers, identified another "deadly menace" in their career-oriented counterparts. His 1963 *Playboy* commentary warned that, left unchecked, the ambitious "single girl" could grow into the "career woman," the middle-aged "ogre" who wields her sexuality like a "Siren" and uses her professional clout to "cripple masculinity and manhood on earth." The "career woman" was symptomatic of a "disastrous confusion" of gender roles, Wylie wrote: "The instant [men] lost their hold on the qualities that truly describe maleness, women grabbed them."[75]

These generalized anxieties were echoed in *Ebony*'s 1963 report on "The Negro Woman." This article offered mixed perspectives on female dominance in African American communities, suggesting that the legacy of strength that had historically sustained family relationships and advanced civil rights "pose[d] new problems" for relationships. *Ebony* claimed that "sexual antagonisms" between African American women and men "run at a fever heat," as strong women evoked feelings of "mistrust and hostility" from men. The article argued that the dominant black woman was "in conflict with her innate biological role . . . in an age when Negroes and whites, men and women, are confused about the meaning of femininity." However, in contrast to *Playboy*'s tone, *Ebony* urged women toward partnership rather than submission.[76]

The threat that career women posed to masculinity is evident in the often-militaristic language used to describe Brown's book and the behavior of unmarried women. One study described unmarried secretaries as "frantic huntresses" who perceive male coworkers as "game" and "prey" and home in for the kill.[77] This aggression could surface in aberrant sexual behavior, as in the case of "Mary P," a promiscuous woman who used her perverse talents to "cut [men] down to size." As she bragged to one sexologist: "I've never yet met a fellow I can't handle by just reaching inside his pants."[78]

Reviewers often expressed discomfort with the cavalier approach to sex and dating advocated in *Sex and the Single Girl*. "I detect a thorough contempt for men, who are the marionettes of this manipulation," wrote a male *Los Angeles Times* reviewer. "There is the assumption that [men] are blind to artifice and shrewdness, and that they are pushovers for the clever and designing woman."[79] A female reviewer for the *London Sunday Times* compared Brown's single women to an "army of occupation" who perceived men as "a set of opponents to be exploited, outwitted and finally taken over."[80] In these reviews of Brown's work, and in the popular press reports and sexological studies referenced earlier, the single woman evoked wider concerns about changing sexual mores and gender roles.

However, these concerns were not confined to print media. Popular film acknowledged and negotiated these anxieties and helped align the threatening figure of the "single girl" with more traditional values. In film narratives, the single woman's decisions about sex were largely individual, cast against a backdrop of promiscuity and peer pressure. Like the study subjects referenced earlier, she often assumed a false air of sexual knowledge and experience to mask her virginal status. While films reserved their harshest punishments for sexually active women, their dialogue also mocked characters who were sexually uptight or frigid. And even the most charming heroine bore the stigmata of neurosis and masculinization that were associated with single women's independence and assertion in this time period.

Single Heroines, Censorship Standards, and Whiteness

The independent woman was not a new figure in film. Scholars and critics have documented a lineage of strong heroines in "women's films" of the 1930s through the 1950s. While characters portrayed by Katharine Hepburn and Rosalind Russell, among others, demonstrated career ambition and assertion within companionate marriages and relationships, other heroines pursued solo career ambitions and surrendered their careers for marriage in the final scene.[81] However, there were key differences between the single women of 1960s films and earlier heroines. While the earlier genre was largely directed at female audiences, many comedies featuring single women in the early 1960s were designed to have cross-gendered appeal: the single woman served as both an object of desire (for men) and identification (for women). Also, films of the early 1960s dealt more directly with sex than the earlier "women's films," in line with the increasingly sexualized nature of popular culture in general.

Many of the films I analyze follow the conventions of the "sex comedy" genre, which reigned in Hollywood in the late 1950s and early 1960s. These films usually foregrounded consumer goods, colorful sets, and stylish wardrobes. Doris Day's character in *Pillow Talk*, for example, was an interior decorator who wore chic suits and backless designer gowns; her suitor lived in a sleek apartment equipped with the latest gadgets. The surface-level appeal of sex comedies has denied them the critical and scholarly attention afforded to other film genres. But as scholar Kathrina Glitre writes, "beneath the Eastman Color, the chic décor and the fashion-plate costumes, the sex comedy reveals anxieties and contradictions comparable to other genre films."[82] Glitre notes that the typical sex comedy centers on the "twin themes of virginity and seduction," pairing a virginal career woman with a charming bachelor.

She wants love (and marriage), he wants sex (without commitment). Courtship patterns are confused: in most cases, the woman thinks she is taking the lead, but only because the playboy has resorted to devious methods of seduction, including masquerading as someone else. These deceptions are inevitably found out (just) before the virgin gives in to his charms. In the meantime, the playboy has fallen in love with the heroine, usually because she is marked out as "different" from other women: her virginal status functions to signify her "worth" and the rate of sexual exchange is marriage.[83]

As I will discuss throughout this chapter, the use of seduction as a source of humor often did not sit well with censors. However, these movies also had moralistic elements as they equated seduction with manipulation, distinct from the authenticity of true love.[84]

Although *Where the Boys Are* contains comical elements, this film and its predecessor *The Best of Everything* fall more naturally under the category of melodrama. The classic melodrama (sometimes equated with the "women's film") is characterized by a female protagonist, female vantage point, and a plot that centers on family, romance, and the domestic sphere. Like sex comedies, melodramas have traditionally been devalued by critics and scholars due to their feminine themes and heightened emotional tone.[85] In the early 1960s, melodramas merged with youth films to spawn what Susan Douglas calls the "pregnancy melodrama." Although these movies often reinforced traditional morality, they acknowledged that "young people were fed up with bourgeois hypocrisy about everything from status seeking to sex, and that they were struggling with often irresistible sexual urges."[86] Most important, Douglas writes, these films offered multiple female vantage points on sex, ranging from prudish to promiscuous: "There were stark differences between the female characters in each film, but there were also contradictions within the same character. It was this latter type of character, deeply conflicted and unsure about whether to act on her sexual impulses or obey the double standard, a girl inclined to rebel yet still every bit a 'good girl,' who was held up as the new role model."[87] Thus the pregnancy melodrama, while it values virginity and punishes wayward women, also encourages ambivalence in viewers. Suzanna Danuta Walters similarly argues that the contradictions inherent in classic melodrama may inspire viewers to take a resistant stance toward their subordination in the home and workplace.[88]

Across genres, films became increasingly sexualized in the early 1960s to meet audience expectations and industry demands. Given the increasing sophistication of youth and popular novels that positioned sex as "a possible and probable part of a single girl's experience," producers sensed that audiences would no longer accept the unquestionably chaste heroine and vague allusions to sex and pregnancy.[89]

American films were also becoming increasingly explicit in the early sixties as filmmakers competed with foreign and art-house cinema that offered more daring depictions of sexuality.

The Production Code Administration—the entity charged with regulating sexuality, violence, and other objectionable material in Hollywood films prior to the rise of a film ratings system—gradually loosened its standards, partly to accommodate filmmakers who might otherwise be tempted to release films without code approval. One pioneering film that inspired changes in the code was *The Moon Is Blue*, a 1953 adaptation of a stage play featuring a virginal single woman who verbally spars with male suitors. Code officials objected to the story's frequent use of words such as *seduction* and *virgin*, its reliance on sexual situations for humor, and its seeming mockery of traditional morality. When the Production Code Administration refused to approve the film adaptation, producers distributed the movie without the code seal. The unexpected success of *The Moon Is Blue* prompted debates on whether Production Code standards were out of touch with changing times and a changing industry.[90]

In 1956 the Motion Picture Association of America announced the Production Code's "first major overhaul in a quarter-century," which lifted the ban on previously taboo topics, such as prostitution, abortion, and childbirth, provided such themes were treated with "good taste."[91] By 1958 *Time* noted that the same censorship code that "once bulldogged producers and exhibitors is being observed these days about as often as the whooping crane," citing the presence of adulterers, strippers, "implicit homosexuals," and references to masturbation in recent popular films. "Hollywood, faced with the stinging competition of TV and foreign films, is in the mood to shed any garments that seem to get in the way at the box office," *Time* surmised.[92] *Saturday Review* concurred in 1962 that "what motion pictures can show and what they can say have been revolutionized in the past decade."[93]

The weakened Production Code still held power, however, as code approval enabled filmmakers to secure bookings and avoid challenge by local censorship boards. In particular, filmmakers depended on code approval of the initial script to obtain a production budget.[94] Geoffrey Shurlock, who had assumed leadership of the Production Code Administration in the mid-1950s, was more flexible than his predecessors in approving films; he believed that there were no "hard-and-fast rules" and that each script should be judged on its own merits.[95] Thus, the code had a somewhat uneven approach to censoring sex in film in the late 1950s and early 1960s. Dramatic films featuring premarital sex—such as *A Summer Place* (1959) and *Splendor in the Grass* (1961)—were approved but usually contained negative consequences or a voiceover condemning the action. Shurlock was able to make an argument for literary merit as he worked with filmmakers to bring a toned-down version of Vladimir Nabokov's *Lolita* to the screen in 1962—although screenings of *Lolita* were restricted to adult audiences. Comedies aimed at general audiences were a touchier subject, as they appeared to be making light of sexual mores.[96] Censors and critics were also concerned that young viewers would flock to films such as *Where the Boys Are* and emulate the behavior depicted onscreen.[97] Thus, comedic films and those aimed at youthful audiences may have come under closer scrutiny.

Despite the increased flexibility of censorship standards, the very notion of the unmarried woman as a sexual being challenged a code that had pledged to "uphold the sanctity of the institution of marriage and the home" and forbid representations of "casual or promiscuous sex relationships."[98] A 1963 letter regarding the film adaptation of *Sex and the Single Girl* typifies the Production Code Administration's stance. The film's initial script, censors warned producers, fundamentally violated the code and community mores by "giving the impression of offering to unmarried girls an encouragement in sexual freedom, or, to use a more unpleasant word, promiscuity." However, censors indicated that if the script were amended to include a "strong rebuttal of the notion that sexual freedom is quite acceptable for unmarried girls," it could be deemed acceptable.[99] This censorship process reinforced societal anxieties and taboos governing female sexuality while also heightening the contradictory nature of popular films. (Some sixties viewers were surprised that a film brazenly titled *Sex and the Single Girl* actually reproached women who sought "sexual freedom.")[100]

The centrality of white, middle-class women in these narratives reflected a broader valuation of whiteness in media. As Wini Brienes describes the 1950s female beauty ideal: "The lighter the skin and hair, the straighter the hair, the more attractive one was considered."[101] Hence, the fact that Kim Novak, Doris Day, Dolores Hart (*Where the Boys Are*), and Hope Lange (*The Best of Everything*) were not only white but also fair-skinned blondes may have amplified their desirability.

Also, although themes of virginity, frigidity, marriage, and the dangers of career ambition were not unique to white middle-class culture, they were defining aspects of white female identity. As Brienes argues, "'Virginal' was compounded by racial meanings; it was the white girl who was expected to be a virgin. Testing gender boundaries implied testing racial boundaries as well."[102]

The dominance of white actresses in film also reflected the historical workings of the Production Code. In *Performing Whiteness,* Gwendolyn Audrey Foster reads the Production Code as a document designed to control sexuality as well as "maintain the borders of whiteness." She argues that the code, by banning miscegenation and advancing the archetype of "the white woman as virginal angel" simultaneously prohibited onscreen sexuality and racial hybridity.[103] Lily-white heroines of the 1950s and 1960s both adhered to the code's conventions and made films more marketable to mass audiences in an era before niche marketing to minority groups.

However, women of color were not wholly absent from films featuring single women: African American actress Perry Blackwell played a brief role in *Pillow Talk* as pianist and confidante to Doris Day who sees through Rock Hudson's deception. However, Judith Roof argues that her character is a "holdover from the mammy's quiet wisdom" and that her presence in the film primarily serves to "spur discernment among a confused mass of white people."[104] Beyond stereotyped characters, we should also consider the role of minority viewers in the early 1960s. While Brienes argues that the stark whiteness of popular culture spurred self-abnegation among both women of color and ethnically marked white women, reviews in the African American press suggest that some black audiences responded enthusiastically to the book *Sex and the Single Girl*.[105] How minority audiences responded to the cinematic "single girl" is a topic largely unaddressed in primary sources.

My analysis centers on popular films about college students and young career women, two groups central to cultural debates about unmarried women's changing desires and career ambitions. The multiple drafts and censorship decisions that shaped these films—as well as the daring books that inspired them—provide insight into how the single woman's sexuality and independence was carefully negotiated in popular culture. Previous studies of early 1960s film have often charted the rise of the single woman through ultrasexualized or aberrant figures, such as the "Bond girl."[106] However, I argue that standard sex comedies and ensemble melodramas most directly engaged the moral choices and consequences facing young white women in the early 1960s and thus deserve equal attention. On the surface, the characters portrayed in these films resembled Helen Gurley Brown's idealized "single girl." They were perky, sharply dressed, career focused, and confident in the challenge they posed to conventional morality. However, much like media reports that presented single women's desires and ambitions as alternately pitiable or threatening, these films strategically undermined and unmasked their heroines' independent spirits.

"Does She or Doesn't She?" Undermining Sexual Knowledge

In most of these movies, the single woman assumes an air of experience and authority regarding sex, an authority that is undermined by plot twists and the heroine's own inner conflicts. The attention-grabbing title *Sex and the Single Girl,* for example, was superimposed onto a pre-existing film script about a duplicitous sexologist. The original concept, starring "a thirty-five-year-old virgin in a Peter Pan collar," was amended to incorporate a sexier younger woman. "The idea that the girl who wrote this sex handbook was a twenty-three-year-old punk, a cerebral infant trading on the gullibility of the public—that interested me," director Richard Quine explained.[107] In the film, Natalie Wood's unmarried Helen Brown is not only a best-selling author but also the sole female research psychologist at the International Institute of Advanced Marital and Pre-marital Studies—a step up from the real Helen Gurley Brown's background as an advertising copywriter. The story revolves around the efforts of tabloid magazine editor Bob Weston (Tony Curtis) to reveal the true motivations behind Brown's best-selling book. "I'll bet you this kid has been giving flying lessons and she's never been off the ground," he muses. "Does she or doesn't she? Either way, it's a crummy story." After the magazine publishes an editorial accusing Helen of hiding her virginity, Bob plans to write a follow-up exposé. Posing as a patient with marital problems, Bob schedules sessions with Helen and pries into her personal life. As he gathers juicy material for his cover story, this bachelor inevitably falls for the sympathetic psychologist.

Characters' obsession with virginity and use of masquerade as a

Therapy session: Bob Weston (Tony Curtis) poses as a patient to seduce psychologist Helen Gurley Brown (Natalie Wood) in Sex and the Single Girl. *Courtesy of Warner Brothers/Photofest.*

means to seduction fits with the standard sex-comedy formula. Both the plotline and visuals emphasize male aggression, in contrast to Helen Gurley Brown's emphasis on female initiative. In an opening animation sequence, a male symbol sprouts devil horns and pursues a reluctant female symbol across the screen to an upbeat Count Basie tune. Similarly, when Bob approaches Helen in her office, the camera positions them on either side of a large archer statue, the archer's arrow pointing straight at Helen's guarded heart.

Natalie Wood appears youthful in the film. Sporting a pageboy haircut, she often wears a white lab coat, deepens her voice, and hides behind thick glasses to assume greater stature and authority. Wood's previous roles as a single woman who becomes pregnant and finds true love in *Love with the Proper Stranger* (1963) and as a sexually frustrated teen in *Splendor in the Grass* (1961) cemented her association with youthful indiscretions. Tony Curtis, too, assumes the masquerade of an insecure, impotent man, much like his dual identity in the earlier comedy

Some Like It Hot (1959). A running joke throughout *Sex and the Single Girl* reminds viewers of Curtis's earlier movie role.

The fictional Helen is conflicted and two-faced, often assuming a brisk, clinical demeanor that masks her insecurities. While she claims to be beyond "the double standard you men keep trying to impose on us women," she is angered at the accusation that she is either "a 23-year-old virgin" with no claim to sexual knowledge or "*that* kind of girl." At the beginning of the film she storms into the office, tabloid magazine in hand, to dispute Bob Weston's claims that her book is a "hoax" written by a virgin intent on "filling frustrated feminine minds with dirty delusions." She quivers and paces, her voice rising to a fever pitch, as her older male colleagues look on with a mixture of concern and amusement.

"This filthy rag is using sex and me for no better purpose than to make money," she complains. "The gall, to call *me, Doctor* Helen Gurley Brown, a 23-year-old *virgin!*"

A coworker gently reminds her: "Traditionally, Helen, the term is considered a compliment."

"Well, not by me!" she snaps back, informing them she's just lost six clients.

When she exits in a huff, one psychologist remarks to the others: "We have just been told off by a 23-year-old . . . [long pause]. You know, that comment about Helen raises some rather interesting questions about her. Either way."

Censors initially raised concerns about this scene, warning the studio that Helen's "indignant" reaction over being called a virgin was sure to be "looked on unfavorably by powerful, religious reviewing groups."[108] (The term *virgin* itself carries particular weight in this scene, as only Helen actually utters the word.) However, the scene ultimately supports conservative ends. By calling Helen's expertise into question, the film undermines the authority not only of her character but also the advice she dispenses.

For the fictional Helen, being accused of virginity poses a professional liability, causing her to lose clients and professional clout. However, her indignation also reflects the attitudes of many young women who were reluctant to admit their lack of experience in sex surveys lest they be labeled "square" or old-fashioned.[109] The scene sets into motion the increasing divide between the fictional Helen's public stance on sex and her private proclivities. She balks when Bob Weston, posing as a client, proposes they have an affair, explaining that her book is "a research study, not an autobiography," and that her chapter on relationships between single women and married men "was an observation, not a recommendation." At one point she frantically flips through the pages of her own book, as if she were a clueless reader seeking guidance.

Although Helen brags that she plans to remain unmarried to pursue her career and "the right to have as many love affairs as I please," she is pleased to learn that Bob is both unmarried and smitten with her. The film's final moments find her tearfully renouncing the "single girl" life and ditching her career to marry the tabloid journalist. Meanwhile, Helen's workplace is reduced to rubble by a wrecking ball, ensuring the end of her psychology practice.

This fictional tale of a sexologist, then, at least momentarily diminished the image of the real-life Helen Gurley Brown, who dispensed sex advice from her own personal experience and retained her career identity after marriage. Critics largely panned the film in reviews riddled with words like "dull" and "snore." The *Washington Post*, citing Natalie Wood's inability to disguise her inexperience or her age in the film, declared in a headline that "Helen Gurley Brown Is Not This Stupid."[110] The *New York Times* complained that *Sex*'s lead characters hit a "dull, sour snag" in their "fumbling near-seduction," and that the "simpering title [is] all that's left" of Brown's best-seller.[111] However, the film also spoke to the discrepancy emerging in sex studies between what women professed and what they did and reassured viewers that even the most brazen advocate of sexual freedom was a nice girl underneath. In a rare positive review, *Life* noted the discrepancy between appearance and reality, remarking that "the [movie] with the most leering and notorious title of them all stands out as a film of surprising fun, and about as sexy as a wink."[112]

The question "Does she or doesn't she?" also animates the 1962 comedy *Boys' Night Out*, in which single character Cathy (Kim Novak) blurs the lines between sexologist and sex worker. The film followed a trend in early 1960s cinema to feature prostitutes with "a heart, as well as hair, of platinum."[113] Inspired by a philandering boss, three bored married men in grey-flannel suits and their handsome bachelor friend Fred (James Garner) pool their resources to rent an apartment—and a female companion—to which they each can escape one night a week.[114]

Fred finds the perfect bachelor pad adorned with bold red walls, a built-in bar, and even a mirrored ceiling in the opulent master bedroom. He is surprised when fellow apartment-hunter Cathy appears at the door to see the place, then agrees to serve as the men's companion instead. "It isn't every day a girl gets a chance to meet men who know how to share," Cathy explains. Her glowing blonde tresses, deep seductive voice, and fur coat mark her as an upscale escort.

"Hello, boys," she croons to the men, sashaying through the modern living room in a form-fitting green dress. "When would you like me to begin?"

Given that Cathy wandered into the situation and never discussed money, Fred perceives her as a misguided "good girl" and becomes obsessed with saving her reputation. The audience is invited into another layer of deception: Cathy is a sociologist on the sly, researching her thesis on "the adolescent sexual fantasies of the adult suburban male" and using the men's love nest as her laboratory. This movie thus inverts the typical sex-comedy formula by having the *woman* perform the masquerade, although her aim is not seduction. Interestingly, the trailer for the film downplayed this unusual aspect of the comedy, presenting the men as virile wolves who capture a "chick" in their swanky lair—a more familiar scenario for early 1960s audiences.[115]

As Cathy assumes her scholar role, her appearance changes: she puts on large glasses and wears baggy shirts that downplay her physique, and she pulls out her typewriter and tape recorder to analyze her findings. The costume changes and research tools reinforce the masquerade and remind us that her sexiness is an act rather than an identity. That Cathy often acts like a teenage girl—talking on the phone while stretched across the bed, or slamming doors and weeping when she argues with Fred—reassures viewers that she is not really the sexual sophisticate she pretends to be.

Her decision to gather data through case studies rather than surveys worries her paternalistic professor. "You're a student, a sociologist—not a courtesan!" he warns in his thick German accent. "Can you look like *yes*, and act like *no?* Can you entice them; lure them; then postpone, evade, delay? This needs a special kind of experience and skill. This, a nice girl hasn't learned."

"No?" Cathy responds with a smirk. "This, a nice girl has learned best."

This dialogue firmly establishes Cathy as a "nice girl" and also calls upon Helen Gurley Brown's avocation of the tease as a way to wield control over dates. "For a female, getting there is *at least* half the fun," Brown observes. "A single woman may promote the attraction, bask in the sensation . . . with never a guilty twinge. She can promise with a look, a touch, a letter or a kiss—but she doesn't have to deliver. She can be maddeningly hypocritical and, after arousing desire, insist that it be shut off by stating that she wants to be chaste for the man she marries."[116] Accordingly, Cathy uses her sexual appeal to lure male study subjects but stops short of fulfilling their fantasies.

Throughout *Boys' Night Out*, the men spice up their subway commute by telling off-color jokes, the prurient parts conveniently covered by the roar of an oncoming train. The men's relationship with Cathy also plays out as an interrupted dirty joke. Although each man assumes the others are indulging in illicit affairs, what goes on behind closed doors is innocuous. Armed with a hidden tape recorder and low-cut, backless dresses, Cathy plies her study subjects not with sex but with what they are truly lacking: a listening ear for the man ignored at home and abundant meals for the man forced by his wife to eat health food. The film thus domesticates the single woman while providing a corrective to the female-dominated households that were thought to stifle men's happiness. As Novak herself explained in a 1962 interview: "When Cathy meets each of the guys she senses their frustration. But in each instance, it's something other than sex. . . . Men want a chance to express themselves. And marriage, with its endless adjustments, suffocates instead of inspiring them."[117]

That Novak's character functions more as counselor than courtesan counters the licentious nature of the film's premise. As one reviewer noted, "nothing happens" sexually in the shared apartment, and the movie's function was "satirizing present-day attitudes more than pandering to them."[118] However, at least one reviewer was frustrated by the film's conservatism. Calling Cathy an "upstanding" character, a *Variety* reviewer predicted that "red-blooded male audiences" would be disappointed to discover that "boy one does nothing but gab, boy two nothing but putter, boy three nothing but eat, and that boy four ups and marries the girl."[119]

Having proven herself to be a nurturing, understanding wife, Cathy lavishes her romantic passions on the unattached Fred, who sees

Double identity: When not posing as a courtesan, Cathy (Kim Novak) conducts academic research on men's sexual behavior in Boys' Night Out. *Courtesy of MGM/Photofest.*

through the veneer. "I just can't figure you out. I know you're one kind of person, but yet deep down I feel you're another kind of person, too," he tells her. Although the two kiss passionately, interactions between Cathy and Fred were carefully edited to remove any impression of a "sex affair" between them.[120] These subtle script changes preserved Cathy's purity, as well as the film's emphasis on duplicity: Cathy and Fred may pretend to be sexually liberated, but they really desire an old-fashioned courtship.

Fred soon proposes to Cathy at a children's baseball game; bells chime when he mentions the word *marriage*, and the couple kiss as a soft rain falls around them. While Cathy struggles to explain her masquerade, Fred still assumes she's a prostitute and makes a grand gesture of forgiving her sordid past. As a script outline explains: "He knows that she has strayed from the straight and narrow, but this is because of her youth and naïveté, and she can be redeemed by the love of a good man."[121] However, when Cathy's cover is blown after a series of comedic twists, Fred becomes uncomfortable with her superior knowledge. "It is one thing for a girl to go wrong . . . but to use a guy for an experiment," he mutters, makes Cathy a "dirty, contemptible sociologist." The scriptwriters initially were equally uncomfortable with Cathy's knowledge. An unpublished early script outline cast Cathy as delusional: "Cathy just *thinks* she is studying for her Ph.D. . . . . Actually, she is a patient of [Professor] Prokosch's. . . . [The professor] assures Fred that as soon as she starts living her real life, she will stop studying, lose her fantasy, and become a normal healthy female."[122]

Although the final film moved away from making her a mental patient, Cathy *does* stop studying and gives up her fantasy of an academic career to serve as a doting wife in the end. (As she explains to the men, her research project was already ruined when they discovered the ruse.) The academic and sexual knowledge she assumes earlier in the story are channeled into her "normal, healthy" married identity. This plotline confirms the perceived incompatibility of career ambitions with marriage and reinforces the idea that single women with careers are only biding time before their weddings. As in *Sex and the Single Girl*, the heroine is only playing at sexual experience and ultimately gives up the pretense to become a full-time housewife. Once married, Cathy stifles rather than stokes Fred's fantasies — the film's final joke is that she and the other wives must accompany their men on "boys' night out" to keep them from cheating again.

"Women Aren't Women Anymore": Frigidity and Masculinity

The filmmakers' original conception of Cathy as a mental patient corresponds with the tendency of popular press and sexological studies to credit the single woman's sexual assertion and career ambition to neurosis or psychosis. The original script for *Boys' Night Out* contained a confrontation between Fred and Cathy in which he calls her "sex-crazed" and "a sick girl," and "suggests she see a head-shrinker." Even smooth-talking Cathy could not maneuver her way out of that conversation: "Every time she makes a point, she merely proves [Fred's] point that women aren't women anymore," the script explains.[123] This scene equates sexual assertion with masculinity and suggests that Cathy's sex drive is a problem to be cured. Although this condemning language was left out of the final film, Fred does perceive Cathy as a misguided damsel in distress—not a woman who authentically enjoys the company of multiple men.

The idea that the unmarried women used sexual assertion and career ambition to compensate for sexual inadequacies, and needed to be reeducated into a proper feminine role, surfaced strongly in other sex comedies of the late 1950s and early 1960s. While Fred feared that Cathy was too forthcoming with her sexual favors in *Boys' Night Out*, a more common comedic plotline featured a "sexually repressed career woman" seduced by a bachelor who "conceals his virility."[124] In the 1959 Doris Day comedy *Pillow Talk*, for example, Jan Morrow (Day) is a successful, sharply dressed New York interior decorator who claims to be contented with being single. However, the film's dialogue and plot twists suggest Jan uses her career to compensate for her failed romantic life. The film contrasts Jan's chastity with the philandering nature of neighbor Brad (Rock Hudson), who happens to share her party phone line. While Jan complains to the phone company about the "sex maniac" who croons love songs to his dates over the phone, Brad teases her about the lack of action on her end of the line. Jan's wise-cracking maid, Alma (Thelma Ritter) concurs with Brad that there is something suspicious about Jan's single status: "If there's anything worse than a woman living alone, it's a woman saying she likes it!"[125]

When Brad first encounters Jan in person, he conceals his identity by pretending to be "Rex," a mild-mannered, old-fashioned Texan. His charade reveals the romantic side of Jan, who both welcomes Rex's chivalry yet becomes impatient at his hesitance to make a move, even after several dates. In a moment of assertion fueled by frustration, she takes the reins and suggests the two escape for a romantic weekend.

"Ma'am, that wouldn't be proper!" Rex protests in a mock Southern drawl.

"Rex, we're both over 21," she reasons, as the two head toward a country cabin.

Their affair, and Jan's assertion, is thwarted when Jan discovers Brad's identity, and she quickly returns to being her uptight and indignant former self. The film's final moments feature Hudson humbling the haughty career woman by barging into her apartment, "hauling her bodily out of bed," and carrying her over his shoulder to his place.[126] As I will explore later in this chapter, the scene was originally set up as a prelude to a sexual tryst but was transformed into an aggressive "carrying across the threshold." In the following scene the couple are married and expecting a child, the career woman successfully conquered and restored to her proper place.

The film *Sex and the Single Girl*—which more directly engages reigning theories about sex—also presents the single career woman as neurotic and not appropriately feminine. Throughout the film, Helen Brown's bravado is shown to mask deeper insecurities. "I made up my mind very early that I was going to learn all I could about love and marriage before I made my mistakes," she tells Bob in a moment of drunken confession. Her insecurity is underscored by nervous tics and volatile emotions. While fuming over the magazine exposé, she repeatedly cleans her glasses in a frenzy; when she first falls for Bob Weston, she phones her mother, weeping uncontrollably.

Much like bachelor Brad in *Pillow Talk*, Bob assumes a false identity to gain access to Helen's private life. He poses as a client struggling with impotence and a failing marriage. And, as with *Pillow Talk*'s heroine, Helen's brisk, professional exterior hides an inner softness and vulnerability that surfaces during her sessions with Bob. After he gains her sympathy, Bob phones Helen at home, threatening to commit suicide,

*Sweet revenge: After Jan (Doris Day) lashes out at Brad (Rock Hudson),
he carries her back to his apartment in* Pillow Talk. *Courtesy of Universal
Pictures/Photofest.*

and she rushes to his rescue. The two tumble off an ocean pier, requir-
ing them to change into dry clothes back at her apartment. While Helen
changes from her white evening gown into a white nightgown — her
preference for white accentuating her purity — Bob is given a flowered
woman's robe to wear. After a few cocktails, the two are intertwined,
the lights are dimmed, and Helen instructs Bob on scientifically proven
seduction techniques. "There are certain erogenous areas of the body —
the back and sides of the neck, for example," she informs him, as he
kisses her neck. "Do not get discouraged if you get no response from
me — my neck is a dead area. However, it's very much alive in over 90
percent of all women — I've made a statistical study." As in the earlier
scene, in which Helen countered claims of her virginity by emphasizing
her earned doctorate, this dialogue suggests that Helen is compensating for sexual inadequacy through her "over-investment in scientific
discourse."[127]

Her eyes wide with unanticipated desire, her speech slurred, Helen

45

shares her dating philosophy with Bob. "No sir, I'm not going to gamble with my life, particularly when it comes to men," she declares.

"But gambling can be part of the fun," Bob insists. "Don't you ever go and experiment on your own as a woman—or aren't you that kind of a girl?"

Helen rises to her feet: "*What* kind of a girl?" she asks, accusingly, as the soundtrack skips a beat. Bob apologizes, and the two resume the therapy session, this time with him on top and her continuing to moan about her lack of sensation—her frigidity apparently cured and the questions about her reputation finally answered.

The original script outline for this scene, however, cemented the link between Helen's frigidity and her assumption of a masculine role. In that unpublished outline, Helen is angered over being called "that kind of a girl," and Bob lectures her about her hypocrisy. He informs Helen that it is she, not he, with the sexual dysfunction:

> *You're* the one who feels inadequate. Sex is for *married* girls—but you have to go running all over the country saying it's for single girls, because you're afraid you can't get it any other way. . . . Your problem's not men. It's other women—other women who can get their fulfillment normally, in marriage. And since you're afraid to compete with other women, you have to adopt . . . a man's attitude toward sex, the attitude man has to be tamed out of, by a real woman who knows what sex is for. I thought I was falling for you, but I'm glad I found out in time. I wouldn't like to be married to a *feller.*[128]

The fact that Bob delivers this invective while dressed in an ill-fitting, frilly, flowered women's robe accentuates the gender-role reversal suggested in the dialogue. Helen—much like the promiscuous women at the center of 1960s sex studies—is said to be assuming a masculine attitude toward sex to compensate for her insecurities and frigidity. This perception of her character is supported by earlier dialogue ("I want single women to stop acting like mice—and start acting like men," Helen tells her colleagues) and a print advertisement for the film in which Natalie Wood poses atop a perplexed Tony Curtis, clearly dominating him. Her low-cut dress and crazed expression add to the advertising image's sexual charge.

However, this scene may also have been scripted to meet another need. Censors had warned that in order for the Production Code

Administration to approve the film, it needed a "strong rebuttal of the notion that sexual freedom is quite all right for unmarried girls."[129] This early script provided that rebuttal by calling upon stereotypes of single women as abnormal and emasculating. Although the dialogue castigating Helen Brown as a "feller" was removed from the final picture, Helen's volatile emotions and apparent frigidity still suggest that her sexual philosophy stems from deep dysfunction and insecurity.

"We're Practically the Same Girl": Consequences and Cautionary Tales

While Helen's emasculating stance and Cathy's provocative posture are revealed to be more talk than action—and thus more pitiable than threatening—the single women who actually do engage in affairs in early sixties films do so out of misguided aims, suffering mental and physical anguish as a result. Ensemble films in particular dole out punishments to naive secondary characters who are too easily swayed by peer pressure and too desperate to attract a husband.

Where the Boys Are, a 1960 film adapted from Glendon Swarthout's risqué novel, centers on a group of college women who journey to Florida for spring break. The novel was originally titled *Unholy Spring*; early reviews compared the book to the writings of Jack Kerouac and J. D. Salinger and called the story "amusing and sometimes appalling."[130] The novel's brash narrator, Merritt—a midwestern college student who quipped, "If parents think their daughters can attain young womanhood in 1958 in a state of pristinity, they are really out to lunch"[131]—must have seemed an unlikely heroine for the silver screen. Furthermore, a portrayal of young people focused largely on "drinking and sex," censors warned, had the potential to create "a storm of protest against the picture industry."[132] Filmmakers countered the film's licentious setting by undermining the main character Merritt's assumed sexual knowledge and introducing the cautionary tale of Melanie, a character largely created for the film. Susan Douglas argues that the film presents a range of stock characters, from the "committed virgin to the fallen angel to the tomboy type," but encourages viewers to identify with Merritt (Dolores Hart), a smart, well-spoken student who is both attractive and relatable.[133]

From its opening theme song—a romantic ballad in which a woman

Fun in the Sun: The cast of Where the Boys Are. Left to right: *Paula Prentiss, Dolores Hart, Yvette Mimieux, and Connie Francis. Note that Mimieux, as Melanie, strikes the most seductive pose. Courtesy of MGM/ Photofest.*

pines for one boy—the film recasts the book's sexual experimentation as women's search for love. However, shades of Merritt's challenge to sexual convention remain. The film opens with a verbal duel between Merritt and her "middle-aged spinster" professor, ironically named Dr. Raunch, in a college courtship and marriage class.[134] Dressed in a prim black suit, her hair upswept, Raunch calls on a dozing Merritt to give her interpretation of the textbook. Merritt, her judgment impaired by a head cold, gives an impromptu speech on sexual morality. She briefly references the Kinsey reports and suggests some degree of intimacy is essential to dating: "If a girl doesn't make out with a man once in a while, she might as well leave campus—she's considered practically anti-social," she tells Dr. Raunch as her classmates giggle. The curriculum, she contends, evades "the jackpot issue": "Should a girl, or should she not, under any circumstances, play house before marriage?" Her blue eyes blazing, Merritt offers: "My opinion is yes."[135]

The Production Code Administration feared the provocative potential of this discussion. "At no time should there be any feeling that premarital sex relationships are right or generally acceptable," censors reminded the film's producers.[136] (Indeed, few college students in the early 1960s would take such a public stance on premarital sex, for fear that their statements would ruin their reputations and scandalize their parents.)[137] In the film, rather than being "delighted" and "yelping happily" at Merritt's pronouncement—as they had in earlier versions of the script—the class responds with stunned silence: "We get the impression that Merritt has gone too far, even for them."[138] Merritt is sent to the dean to account for her insubordination and sincerely apologizes. As she exits the dean's office, her sole admirer, Melanie, asks whether she stands by the statements she made in class. In the original script outline, Merritt answers affirmatively; in the film, she evades the question and gripes about the wintry weather.[139] These changes allow the film to voice bold ideas about sex without endorsing them.

To escape the snow and her academic woes, Merritt joins Melanie and two other friends on a spring-break trip to Fort Lauderdale. The movie initially takes a lighthearted and escapist tone: The students drive south in a bright blue convertible, pick up a wisecracking but harmless hitchhiker, and check into a cheerful hotel with a turquoise pool. The brassy soundtrack and tropical setting amplify the film's popular appeal, and the story often makes light of youthful rebellions. Masses of students crowd the streets near the beach, causing a traffic hazard; the promise of free beer sends them running for the nearest bar. A fancy restaurant erupts in chaos when drunken students disrupt a burlesque performance. Elsewhere, police radios buzz with reports of students caught skinny-dipping.

Our heroines, however, seem less concerned with youthful rebellion than with questions of love and chastity. Merritt quickly attracts the attention of Ryder (George Hamilton), a tan, tall, and wealthy senior from Brown University. She succumbs to lengthy make-out sessions on his private yacht but interrupts and deflects his sexual advances, seeing straight through his seduction schemes. Although their verbal sparring references her high IQ and initially marks her as sexually knowledge-able, her inexperience is ultimately revealed. "I've never done anything like this before," she nervously admits to Ryder as the two caress on a beach.

There is little question about the sexual status of fellow traveler Tuggle (Paula Prentiss), a tall ROTC inductee with a deep voice who defends her virginity with military force. "I promised myself I'd try for a man the chaste way, and so help me I'll keep it if I have to drop in at the local blacksmith and buy a belt," she boasts before heading out on a date. In contrast, Melanie, whose apparent lack of IQ and physical stature led one reviewer to call her a "bird-brained little blond,"[140] is far less discriminating. Melanie meets two college men, Dill and Franklin, as soon as she arrives and is thrilled to learn they are "Ivy Leaguers." Melanie shrieks as the men toss her into the hotel pool and flip a coin to determine who will be her escort for the evening. Her playful screams hint at the dangerous side of pleasure, and the men's cavalier treatment of Melanie foreshadows her disastrous dating experiences.

While her friends fight off their dates' advances, Melanie too quickly surrenders her heart and her purity, sleeping with Dill and then Frank-lin. Yet she has not given up her romantic ideals. "A girl from U got married down here last year, did you know?" she says wistfully.

"Two jumps ahead of the obstetrician," Merritt responds with a smirk.

Other scenes characterize Melanie as both impressionable and fallen. She falls prey to the licentious behavior that seems not to tempt her roommates—trying cigarettes one day and staggering home drunk the next. Twirling in a lacy pink dress, she jubilantly announces she is in love with Franklin and thanks Merritt for her sage advice. Merritt ap-pears alarmed that her theories on sex were taken to heart and douses Melanie with cold water to bring her to her senses.

Predictably, Melanie's fling ends not in matrimony but in date rape and near-suicide. While waiting in a hotel room for Franklin, she opens the door to find his friend Dill standing there. He advances on Mela-nie menacingly as she tearfully shakes her head and whispers "no."

Afterward, the desolate Melanie wanders onto a busy highway, where she is struck by a car. Although she has been sexually victimized, visual effects and the soundtrack cast judgment on her choices. As Melanie prepares for her fateful date, her figure dissolves into the neon sign advertising a loose woman's burlesque act, and bawdy music accompanies her drunken, suicidal saunter down the highway.

Although a student suffers gang rape in the novel version of *Where the Boys Are*, she is not one of the main characters, and her friends' immediate response to her violation is to angrily confront the men who committed the crime.[141] In adapting the story to film, the filmmakers created dialogue that places the blame largely on the two women: both Merritt, for recklessly espousing sexual freedom in the first place, and Melanie, for bad decisions that made her easy prey. The film illustrates for impressionable viewers the social costs of promiscuity. In a pivotal scene, Melanie lies deflated in her hospital bed, the soft lighting and white pillow highlighting her childlike qualities. She insists that she is ruined for marriage and laments that her lecherous love interests "weren't even Yalies," then passes out. Merritt weeps uncontrollably, cradling Melanie's face in her hands. Merritt initially turns on Ryder, telling him she blames men for treating women as "cheap and common." He offers an alternate explanation: "She got mixed up with the wrong people."

Merritt and Ryder part ways at the hospital, then reunite in a more romantic setting. They sit alone on an empty, pristine beach, after all the spring-break revelers have returned home. Melanie's tragedy is still foremost on their minds. "I keep thinking it could have been me," Merritt admits to Ryder. (In an earlier script for the film, she takes this comparison even further, declaring: "We're practically the same girl, do you realize that?")[142]

The final script drew a firmer distinction between the women, emphasizing Merritt's moral superiority. "You're a pretty strong girl, Merritt," Ryder assures her. "You'd never lose your grip." In the end, the chaste girl reaps the rewards, as Ryder pledges his love and his desire for a long-term relationship. The two walk off hand in hand toward the sunlit shore as the romantic ballad "Where the Boys Are" plays.

The studio billed the film as a comedy, chirpily dismissing Melanie's rape and suicide attempt as a "near tragedy" that fails to overshadow her friends' fun and success in finding lasting romances.[143] However, her cautionary tale had a chilling effect on viewers and critics, as it corresponded with alarmist reports of naive college girls ruined by promiscuity.[144] Experts warned that the undiscriminating woman who sleeps with a date too soon not only risks being treated as "cheap and common," but also misses the boat for marriage. While the film dramatically illustrated the dangers of carrying new attitudes toward sex to their logical conclusions, it also provided viewers with a point of identification and reassurance in level-headed Merritt.[145]

Douglas argues that the film left sixties viewers with an ambivalent message. Merritt, she notes, only narrowly averts going all the way and at the end of the film accepts an invitation to visit Ryder at Brown, leaving open the possibility that the couple will have premarital sex. As Douglas interprets the film, Melanie's mistake was having sex before determining that the boy loved her. "There are so many contradictions about girls and sex that the final message is that 'Every girl must decide for herself,'" Douglas writes.[146]

Critics and audiences were similarly cognizant of the movie's mixed tone and moral messages. Many viewers recognized the role that censorship played in the adaptation of Swarthout's risqué novel. As *Time* crassly summarized the plot: "Two of the girls play it safe, and though they miss their fun, they get their men. The third plays 'backseat bingo' and in the last reel finds herself all smashed up by an automobile. Not very subtle, but it squares the censor."[147] A Spokane reviewer remarked that the film's bright tone "clobber[s] the somber morality with which the tale has to end in order to pass as an acceptable motion picture."[148] The *New York Times* called the film "shocking and sad," remarking that "there is not much to laugh at in this film."[149]

Other critics felt the film promoted promiscuity. *Where the Boys Are* was deemed "as much an incitement as it is a warning" about licentious behavior, and critics complained that "any moral message appears to have been dragged in by the ears."[150] The film may have been more controversial than the average motion picture because it featured college-aged women. As a *Variety* reviewer commented, "The illusion of wholesome youth becomes the latest illusion to be stripped away as filmdom's mushrooming preoccupation with illicit sex continues."[151]

A 1960 Los Angeles preview audience held similarly mixed opinions. While a few of the 277 viewers who filled out comment cards felt the movie overemphasized sex and was "too much for youngsters," others reveled in the film's more rebellious moments. "It was hysterical to hear [Merritt] say 'barf,' and talk like we do," one female viewer wrote. "The scene at the school where she tells off the teacher was very realistic . . . something we'd all like to do."[152]

The audience comments also reveal different interpretations of the film's ending. "A lot of truth is brought out about so-called summer romances," one woman wrote. A male viewer recommended the film be screened in high schools "for benefit of teen-agers that may get into similar trouble." A mother claimed she was "thrilled" with the picture and planned to watch it again with her teenagers. However, other viewers found the moral message forced. A male viewer referred to Melanie's assault and accident as "emotional tripe." While many female viewers praised the film's truthfulness and realism, a few complained that Melanie was not believable—that she was "shown as too much of a 'chump'" or "too naïve for a college girl." One male viewer flatly stated: "If the ending would have left the message out, it would have been O.K."[153]

The Best of Everything, a 1959 ensemble film about young career women who work at a New York publishing firm, took a more somber tone than *Where the Boys Are*. It was based on the best-selling novel by single, twenty-six-year-old Rona Jaffe. In a 2005 commentary, Jaffe claimed the book was based on interviews with dozens of female office workers and was designed to counter male assumptions about working women. The novel, she said, was "very comforting to a lot of girls, because they saw their lives in it."[154] Jaffe took some personal risks in truthfully representing women's sexual lives—she reportedly moved out of her parents' house while writing the book, fearing its frankness would shock them. After the novel sold 30,000 advance copies, producer Jerry Wald (whose earlier credits included the film adaptation of *Peyton Place*) purchased the movie rights.[155]

Despite the novel's attempts at realism, the film was critically received as a Hollywood fiction. "There is no office in New York City quite as lush . . . no street as clean as Eastman Cinecolor makes it seem," a Florida reviewer wrote, arguing that *Best* "gives the impression that every big office in New York City is a veritable harem of luscious females." He also mocked the film's moralism: "As is usual with Hollywood, the girls seem to get in trouble over night or simply by interlocking glances or hands with a male."[156] A Pittsburgh reviewer panned the film as a radio soap opera with clichéd characters and "unsatisfactory suds and tears."[157] While the heightened emotional tone was characteristic of melodrama, the beautified images of New York and exaggerated moral consequences helped to counter a potentially sordid narrative. *Variety* stated that the film took Jaffe's novel and "simmered it down somewhat" and that the film's skillful director "[kept] the over-wrought story from getting over-heated."[158]

Best opens with a panoramic shot of the New York skyline. Young women in long skirts and high heels stream from buses and subway stations, hurrying to work. Their motion is countered by Johnny Mathis's crooning ballad, which asserts the primacy of love: "We've proven romance is still the best of everything," he sings. Among the women is Caroline Bender (Hope Lange), who clasps a help-wanted ad in her white-gloved hands. She surveys her new workplace: a sleek black high rise that houses the offices of Fabian Publishing. Once she's inside, her elegance and poise distinguish her from the other secretaries, who engage in gossip and last-minute wardrobe adjustments. The head of the typing pool correctly guesses Caroline has an elite college degree.[159]

Like Merritt in *Where the Boys Are,* Caroline serves as the balanced counterpart to her single roommates, acting sensibly in dating while the others fall prey to romantic tragedies. While roommate April romances a devious bartender and aspiring actress Gregg beds a womanizing director—their mistakes meeting with harsh consequences—Caroline dreams about her fiancé overseas. Her workday daydreams are rudely interrupted by her boss, Miss Farrow (Joan Crawford), who summons the new secretary into her office. Caroline and Farrow initially seem to have little in common, but the film repeatedly suggests that Caroline's career ambition will turn her into a bitter, adulterous woman just like her boss. Although Miss Farrow is a memorable character in the novel that inspired the film, many of her interactions with Caroline—and dialogue that suggests Caroline is in danger of becoming her—were created for the movie.

Miss Farrow's reputation precedes her. Other employees refer to her as a "witch," she has gone through twelve secretaries in three years, and she is known to be sleeping with a married vice president. Her appearance is severe, with her upswept, dyed hair accentuating strong facial features, and she appears to spend her day painting her nails and rudely rejecting scripts. On Caroline's first day on the job, Farrow barks contradictory orders at her and openly resents her ambition. "You young

Self-satisfied: Joan Crawford as Miss Farrow, the hardened career woman in The Best of Everything. *Courtesy of Twentieth Century Fox/Photofest.*

college things are all alike," Farrow mutters. "You think everything's so easy." In her outward persona, Farrow resembles author Philip Wylie's "ruthless," middle-aged, masculine career woman who "hands out holy ordinance without ethic or principle" and treats employees "according to whether they advance her name or threaten her idiot eminence."[160] As a reviewer interpreted Farrow's character, "she browbeats female underlings because of an affair she can't have with her already-married boss."[161]

Amanda Farrow has clearly relinquished her femininity not only through her single-minded focus on work but also through her eagerness to indulge in office affairs. However, the film also encourages us to see her sensitive side. She is pained when a young secretary rebuffs her advice on romance and reacts angrily when invited to a bridal shower, holding her head in her hands and tossing the invitation in the trash. As an early film synopsis explains Farrow's inner turmoil: "What went wrong? What wrong button did she push? She started out with the best of everything."[162] As Jaffe herself explained the struggle at the heart of her novel: "What [women] really want isn't a career but someone to love who loves them." The work world, she claimed, made women "more and more demanding, cynical, and harder to please."[163]

At the time that *The Best of Everything* was released, Joan Crawford shared more than a desk in common with Amanda Farrow. Crawford's husband had recently died, and she assumed corporate responsibilities in his absence, becoming the first woman elected to Pepsi Co.'s board. She boasted that work was her life and that her personal motto was to "look like a woman and act like a man." As Crawford toured the country to promote the film, her personal story may have lent realism to the character she portrayed.[164]

Initially, Caroline's ambitions are distinct from Farrow's. Like many young women of her generation, she plans to work for only a year or two and then leave her job to marry. However, when fiancé Eddie calls with the sudden news that he has married another woman overseas, Caroline is devastated. After a night of drunken wallowing, she channels her desires into her work, neatly avoiding the romantic catastrophes that befall her roommates. But she's still in danger of becoming a hardened career woman like her boss. As Wylie warned in *Playboy*: "There are in business today many charming, chic, sexy women—but the man who is sharp of eye can detect . . . the signs of burgeoning harridanism, and perceive premonitions of the horror that is yet to be."[165]

Mike, a charming older coworker who admires Caroline, detects in her a dangerous tendency. "Get out quick," he advises. "Work six months or a year. Prove whatever you have to prove. Then marry the med student, or the law student, and 'love' happily ever after." When the Radcliffe-educated Caroline instead takes on extra work and begins to impress the higher-ups with her editorial expertise, Mike accuses her of seeking to replace Farrow.

A company picnic serves as the backdrop for Mike's intervention. While other Fabian females cheer on potato-sack races, Caroline joins a cluster of men to talk about paperback sales. Mike grabs her by the arm and forcefully pulls her away from the business talk, leading her down a wooded lane to sit beneath a shady tree. He strips off his suit jacket and the two share a cigarette. Their initially flirtatious banter becomes heated when Mike accuses Caroline of pursuing Amanda Farrow's job. "Maybe," she admits breezily. "Anything wrong with that?"

"Not a thing. That is, if you want to become a ruthless, driving, calculating woman," he retorts and informs her: "Do you know why you're doing all this? It's because a man you thought loved you really loved somebody else. Being a woman is too painful, so you're not going to be one. Men aren't lovers, they're competition. Let's not join 'em, let's lick 'em." He pins her against the tree, and she struggles to get free, expressing anger and grief as he walks away. This bit of dialogue—which resembles Bob Weston's upbraiding of Helen Brown in the *Sex and the Single Girl* script—again blames the single woman for assuming a masculine role in order to compensate for her romantic failings. (Significantly, it also places the dedicated careerist outside the category of "woman.")

According to Jaffe, the character of Mike was amplified for the film and serves as the "voice of morality" in a way he never did in the novel. "Actually he was quite a reprobate in the book," she says. "All through this movie he's her conscience . . . in the book everybody had to be their own conscience."[166] By shifting the moral decision making from Caroline to a paternalistic coworker, the film diminishes the more daring elements of Jaffe's novel and reinforces traditional ideas about women's ambition and sexuality.

As Mike predicted, Caroline is chosen to replace Miss Farrow, and she jubilantly races down the rows of secretaries to announce, "I'm an editor!" Farrow explains to Caroline that she's leaving the firm for a belated chance at marriage. Her new husband is a plain, small-town man whose marriage proposal she rejected fifteen years earlier. "He treats me as if he believes I'm the gentlest, softest woman in the world," she tells Caroline. "Maybe, with enough time and tenderness, if it's not too late, maybe I can get to believe it myself." Her romantic problems finally solved, she focuses her attention on Caroline. "I'm going to worry about you *very* much," she says gravely, as she exits the office.[167] The young woman is unfazed, instead looking smug as she sits at Farrow's desk for the first time and happily spins in the desk chair.

Mike stops by to offer sarcastic congratulations. "You have everything you want now, haven't you? Miss Farrow's job. Miss Farrow's office. And in another month or so you'll have the rest of Miss Farrow's life." Caroline is crestfallen, but we see Mike's prediction come to pass. Caroline's wardrobe becomes darker and more austere, her mood more volatile,

Voice of reason: Carolyn (Hope Lange) initially resists Mike's (Stephen Boyd) moral authority in The Best of Everything. *Courtesy of Twentieth Century Fox/Photofest.*

and her treatment of authors and secretaries more demanding. When her married ex-fiancé Eddie comes into town and calls her for a date, viewers suspect Caroline may adopt Farrow's loose morals as well.

However, Caroline's sexual purity and ultimate preference for marriage distinguish her from the opportunistic Farrow. She meets Eddie in a lavish hotel room wearing a formal black dress; a romantic record spins on the turntable as he professes his love. Caroline assumes he will leave his unhappy marriage to marry her. Instead, Eddie gets down on one knee to propose adultery, suggesting that Caroline serve as his mistress when he visits New York. "You'll have your own life, your career, and I'll have mine," he reasons.

Incredulous, Caroline turns away from him, fingering her pearl necklace. "What is it about women like us that makes you hold us so cheaply? Aren't we the special ones from the best homes, the best colleges?" she asks, her voice tinged with sarcasm. As in *Where the Boys Are*, which distinguished its (mostly) moral heroines from the licentious youth that surrounded them, Caroline's monologue draws a line between herself and the "plenty of other girls" who would happily accept Eddie's offer out of a sheer desire to be loved.

"I won't be your mistress!" she shouts. "I'm too square for you, Eddie." As Caroline firmly rejects Eddie's proposal to be a kept woman — slamming the hotel-room door as she leaves — she also loosens her grip on the career that might interfere with her possibilities for true fulfillment as a woman.[168] For, as experts warned and as Farrow aptly illustrates, a woman who has been independent too long loses her ability to fill a more feminine role.

Toward the end of the film, Farrow returns to work. She pleads with the publisher and with Caroline to return to her old position, as gossip-hungry secretaries press their ears to the office door. Seated behind a desk, her once-haughty stature humbled, she confesses to Caroline: "It was too late for me. A lonely man, two children — they needed too much. I found I had nothing to give. Nothing. I'd forgotten how." Her failure corresponds with the findings of a 1962 study on single women, tellingly titled *The Lonely Sex:*

> The career woman may have trouble finding a suitable husband when she decides to marry. . . . She is accustomed to lead, to make decisions, keep her own hours, mingle with her own friends, and plan for her future. She may have looked forward to a more feminine role. . . . If she carries her executive attitudes into marriage, she must either find a man strong enough to hold her respect, or one weak enough to let her continue her completely independent psychology of existence.[169]

Farrow, apparently, was too hardened to make the transition from head executive to subservient wife and mother.

By day's end, Farrow has made another date with a married executive. But the film implies it is not too late for Caroline, who graciously gives back her position to Miss Farrow. "You know, I never really belonged in [your office] anyway," she concedes. The film's final scenes portray Caroline as a lesser executive with a balanced approach to work. She leaves the office early on a Friday, strolling the rows of secretaries in a tailored blue suit and netted hat that shields her face. While the secretaries look up at Caroline with a mixture of envy and admiration, the script characterizes Caroline's expression as "thoughtful and sad."[170] The theme song swells when she walks out of the skyscraper and spots Mike waiting for her on the corner. She removes her formal work hat, freeing her tresses, and the two walk off into the soft-hued city, suggesting that success in love, not publishing, promises "the best of everything." As Jaffe herself interpreted the message: "He had saved her, because she didn't have to be Miss Farrow and be all alone." In the novel, she argues, Mike was merely a transitory affair for Caroline. In the movie, he's the source of a Hollywood happy ending.[171]

Purified Heroines and Perennial Virgins

As *The Best of Everything* illustrates, ensemble films about single women often imbued their primary characters with a sense of moral integrity that enabled them to resist the temptation that led to the downfall of others. Here in particular the filmmakers and censors were hard at work. In contrast to the films' chaste heroines, the novels on which *Where the Boys Are* and *The Best of Everything* are based featured brash-talking characters who eagerly relinquished their virginity and reputations for a taste of experience, each sleeping with no fewer than three men. (Case in point: in the novel *Where the Boys Are*, Merritt returns to the Midwest bearing not a fraternity pin but an illegitimate child.)[172]

In the original script for *Where the Boys Are*, Merritt checks into a hotel with her date Ryder, feeling ashamed and leaving only when she overhears Melanie's drunken laughter in the next room.[173] In the film she is far less calculating about sex: her momentary lapse of morality on a moonlit beach—in which she considers sleeping with Ryder when he professes his love for her—is conveniently interrupted by news of Melanie's downfall, and the sight of Melanie's broken body and spirit builds her resolve. This strategic script change emphasizes that Merritt is a "nice girl" who might have yielded to temptation in a particularly romantic moment. The pairing of her uncharacteristic lapse of judgment with Melanie's rape and car accident reminds viewers that casual sex can lead to harsh consequences.

In an early script outline for the film *The Best of Everything*, Caroline seriously considers the offer to become the mistress to her ex-fiancé Eddie, even packing a suitcase to join him for a weekend rendezvous. However, the script outline was amended to make Caroline morally upright. The lines that reference Caroline's ambivalence have been crossed out and replaced with the directive "She firmly rejects him."[174] Caroline's solid decision is supported by the film's next scene, in which her promiscuous roommate Gregg loses her mind over an affair and tumbles, disheveled, from a balcony to her death. (Caroline's other roommate, April, suffers an illegitimate pregnancy and violent miscarriage earlier in the film.) By firmly refusing the affair, Caroline affirms her own worth and avoids the tragedy that befalls her roommates. She also distinguishes herself from a woman like Miss Farrow, who engages in extramarital affairs without remorse. Caroline, we learn, is determined to achieve "the best of everything" and is unwilling to settle for second best, even if it means turning away her beloved ex-fiancé.

While Merritt and Caroline narrowly resist the allure of affairs, relying on their friends' failures to keep them on the straight and narrow, Doris Day's inner constitution makes the decision for her: Her character, Cathy Timberlake, hallucinates and breaks out into a rash when she contemplates bedding Cary Grant in *That Touch of Mink* (1962).[175] Indeed, Doris Day has been roundly mocked by critics and scholars for her implausible purity; some have even read her as an exception to the increasing sexual frankness of sixties films.[176] However, Day's status as the top-grossing actress of the early 1960s indicates she is central to popular representations of the single woman. Her films illustrate the social conventions that kept women's sexuality in check and the censorship process that purified single characters in their transition from script to screen.[177] Day appeared older than the college kids and the young working women of other single-girl films: The actress was in her late thirties when she starred in *Pillow Talk* and was pushing forty in *That Touch of Mink*, making her virginal image seem especially contrived. In *That Touch of Mink*, Day plays a much younger character: a cash-strapped working girl who relies on an older female mentor.

While Day is remembered for playing the perennial virgin, scholar Tamar Jeffers McDonald argues this perception was more accurate of her later film career. In *Pillow Talk*, the thirty-seven-year-old Day portrayed an established, self-assured interior decorator, and the film's dialogue and daring song lyrics hinted at her sexual experience. Day's character inwardly sings the song "Possess Me" as she heads to a possible tryst with Hudson, and the affair is interrupted only when she discovers Hudson's deception. As McDonald argues, her character's dilemma is not whether to have sex, but whether Hudson is worthy of her affections. However, in Day's subsequent sex comedies, such as *Lover Come Back* (again starring Day and Hudson as dueling ad executives) and *That Touch of Mink*, she is more clearly marked as virginal. Thus, it is important to consider not only the censorship of individual films but also the differences among Day's comedy roles as evidence of how the "single girl" was subdued in popular film.[178] While I agree it is possible to read Day in *Pillow Talk* as embodying both sexual experience and careerist confidence, the dialogue in this film still plays upon reigning stereotypes of single women as frigid and neurotic.

In contrast to *Pillow Talk*, which presents Day as a sexually repressed career woman in need of a romantic cure, *That Touch of Mink* positions her as a naive, corruptible, unemployed single girl. Cathy Timberlake is swept off her feet by a sex-minded millionaire, Philip Shayne (Cary Grant), and agrees to travel to the Bahamas with Philip largely to prove that she is not the prudish "girl from Upper Sandusky" that he assumes her to be. Comments by her older, more cynical roommate Connie (Audrey Meadows) both warn Cathy of Philip's intentions and reassure the audience of her purity. "It's like watching Joan of Arc on her way to the fire," Connie laments, as she watches Cathy, clad in a mink coat, boarding Philip's private plane.

Visual and auditory cues keep the saintly Cathy from being consumed by temptation. As the couple step into the Bahamas hotel, a wedding party walks out, and the movie's orchestral soundtrack chimes "Here Comes the Bride." Entering the elevator, Cathy and Philip stand alongside a different kind of couple: a garishly made-up younger woman clutching the arm of a wealthy older man, giving Cathy a knowing smile. The wedding march chimes again, this time in a sinister minor key, as Cathy beholds the lone canopy bed in their luxury suite.

As the two leave the hotel to explore the island, the prospect of

premarital sex hangs over Cathy's head, quite literally. In her imagination, the horse-drawn carriage she and Philip are riding in turns into
the canopy bed, their planned indiscretion obvious to all. "Everybody
knows!" she realizes, alarmed. The visual gimmick and soundtrack
present the viewer with two choices: either you are a prospective bride
or the kind of woman for whom the wedding march will never chime.
That night, faced with the specter of shame and ruination, Day does
what any decent comic heroine of 1962 would do: She breaks out into
a contagious rash, forcing Grant to sleep on a sofa in the next room.
The *Hollywood Reporter* noted the story's improbability, praising the
leads' "charming" performance of "gyrations that nobody in all the
world—including them—believes for a moment would prevent the final
clinch."[179] Although the film followed Day's tradition of going "into the
bedroom, but never into the bed," the Catholic Legion of Decency still
frowned upon its glamorization of illicit sex.[180]

That Touch of Mink—which predictably ends in marriage for its
leads—comically illustrates the consequences of premarital sex for
the young working woman. As communicated in *Where the Boys Are,*
a woman who shows herself available risks becoming "cheap and common," ruining her reputation and chances for marriage. (For Day,
merely the *appearance* that she is sleeping with her millionaire boyfriend is potentially ruinous.) Yet the lead character is imbued with an
inner purity that allows her better impulses to triumph.

The film *Pillow Talk* granted Day greater sexual assertion, perhaps
because of her character's greater maturity and the film's emphasis on
curing the sexually repressed career woman. However, the film's closing
scenes were edited to protect her character's purity. After Jan discovers Brad's deception, he attempts to win back her affections by hiring
her to decorate his apartment. She is aghast at evidence of a playboy
lifestyle, particularly wiring that enables Brad to set up a seduction scenario. With a flick of a switch, the lights dim, the record player kicks
up, a bed folds out, and the door locks. She angrily acquiesces to decorating the apartment and does so in garish fashion.

As referenced earlier in this chapter, Brad responds to Jan's ploy in
a possessive manner. The script synopsis describes the confrontation:
"Brad storms over to Jan's apartment, kicks in the front door, hauls
her bodily out of bed. When she refuses to get dressed, he throws a
blanket around her and carries her to his apartment. Dumping her

Bachelor pad: Brad (Rock Hudson) begs interior designer Jan (Doris Day) to decorate his apartment in Pillow Talk. *Courtesy of Universal Pictures/ Photofest.*

unceremoniously on the sofa, he tells her that she decorated the place and she can keep it."[181] Here the script synopsis differs markedly from the final film, granting Jan sexual assertion: "Then he storms toward the door, but before he can reach it, Jan flips a switch that snaps the lock. As he turns toward her, she smiles, turns out the light and says, 'All apartments look alike in the dark.'"[182] While the Production Code granted the film other flirtations—such as a "sex suggestive" split-screen trick in which Brad and Jan face each other in separate bathtubs, and even Hudson's jokes about homosexuality—a premarital affair in which Jan appropriated Brad's tools of seduction was out of the question.[183] "The conclusion . . . should not include a sex affair. Specifically, eliminate Jan's line, 'All apartments look alike in the dark' and the subsequent action of the camera moving in," censors told Universal executives.[184] In the film, Brad and Jan merely smile lovingly at each other after he places her on the bed in her frumpy pajamas; the next scene cements their desires in marriage.

By curtailing Day's sexual assertion in this scene, the film followed a comedic formula that chastened the uptight career woman and restored her to traditional gender roles. Ultimately, it is Hudson who takes the final, decisive action. However, the debate over this scene illustrates how Doris Day's characteristic purity was crafted through careful negotiation. Much like Merritt and Caroline of the ensemble films, her character strikes a strategic balance. She learns to prioritize romance above her career, yet she successfully preserves her virtue for marriage. The edited ending also subdues the daring nature of Day's character, whom viewers could read as sexually experienced. As with *Boys' Night Out*, critics observed that "nothing really happens" sexually in a film that ostensibly revolves around sex. As *Variety* observed, "the principals seem to spend considerable time in bed or talking about what goes on in bed, but the beds they occupy are always occupied singly. There's more talk than action in this department, titillating but neatly skirting the blatantly sexual."[185]

By undermining the single woman's knowledge, punishing her transgressions, and purifying her moral stance, filmmakers and censors aimed to reinforce traditional morality and counter potential readings of these films as sexually licentious. However, critics and viewers often saw through these strategies. For example, they interpreted *Where the Boys Are* as inciting rebellion, dismissed *The Best of Everything* as too heavy-handed, or joked about the implausible purity of Kim Novak and Doris Day's characters. The disjuncture between the films' intent and their critical reception indicates that movies served multiple purposes in this era of mixed messages and quickly changing ideologies.

The single woman offered a refreshing alternative to the largely domestic media images of women in the 1950s and early 1960s, and her appearance contributed to the increasing sexualization of popular cinema, even if she ultimately abstained from sex. Although sleek wardrobes, soft lighting, and the occasional happy ending glamorized the "single girl," these characters also played into harmful stereotypes about female sexuality and ambition. Both breezy sex comedies and moralistic melodramas insisted that single women desired marriage above all else, that their career ambition was incompatible with feminine pursuits, and that both resolute chastity and reckless promiscuity were symptoms of sexual dysfunction. Even worse, melodramas hammered home that one wrong decision could ruin a young woman's chance for marriage, or even end her life.

Most of these films—as well as the novels and sexological studies that inspired them—were authored and directed by men, revealing the deep fear and suspicion they may have felt toward single women. Although Helen Gurley Brown and Rona Jaffe were notable women who wrote frankly from their own experiences, their radicalism was diminished as their books were adapted to film. Also, although these female authors presented possibilities for professional achievement and sexual pleasure outside marriage, they too emphasized the importance of maintaining one's femininity and finding a suitable spouse.

The weakened Production Code held sway over images of single women, relying on and reinforcing cultural norms in the censorship process. Characters who might have had affairs in film scripts fiercely guarded their purity. Ambition and sexual drive were deemed madness, and marriage the natural vocation for women. As they mocked and humbled their heroines, ultimately pairing them with paternalistic men, these films undermined the viability of female sexual pleasure and career ambition. Yet these sex comedies and sultry melodramas contained contradictions that may have advanced new ideas. As Jan in *Pillow Talk* cheerfully ran a decorating business and Caroline in *The Best of Everything* embraced her dual role as editor *and* girlfriend, these films hinted at alternatives to early marriage and lifelong domesticity. Although Helen in *Sex and the Single Girl* and Merritt in *Where the Boys Are* were ultimately revealed to be virgins, their bold statements against the sexual double standard may have resonated with some viewers. These films thus offered a new kind of heroine who gave credence to women's inner conflicts, presented alternatives to early marriage, and paved the way for more realized film and television representations of single women that would emerge later in the decade.

Leaving Home

Single Women's Perilous Journeys in Late 1960s
Television and Film

In the late sixties, two single heroines set off on parallel but divergent journeys from their humble hometowns to bustling New York, the epicenter of a national "swinging singles" scene. In the montage that opens the ABC sitcom *That Girl* (1966–1971), star Ann Marie (Marlo Thomas) journeys to the city by train, gazing upon skyscrapers with wide-eyed wonder. The city serves as a playground for the well-dressed woman, who peers in shop windows, prances with a parasol, and envisions her name in lights. The series, originally titled *Miss Independence*, established the normalcy of Ann's journey. "Thousands of girls every year do exactly what Ann is doing," Ann's mother reasons as her daughter first prepares to board the train. However, the series' concept also places independent Ann under the watchful gaze of her overbearing father and chivalrous boyfriend.[1]

For Anne Welles (Barbara Parkins), the "nice girl" at the center of the lurid melodrama *Valley of the Dolls* (1967), the journey from small-town New England to New York is far less celebratory. "You have to climb Mount Everest to reach the Valley of the Dolls," Anne intones in the film's opening scene. "It's a brutal climb to reach that peak." She narrates her journey as her train weaves through an austere winter landscape. "I never meant to start that climb," Anne admits as the train carries her from her heartbroken family and fiancé toward an uncertain future. When she approaches the city, the view from her window is not of statuesque skyscrapers but endless graveyards and industrial bridges. A winter haze descends upon the city skyline, rendering it both alluring and foreboding. "When will I return?" the theme song asks, longingly.[2]

Both narratives speak to the symbolic importance that urban life held for young single women in the late 1960s. Moving to the city provided women an escape from provincial mores and enabled them to pursue alternatives to early marriage. New York, in particular, offered chances for one's true talents to be realized. In *That Girl* and *Valley*, single heroines dream of breaking into show business and achieve at least momentary fame. Yet the fact that one narrative offered a promising future, the other ruin, echoes the news media's contradictory accounts of urban singles life.

Prompted by expanded career options and the stirrings of sexual revolution, many single women chose to delay marriage and pursue personal ambitions in the late 1960s. Rural singles often relocated to large cities, which offered not only white-collar jobs but also burgeoning singles scenes. However, as *Time* noted in 1967, the urban singles life offered both pleasures and pains.[3] While some media reports presented singles scenes as sites of personal fulfillment and innocent flirtations, others stressed their predatory nature and ruinous effects on women. Fictional film and television narratives drew from these divergent perceptions of the singles life, often placing an unwary heroine against a dangerous city.

In this chapter, I examine popular press accounts for evidence of the hopes and anxieties surrounding single women in the late 1960s. My analysis reveals that these young women were praised for their ambition and sense of adventure but were warned to expect loneliness, disappointment, and exploitation as they pursued their dreams in the big city. Single women's journeys provided rich material for a range of film and television genres—including domestic comedies, musicals, and melodramas—which I explore in the latter half of this chapter. These popular texts often emphasized characters' purity and femininity and directly addressed the dangers females faced upon leaving home.

Changing Attitudes toward Marriage and Careers

The average age of first marriage climbed only slightly during the 1960s, and media accounts continued to promote marriage as singles' eventual goal.[4] Still, news reports chronicled a wider rebellion against early marriage and domesticity among young women. In 1966 *Newsweek* hailed the rise of the "new feminists," a generation of idealistic, ambitious white college graduates who sought careers before marriage. College presidents interviewed for the article agreed that the "career drive . . . exceeds the mating drive" among their female students, crediting

The single girl steps out: Marlo Thomas in That Girl *(1966–1971). Courtesy of ABC/Photofest.*

this ambition to optimism fostered by the Peace Corps and civil-rights activism. "Young women today are assuming that they eventually will be absorbed in some important work," observed Radcliffe's president.[5] The women interviewed for the article scoffed at the traditional pressure to be engaged by college graduation and the accompanying idea that homemaking constituted their true vocation. "I'm going to have to marry a man who wants me to have a career," one unattached Vassar senior told *Newsweek*. "And should he change his mind, it would probably necessitate divorce."[6] This independent attitude was echoed in *Redbook*'s 1968 article on "women who refuse to marry," and by *Mademoiselle* readers who bragged about their single freedoms.[7]

It was the opportunity to live a little before getting married—rather than opposition to marriage itself—that fueled young women's ambitions. In a 1969 article provocatively titled "Young Lovers of the World Unite! But Don't Get Married Yet," a *Mademoiselle* author argued that couples who married at the typical age of twenty-two were headed toward divorce or unfulfillment. Citing Betty Friedan, she noted that many young marrieds feel dead inside because "they've never lived—not their own lives, anyway."[8] Women who remained single by choice or circumstance similarly emphasized the importance of self-development and career achievement prior to marriage. "I'm learning what I want out of life—and what I want from the future," said a Los Angeles advertising executive, still single at twenty-six. Added a twenty-three-year-old Chicago copywriter, "Until I learn who I really am, I'm not ready to be a good wife or mother."[9]

These new attitudes were facilitated by expanded work opportunities for women in the late 1960s. Growing numbers of women entered the workforce, encouraged by heightened demand for skilled and semi-skilled workers. Labor analysts noted particularly strong workforce participation among women under twenty-five, which they credited to a gradual decline in early marriage.[10] *Time* reported in 1966 that employers were increasingly willing to hire young women given the widespread use of birth control, which reduced the traditional fear that youthful employees would "marry, become pregnant, and quit."[11] The Civil Rights Act of 1964 also opened new opportunities for women of color—and women more broadly—by barring discrimination in hiring and establishing the Equal Employment Opportunity Commission. Although African American women workers continued to be concentrated in service and household work, young, educated African American women began to advance into clerical and professional fields in the late 1960s.[12] The founding of the EEOC also inspired unions and feminist groups to challenge gender-based discrimination, such as newspapers' common practice of listing job classified ads in separate "Male Help Wanted" and "Female Help Wanted" categories.[13]

Single women's increased independence and career ambition also corresponded with the rise of second-wave feminism in the late 1960s. While many single working women identified as feminists, others perceived the movement as too militant and anti-male.[14] However, real-life single women clearly inspired and benefited from second-wave feminist activism, which, as Ruth Rosen notes, addressed the fundamental inequalities that shaped unmarried women's lives—workplace discrimination, sexual exploitation, and lack of reproductive choices among them.[15] As I will explore later in this chapter, women within singles scenes and feminist circles also shared similar misgivings about the effects of sexual liberation.

Consumer Aspirations and Sexual Revolutions

As careers enabled single women to transcend the early marriage and domestic imperatives that had shaped their mothers' lives, these young women also rebelled against moral codes that would deny them sexual experience before marriage. Their sexual freedoms were encouraged and shaped by consumer culture and emerging political movements. John D'Emilio and Estelle Freedman argue that the single working woman of the sixties was "not only an accepted but also a necessary feature of economic life," both providing employees for rapidly expanding retail and service industries and promoting an ethic of consumption.[16] *Time* reported in 1967 that singles constituted a $60 billion market, and that advertisers strategically marketed the singles' image of "youth and glamour" to appeal to young marrieds.[17] According to D'Emilio and Freedman, "The consumer economy of the sixties helps explain how the singles culture could emerge from a period seemingly rooted in a marital ethic and why it won such ready acceptance."[18]

Single women also occupied a distinct place within the emerging sexual revolution, a movement composed of divergent and often contradictory strands.[19] The single girl's accentuated femininity and middle-class aspirations marked her as more conventional than counterculture radicals, who used sexual expression to challenge mainstream political and economic values more broadly.[20] Also, texts such as *Cosmopolitan*, which privileged single women's sexual pleasure and autonomy, were distinct from the messages offered in *Playboy* and counterculture publications, which premised the sexual revolution on male terms.[21]

While the singles culture was celebrated as a middle-class consumer phenomenon, the woman who publicly staked a claim to sexual pleasure was still a controversial figure, subject to harsh critiques from her elders. The revamped *Cosmopolitan*, which featured articles on female sexual response and pictured models with plunging necklines, was castigated by readers for promoting a "sex-sick, money-hungry, prestige-happy philosophy" and "reduc[ing] a woman to nothing but a stupid, idiotic *cow* of a sexpot."[22] One reader asked of the fashion spreads: "Since when are women expected to wear price-inflated . . . clothes, be skinny and look whorish?"[23] Parents used similar language when responding to the controversy surrounding Linda LeClair, a Barnard College student who informed a *New York Times* reporter in 1968 that she was living off campus with her boyfriend. In letters to the college administration, LeClair was publicly branded an "alley cat" and a "whore" for flouting the college's rules and questioning the double standard governing the behavior of college women. Beth Bailey argues that LeClair's critics reacted to not only her overt rejection of traditional moral codes, but also her desire to seek an equal partnership with her live-in boyfriend.[24]

If a fashion model or a monogamous college student could be labeled a harlot or a whore, the woman who truly engaged in promiscuous sex was an even more marginalized figure. The LeClair controversy reminds us that the sexual revolution encompassed not only promiscuous bar-hoppers but also many women who, whether by preference or convention, pursued sex within monogamous relationships. Drawing from studies of sexual attitudes and practices in the late 1960s, David Allyn argues that "modified forms of monogamy, not promiscuity, were the norm" among young adults.[25] Much like Linda LeClair, an increasing number of couples cohabited as an alternative to marriage, satisfying a need for companionship and stability even as they delayed their weddings.[26]

Bailey proposes an expanded definition of the sexual revolution as "a revolution in meaning" as well as behavior: "The sexual revolution was not just about the right to have sex with a stranger met at a singles' bar and to depart the next morning uncommitted and guilt-free. It was also about the right of unmarried people to express love sexually, and centered around a rejection of the understanding that equated a woman's value with her 'virtue.'"[27] Accordingly, the print media, television, and film texts I analyze in this chapter address not only the pleasures and consequences of promiscuous sex but also women's experiments with monogamy outside marriage. For single women who sought fleeting affairs as well as those who sought long-term partnerships, big cities provided sites to meet eligible men and freedom from parental oversight—as well as opportunities to develop new personal and professional identities.

The Allures of Mobility and City Life

An urban setting, which signaled expanded career opportunities and new social and sexual freedoms, was central to narratives featuring single women in the late 1960s. In an era when Americans were traveling abroad in record numbers, and the automobile increasingly served as a status symbol, the single woman was urged to escape the small town and suburbs for the greater adventures and freedoms of the city.[28] Magazines and advice books stressed the need for rural women to relocate, profiling key locales and even offering detailed guides on housing, employers, and social networks that the savvy newcomer might tap into.[29] Although New York and Los Angeles were destinations of choice, news media often presented the "singles scene" as a national trend with expressions in smaller cities such as Miami, Houston, and Seattle.

At a time when white-collar industries were booming, cities offered chances for career advancement and the possibility of pursuing more grandiose ambitions. As Helen Gurley Brown explained in her proposal for *Cosmopolitan*, the magazine would tell the woman who wanted to become an actress "not to stay back home in Lima, Ohio, like most articles on the subject do" but instead offer her "practical advice. Where to live. How much money to save up first."[30]

On a more practical level, moving to the big city was a means for escaping community and parental oversight. As one secretary observed: "Most people don't go *to* New York; they flee *from* their home towns."[31]

One woman justified her move from suburban Chicago to a swinging singles complex in Los Angeles by explaining that staying in Illinois "would have meant living at home—my father wouldn't permit me to live in the parts of downtown Chicago I could afford."[32] Others were attracted to the anonymity of city life, couching their independence in more sexual terms. "In New York you're your own person," a thirty-six-year-old single woman from the Midwest declared. "The druggist and the bus driver and the minister—they're not all looking over your shoulder studying your morals. You're free."[33] Another twenty-five-year-old woman from Missouri credited her new brazenness to urban life: "I would never go to a bar alone back home," she told *Newsweek*. "But here so many other girls do it there's no stigma."[34]

Mobility, and the opportunity to shape a new identity in the city, also held symbolic importance for women who failed to fit the white, middle-class model of the idealized single girl. Media scholar Laurie Ouellette argues that the "Cosmo Girl" philosophy was largely a narrative of class mobility, as Helen Gurley Brown often bragged about her rise from a working-class background and suggested a self-improvement regimen to hide the effects of a poor upbringing.[35] "Class is a state of mind," *Cosmopolitan* reassured readers in 1970. "It goes far beyond finances, all the way to matters of style and character."[36] At a time when young women of color were increasingly moving into white-collar career fields, *Cosmopolitan* offered career advice written by and for African American professionals, and the *Washington Post* reported on the growing number of black single women working in elite Georgetown circles.[37] In both the *Washington Post* report and *Ebony*'s annual feature on successful single professionals, African American single women served as symbols of racial progress and indicated barriers yet to be overcome. As the *Washington Post* reported, African American women working in government jobs "parroted successful whites" in their education and ambition and took advantage of new opportunities to advance in the workplace. Yet, as I will address later in this chapter, women of color often found their mobility and dating options were limited by legacies of segregation and entrenched racism on the part of employers and landlords.[38]

The narrative in which the (presumably) heterosexual single woman moves to the big city, discovering her identity and finding sites for congregation in the process, parallels the dominant narrative of gay and lesbian liberation, which would gain currency in the early 1970s.[39]

Although advice books and media reports presented the "single girl" as distinct from the single lesbian, these authors acknowledged that she was apt to encounter lesbians and gay men in her work and dating life. While some authors warned single women against falling prey to predatory lesbians, others, such as Helen Gurley Brown, urged sympathy for lesbians' "plight" and even permitted the single girl the occasional lesbian affair, as long as it did not preclude the greater goal of heterosexual partnership.[40]

"New Rules for the Singles Game": Balancing Femininity and Assertion

Moving to the city not only offered social mobility and sexual freedom, but also enabled the single woman to shape her identity within and against a commercialized singles subculture. New York City — where single bars proliferated and lines to get in stretched a half block — warranted the most media coverage, but smaller cities offered their own versions of the singles scene. Denver singles mingled at "woodsies," or outdoor excursions; Los Angeles singles apartment complexes compensated for urban sprawl; Chicago college students congregated at hip Laundromats. Computer-driven matchmaking services and private parties offered less public means to connect with kindred spirits.[41]

According to some media reports, these singles scenes transformed dating customs, particularly by putting young women in a more active and aggressive role. *Life* chronicled the national singles scene in a 1967 photo essay, presenting traditional dating arrangements as quaint and outmoded. "Once upon a time . . . a proper single girl attended church socials and mixers, and then waited hopefully by the telephone," the article intoned. "Today, however, there is a whole new set of rules for the singles game, otherwise called the dating-and-mating pattern."[42] An older system of dating etiquette — which had clearly delineated male and female roles and was shaped by community standards — had only limited applications for urban singles.[43]

Time noted that while even the "liberated career woman" might otherwise be hesitant or even embarrassed to walk into a bar and order her own drink, singles saloons "allowed them to enter without trepidation."[44] Alone or in pairs, these women engaged in assertive flirtations. The 1967 *Life* photo spread, for example, shows a single woman trying unsuccessfully to pick up a date at New York's Friday club. Once thwarted, she "plants a [kiss] on the next male she encounters—who happens to be a bartender."[45] Another *Time* article describes women roving the club scene, stopping to talk to eligible men, and moving quickly to the next table if they weren't interested.[46] "After all, there's little time to waste," *Life* reminds us, given the crowd of eligible, attractive women lined up outside.[47]

However, these single women often found their forward approach to meeting men was perceived as unfeminine and off-putting. "The [singles] scene really depresses me," one female newcomer to New York told *Mademoiselle* in 1968. "So many of the girls are hard; there's no gentleness about them." She advised these singles to "just take off some makeup, quit pushing and relax."[48] A bachelor quoted in a New York newspaper complained that the city "ruins women," draining them of "qualities like warmth and sincerity."[49] Female clerical workers interviewed for the book *The Girls in the Office* further questioned whether aggressive attitudes were effective in catching or keeping a man. "A girl can't swing as a single around New York; she'll just turn off all the men," said one thirty-six-year-old secretary. "She might get taken to bed a few times, but she'll never find anything meaningful or real. A woman can invite men out and consciously attempt seduction, but she'll soon find that New York men can't accept this."[50]

Perhaps anticipating this critique, Helen Gurley Brown insisted that *Cosmopolitan* represented "a new return to femininity and softness," and her magazine offered tips on pairing sexual assertion with accentuated femininity.[51] "I am terribly thrilled to be a girl," wrote the author of a 1968 *Cosmopolitan* article on how to pick up men. "I feel feminine through and through all the time."[52]

> I ask men to help me . . . everywhere . . . under all circumstances. They adore it!
>
> I ask men for advice, to explain things to me.
>
> I am soft—in my manner, in my voice, in my touch and smile, in the way I walk, I am not a pal or one of the boys. I am many things he is not—I am *feminine!*[53]

This advice piece emphasizes the importance of maintaining gender distinctions even as single women assumed a more active role in dating. As one Vassar senior quipped in 1966, "Being feminine is just being aggressive without letting men know you're aggressive."[54] Notably, *Newsweek*'s report on the "new feminists" reassured readers that feminine softness usually triumphed over assertion and ambition—the ambitious college students and career women they interviewed hoped to marry "dominant" men.[55]

Singles Scenes: Pure or Predatory?

According to media reports, femininity could serve not only as a dating tool, but also as a form of protection for the single woman. Some accounts eased anxieties about women's dating tactics by implying that sex had little to do with the singles scene—or at least was not a central motivation. When the staid *Ladies' Home Journal* covered the singles scene in 1966, it profiled not a hardened bar-hopper but a gentle kindergarten teacher who only reluctantly moved into a singles apartment complex, Los Angeles' South Bay Club. Describing Janet Hyland as a "sweet young lady who is learning to be a swinger," the article credited her "highly proper" and feminine character with keeping her out of trouble. "What protects Jan in situations that might bring disaster to other girls is her unfailing aura of innocence," wrote author Gael Greene. "When Janet Hyland goes to a man's apartment for a nightcap, that's what she gets."[56]

The bachelors interviewed for the article agreed. "As one of the club's more notorious wolves remarked: 'Jan has a sort of helpless and feminine quality. It makes you feel more protective than you meant to be.'" Said another male resident: "She's so incredibly feminine she makes you feel immensely masculine."[57]

However, the article insisted not only on Janet's virtue, but the essential innocence of the "live-in bachelor playground" where she lived. "Notorious wolves" aside, the most provocative aspect of South Bay Club life was a weekly forum on timely topics like Vietnam and birth control, according to this account. While residents joked about holding a "Roman Orgy," this too turned out to be more talk than action—merely a platonic costume party in which single residents dressed in togas to sip wine and eat grapes.[58]

Other accounts even put a positive spin on singles bars, claiming they were less about sex than fostering meaningful connections. *Newsweek* reported in 1966 that the enclave of singles bars on New York's East

Side were casually referred to as "The Body Exchange" but reassured readers that, "in practice, all that is usually exchanged is chitchat, telephone numbers and the promise of a Saturday-night date."[59]

"No one thinks you are a pickup," a twenty-three-year-old Berkeley graduate told *Time* about the San Francisco singles-bar scene. "The people I would like to meet would be horrified to think of me that way." That same *Time* article informed readers that in the typical singles bar, "The most a girl is expected to yield on first encounter is her phone number."[60] The article suggested that these encounters could lead to something permanent: one Denver singles bar claimed responsibility for facilitating thirty-five marriages. And what could be more innocent than a Chicago's singles washeteria, where young women explain to men "the mysteries of detergents and . . . help the boys fold their wash"?[61]

A *Mademoiselle* columnist announced in 1968 that she was proudly reclaiming the label "spinster," since the term "single girl" was saddled with "misleading *a-go-go* implications." She argued that singles "live clean," compared to their licentious married peers: "Why don't you hear much about premarital wife-swapping? Because it's not a big thing. And compared to swinging-doubles parties . . . those reputedly 'wild singles' get togethers are as innocent as the square dances in Kindergarten 1. (Or am I naïve? Nursery 1?)"[62]

However, another *Mademoiselle* column published the same year characterized the singles scene not as "Nursery 1" but as "Desolation Row." Two male authors of the regular column "Man Talk" claimed that bargoers in particular "are freely and unashamedly indulging in a practice that formerly reeked of sordid overtones—the pickup."

> For single men, it is like being let loose on a playground. The chances of scoring—*and we don't mean finding a wife*—are infinitely greater than they used to be. . . . For girls it's only the *facade* of a playground; underneath all that gaiety is a deeply hysterical quest for Mr. Right. . . . Now there are some nice things about this singles business. For one, it allows girls to go to a place unescorted without feeling like the town slut. For another, it gives you the chance to see that there are hundreds of others as miserable as you are. And that's about it.[63]

The authors' bleak account of the singles bar scene as exploitative and unfulfilling for women generated "a lot of letters" from *Mademoiselle* readers, most of whom vowed to avoid bars and "stop thinking [they] can meet anyone decent that way."[64] Even the libertine Helen Gurley Brown suggested that the single woman might make better use of her time. "When the bar closes at 2 A.M., everybody goes home with somebody, and very warm friendships are undoubtedly formed—at least from 2 A.M. to 9," she wrote. "Can you afford to pass them up? I'd say yes! If that's such a great way to meet men, how come those girls are back the next night forming new friendships?"[65]

These critiques of the singles scene, and singles bars in particular, operated under the assumption that women were looking for long-term romance and marriage, and were vulnerable to the advances of men with baser motivations. As a cab driver summed up the singles scene in *Look*, "The guys are lookin' for action, and the girls all look for marriage."[66] At times, the men vying for women's affections were not even single, but married men on the prowl.

These negative accounts also insisted that men within singles scenes were putting pressure on women to engage in sexual behavior that went against their better impulses—and against their very nature. In a 1969 *Cosmopolitan* essay titled "My Long, Long Night in a Singles' Bar," the author and her friend descend into a New York club that she likens to "a cellar, or a sewer."[67] Her report characterizes the bar as a predatory scene with the capacity to transform people into sexual animals:

> Something had happened to [my friend] Alice. . . . Her nostrils began to flare slightly, like a puma catching a mating scent on a jungle breeze. When I saw where she was looking, I saw men everywhere, a sea of eyes, predatory and insolent. Come on, baby, those eyes were saying. What do you say? Baby, let's go to your place, let's go to mine. . . . "My God," said Alice . . . "I feel like I'm being picked up on a bus. I could go to bed with fifteen men here, twenty men. I've never been through anything like this in my life."[68]

While some women sought sexual liberation by acknowledging their animal impulses and claiming their right to be as promiscuous as men, a growing chorus of critics questioned whether this behavior was truly liberating or healthy for women. (Alice, for her part, left the bar as quickly as she had arrived.) A 1968 *Cosmopolitan* article asked "How Sexually Generous a Girl Should Be," contending that "far too many girls have abdicated an active role in the sexual relationship and find themselves drifting aimlessly, almost lustlessly, from bed to bed out of resignation, routine, habit, passive nonresistance. And all this joyless bedding about is accomplished under the guise of sensuality and free love. . . . It is pitiful to be deluded."[69]

According to this article, these "deluded" single women were emotionally and sexually numb from being "pressured into behavior they *cannot* handle and aren't any good at."[70] As one twenty-four-year-old secretary described the "extraordinary" sexual pressure she experienced in the New York singles scene: "It builds up, date after date, until you can barely handle it. If you haven't gone to bed by the third or fourth date, he starts telling you that maybe you're frigid, maybe you should see a doctor and you start doubting yourself! . . . If you don't 'put out,' they wonder why you accepted the *first* date!"[71] That the fear of being frigid pushed some women into having sex echoes feminist complaints that women's sexuality was still pathologized and defined by male psychologists.[72]

Women within feminist circles, as well as singles scenes, grappled with the realization that "the sexual revolution [had] arrived on men's terms."[73] Much like the women interviewed in *Cosmopolitan,* one former Students for a Democratic Society member confessed in her essay "Sexual Revolution Is No Joke for Women": "I'd been pushing myself into 'freedom'—into sleeping with men I didn't give a damn about and sometimes wasn't even attracted to, because I'd gotten dependent on my notion of sex as fulfillment."[74] Her essay went a step further than *Cosmopolitan's*, however, characterizing the idea that women should mimic men's sexual behavior as one form of oppression of women. Did men's sex drive stem from "real, honest, animal lust," she asked, or was it a false construction contrived to maintain power?[75] In early consciousness-raising groups, feminists admitted to feelings of sexual inadequacy and their realization that "*more* sex did not necessarily result in *better* sex." While some feminist groups began to valorize a feminine ethic of emotional connection and commitment, others responded with a call for celibacy or a "no-sex" position.[76] Women within singles scenes were urged to rethink the terms of their new "sexual generosity." Asked *Cosmopolitan:* "If you are caught in the embrace of a man for whom yours is the most convenient bed, hasn't all meaning been lost? Is that giving? Or are you being taken?"[77]

Psychological and Physical Dangers

Beyond critiques of the commercialized singles scene itself, media accounts warned that the very aspects that attracted single women to the city—anonymity and autonomy—posed a threat to women's psychological health and physical safety. Sheer boredom was a resounding theme in *The Girls in the Office*, a collection of personal narratives that chronicled the experiences of single clerical workers in a New York firm. While one woman characterized her work as "eight and a half hours of painful monotony," others bemoaned their "bleak" dating prospects in a city full of "dullards and homosexuals."[78] As one twenty-five-year-old secretary complained, "Helen Gurley Brown . . . teaches that there's a wonderful, swinging, single life to be enjoyed . . . and she's full of crap. There is no pool of glamorous single men here, and there are damned few interesting single men at all."[79] To compensate for the lack of sexual and intellectual stimulation, most single women in this account resorted to alcoholism and affairs with married executives.

Washington Post columnists writing on the Georgetown singles scene in 1966 painted a similarly dreary picture of professional women's lives. By Judith Viorst's description, Washington was teeming with single women "cracking up from loneliness, being mistresses, living in deadly fear of rapists and purse snatchers, trying to decide which man to marry, or trying to face the dismal fact that they never will."[80] Fellow reporter Dorothy Gilliam noted that desperation and loneliness were particularly acute for African American women, who found that legacies of segregation limited their access to desirable housing and decreased their ability to meet eligible men. "The color problem smacks them in the face as soon as they arrive in the nation's capital and find they can't get the bargain apartments in suburbia," Gilliam writes. "Not anxious for long court fights, some move into Southern high rises which strain their budgets, or settle for apartments in neighborhoods with high crime rates and live in fear."[81] Both the *Post* and African American publications such as *Ebony* emphasized that professional black women's dating prospects were limited by the lack of single African American men, who were underrepresented in professional government jobs.[82] The overall ratio of women to men was also unfavorable. In Washington, D.C., for example, the ratio was four unmarried black women for every three unmarried black men. According to *Ebony*, many of these

81

eligible males "treasure[d] their playboy lives," and some preferred to date white women instead. "It's hard enough to find a nice escort in the capital," *Ebony*'s female reporter lamented. "Catching a prospective husband is almost impossible."[83]

Ebony and the *Washington Post* concurred that African American women who remain single after the fateful age of thirty "react to the loneliness by eventually becoming very nervous, taking tranquilizers and too many drinks," and invariably "become a prime target for the married man on the prowl." As one African American single woman admitted to the *Post:* "The whole thing gets pretty sordid and most of it seems to be predicated on sex. Yet there are many women in the town who are desperate and they do need somebody."[84]

Single women not only suffered poor psychological health, according to these reports, but also risked being victims of urban violence. In *The Girls in the Office,* single women complained of gropers and flashers in the subways, and menacing figures lurking outside their apartment windows.[85] Publications such as *Cosmopolitan* were rife with chilling reports of single women assaulted and murdered, either covertly in their own apartments or overtly on the street, within sight and earshot of indifferent neighbors.[86] Many of these violent reports stemmed from New York City, which struggled with a growing crime rate.[87] Yet these reports also amplified notions of the city as an unsuitable and unsafe place for lone women.

Prevalent images of unmarried women as desperate, drug-addicted, or endangered, spending their spare hours behind double-locked doors, competed with more rosy perceptions of urban singles life. Was the city the source of freedom and adventure for the single woman or primarily a site for sexual and psychological victimization? As they developed new representations that would be relevant to changing audiences, television and film producers drew from these divergent conceptions of the singles life, often deeming women's increased mobility and sexual freedom as a threat to their overall well-being.

Television and Film Trends

The commercial power of the singles market—and new demographic models that emphasized the need to reach youthful, female audiences—enhanced media producers' interest in representing urban singles.

Although the late 1960s series *That Girl* is often credited as the premier representation of the urban single woman on television, it built upon an established lineage of comedic representations. Early sitcoms such as CBS' *Meet Millie* (1952–1956) and *Private Secretary* (1953–1957) centered on dutiful office workers who occupied themselves by meddling in others' affairs. The single characters of *Our Miss Brooks* (1952–1956, CBS) and *How to Marry a Millionaire* (1957–1959, syndicated) repeatedly tried and failed to snag men, hindered by their strong personalities and lack of common sense. *That Girl*'s Ann Marie represented a break from these earlier representations in that she was self-focused and successful in romance, and had her own apartment — unlike earlier heroines who lived with family members or roommates.

Attempts to position the single woman as a dramatic and sexualized heroine on television were met with controversy and cancellation in the mid-1960s. ABC, which aimed to revive its flagging network by courting youthful consumers, pioneered the boldest representations.[88] The popular daytime soap opera *Peyton Place* (ABC, 1964–1969), based on Grace Metalious's best-selling novel about small-town sexual hypocrisy, featured teenagers and young women who pursued affairs within the town and journeyed to freedom in the big city. Although the series was much more tame than the scandalous novel that inspired it — rarely showing more than kissing onscreen — it was roundly denounced by religious leaders and the popular press as "an open sewer" and a "dirty joke."[89] Among the central characters was Betty (Barbara Parkins), whom the network described as "the fastest girl in town." Parkins's character was scheduled to be killed in the series' sixth episode, but her storyline inspired so much viewer interest and loyalty that she was kept on as a series regular.[90]

As Moya Luckett notes, *Peyton Place* offered one of the first storylines on prime-time television in which a young woman ventures to New York from a small town. Early in the series, Betty uses an unplanned pregnancy to persuade boyfriend Rodney to marry her. When Betty miscarries and the hasty marriage falls apart, she flees for New York City. Originally, producers planned Betty's departure as the start of a new spinoff series, "The Girl from Peyton Place," which would center on her adventures in New York. In early promotions, ABC executives described the series as "a well-told, well-acted story, not based on sex in any way."[91] When the series idea was shelved, producers turned

Betty's brief departure into a lesson on morality and the dangers of city living for young women.

Betty claims hers is a journey of self-actualization: "I want to prove I can be someone on my own," she tells her roommate. We watch as the dark-haired beauty enters an employment agency wearing a prim suit and expresses her desire to become a department-store model. "My dear child, the streets of New York are filled with girls who thought they could become models," the interviewer sighs. She chides Betty for expecting miracles and commands her to "go home" to Peyton Place. The tearful, penniless Betty is taken in by Sharon, a svelte, sophisticated single woman who possesses expensive furs and a spacious apartment. However, she begins to see the dark side of her roommate's lifestyle, as Sharon depends on a married man for her wealth and fulfillment, and has a medicine cabinet resembling a small pharmacy. "Sometimes a girl can go a long way on the right pill," Sharon admits.[92] The series' creators intended Sharon's depravity as a moral message. As a producer wrote in a memo: "To many youngsters in the audience, [Betty and Sharon] may well seem like a delineation of their own secret dreams of leaving Des Moines for the big time, and it is properly in our province to hint, at least, that the streets of New York are not necessarily paved with gold."[93]

Sharon sets up a blind date for Betty, which she accepts against her better judgment. Wearing a black dress and pearls, Betty gulps a strong drink and goes to dinner with businessman Roy. She is reluctant to reveal much about her past or her Peyton Place roots, which leads to a frightening miscommunication back at the apartment. In a dimly lit scene, Roy makes his move, first forcing Betty on the bed and then chasing her around the couch. By the time it dawns on him that Betty is not having fun, she is crying and cowered against the door, her hair wildly unkempt. Roy apologizes, then concedes: "Betty, you don't belong here. If you're smart, you'll pack and go home. The next man might not be as reasonable as I am." He places money in her trembling palm for train fare. She returns home in the next episode, the male voiceover declaring New York "not a dream, but a nightmare" for girls like Betty. Besides nearly being raped and befriending a kept woman, Betty causes her family members great concern, as they fear for her safety in the big city.[94]

The year after *Peyton Place* debuted, ABC offered a more direct representation of swinging singles culture in *Honey West* (1965–1966), an action series about a single spy. However, this autonomous, sexualized single heroine failed to capture an audience, and the series was canceled after one season. As Julie D'Acci describes the dilemma faced by ABC: "It was, in 1965, and has been ever since, extraordinarily difficult to portray the new (hetero)sexual woman in mainstream network prime time. From the outset, she could not be permanently bonded to one man; could not be seen as a 'sleepabout'; and could not be part of a traditional 'family.'"[95] The failure of *Honey West* bolstered existing fears that the single woman would alienate viewers and could not be taken seriously as a dramatic heroine. According to D'Acci, "The networks found it more fiscally sound to channel their efforts involving the new single woman into cheaper, more formulaic, and more predictable situation comedies."[96]

Television's need to appeal to a broad audience limited networks' ability to keep pace with changing sexual mores. In contrast, movies — which could be designated "For Mature Audiences Only" — offered a more modern take. Competition with foreign and art-house cinema led to greater explorations of sexuality in 1960s film, eventually leading to the demise of the Hays Production Code and the rise of a film ratings system in 1968.[97] "People today are insisting upon realism," Mark Robson, director of the film adaptation of *Valley of the Dolls*, told the *Los Angeles Times* in 1967. "They're more cynical, more sophisticated, less sentimental. They want the truth to be portrayed. They want to see sex on the screen and read about it."[98]

However, filmmakers still submitted scripts for approval by the Production Code Administration through 1968 and were conscious of concerns from some viewers about gratuitous sexuality in film. A 1967 *Redbook* survey reported that the majority of female filmgoers claimed to be offended by explicit sexual content, but that most viewers understood the difference between "sex as a natural and harmonious part of the plot and sex when introduced without relevance and strictly for shock value."[99] Robson, for his part, reassured audiences that *Valley of the Dolls* would not be "laundered rinso white" in its adaptation, nor would he take advantage of loosening censorship standards to make "something dirty." He insisted that *Valley* went beyond representing "sex for sex's sake" and could convey to young people "the pitfalls of certain ambitions."[100] As Robson's stance suggests, popular film narratives used the single woman's move to the city as an opportunity to broach sexual topics and to represent pleasures and dangers associated with the singles scene. Yet representations of independent and ambitious heroines served to reinforce moral messages that were similar to those conveyed in sex comedies and cautionary melodramas of the early 1960s.

The television and film narratives that I analyze were clearly shaped by genre conventions. As a situation comedy, *That Girl* used humor to soften controversial themes, situated the "single girl" within a traditional family structure, and resolved conflicts in the course of a half-hour episode. Much like the earlier "pregnancy melodramas," films such as *For Singles Only* and *Valley of the Dolls* often punished wayward women and offered ensemble casts who took different approaches to love, sex, and careers. As a film musical, *Thoroughly Modern Millie* did not promise realism, instead relying on its stars' theatricality and stereotypical supporting characters.[101] However, even this glib narrative addressed serious concerns about women's safety and gender expression. Despite their differences, these films and television programs explore common themes: the single woman's journey into the city, her negotiation of urban singles life, and her often perilous experiments with sexual liberation.

Television's *That Girl:* Innocent Ambitions and Sexual Stirrings

In *That Girl*, ABC introduced a comedic heroine more glamorous than many earlier television characters, yet far less daring than the single sleuth on the canceled series *Honey West*.

A youthful female lead posed a challenge for network executives who feared that a single woman could not carry a series, and the urban theme of *That Girl* clashed with the rural setting of most successful sixties sitcoms.[102] The series countered such concerns by placing the urban single woman squarely within a family dynamic. As a chaste, monogamously partnered working woman within arm's reach of her parents, Ann Marie clearly supported perceptions of the single life as essentially innocent. Yet, in comedic fashion, the series also addressed the threats that the city posed to the single woman's safety and morality.

Early promotions for the series emphasized its modern aspects. In a

1966 press kit, ABC promoted *That Girl* as a "sparkling" comedy offering "now-ness" and a "real-life touch." The network described Ann as a "high-spirited [woman] who seeks independence and an acting career in New York City," much like other young women who longed to "break away from home."[103] Thomas herself commented on the show's contemporary appeal, telling a reporter in 1966, "The time is ripe for this kind of format. The single girl is a subject that television has avoided. Just in the past few years has the young girl tried to find herself, to learn what she's all about before getting married. . . . She's much more intent on finding herself than in my mother's day."[104]

Although *That Girl* was largely created by men, Thomas wielded creative control behind the scenes as the head of Daisy Productions. In interviews, Thomas has taken credit for pitching the series to ABC and enhancing the realism of scripts and settings. For example, she helped male scriptwriters interpret how a young woman would behave during an argument, and she urged the set designers to furnish Ann's apartment with mismatched furniture to convey that she was newly on her own.[105] "You can't do a show about a young woman and not have a young woman part of the conversation," she flatly stated in a 2007 interview. From the second season onward, Thomas collaborated with a female story editor, Ruth Brooks Flippen, who had earlier penned scripts for the teen series *Gidget*.[106]

While Thomas's charisma and insight made the series "sparkle," so did the series' visual elements. Thomas's decision to film a single-camera series with a dubbed laugh track, rather than a staged comedy in front of a live audience, gave the show a cinematic quality. The series' opening scenes were filmed on location in New York instead of on a studio set. Also, *That Girl* debuted in the very season that ABC converted its full prime-time lineup to color, making Ann's colorful mod fashions and strolls through the city more vibrant for viewers.[107] Thomas's flip hairdo, designer wardrobe, and rising hemlines marked the star as a modern woman, even if her fashions were improbable on a working girl's income.

However, ABC emphasized that Ann was traditionally minded as well as modern, and that much of the series would focus on her romantic and familial relationships. "Ann Marie isn't all career girl," the 1966 press kit explained. "The idea is as ridiculous as spending the rest of her life at home with her parents." The network also reassured viewers that Ann remained "emotionally close" to her parents: "She's growing up but not away from them." Indeed, *That Girl* rose to fame as part of ABC's Thursday "Ladies' Night" lineup, following the established domestic hit *Bewitched.*[108]

Early episodes emphasized Ann's efforts to achieve independence yet remain in her family's good graces. The series' second episode, in which Ann makes her journey to the city, explains her voyage as both natural and common. A narrated cartoon sequence at the beginning features a family of birds, in which a "fledgling tries its wings and flies away from the nest"—comically plummeting to the pavement below. The scene then switches to urban New York. "This is Manhattan island, the destination of many modern American fledglings," the narrator informs us. "No matter what they're seeking, young people seem to feel this is the place they can find them."[109] However, the series is curiously devoid of the singles culture that attracted those flocks of "modern American fledglings." The original, unaired pilot episode placed Ann in a women's boardinghouse, where three single friends—one of them a stewardess—were her closest companions.[110] The revised concept granted Ann a lone apartment with only one married woman as her neighbor, and later in the series she is denied even this female camaraderie. While this absence of community made *That Girl* less politicized, it also reflected the tendency of sitcoms to address social change through exceptional, individual characters rather than emphasizing collective struggles.[111]

Unlike the real-life single women who drove cross-country to sever their ties to overprotective families, Ann keeps in close contact with her parents, who often drop in unannounced. "New York is only 40 miles away," she reminds her tearful mother, as she leaves for the first time. "I'll call you tonight." Her father phones three times soon after she arrives in her new apartment; she graciously accepts his calls but mutters to herself, "I didn't talk to him *that* much when I *lived* there." The inclusion of her parents as series regulars broadened the appeal of the series to swinging singles and sedate marrieds alike. In the tradition of domestic situation comedy, *That Girl* emphasized the importance of family unity. Ann pursued her goals but sought to preserve her relationship with her parents and boyfriend.[112]

While early episodes dramatize Ann's efforts to achieve independence from her worried parents, she also demonstrates her loyalty to them. In the episode "What's in a Name?," Ann decides to keep her father's less-than-marketable surname, Marie, rather than change her name to further her budding acting career. The plotline may have been a veiled reference to Thomas's own career. Marlo was the daughter of established television comedian and producer Danny Thomas, and she struggled to prove that "she is a capable performer in her own right, not just the daughter of a big star." Before she got her big break in a London theater production, she had considered changing her surname, and she reportedly rejected her father's help in pitching the series to ABC.[113]

Ann's escape to the city, the opening episodes clarify, is more about pursuing acting jobs than sexual freedom. The first episode pairs Ann with a steady boyfriend, Donald (Ted Bessell); from their first date onward, the two are inseparable. The couple frequently meet with Ann's parents, who comment on the unconventionality of their relationship. In the first-season episode, "What Are Your Intentions?," Ann's father insists that eight months of dating should lead to a marriage proposal. "Do you want to marry my daughter?" he asks Donald as Ann eavesdrops from the neighboring kitchen.[114]

Before her boyfriend can answer, Ann rushes in to inform her father she's not waiting for a proposal. "Don and I are very fond of each other, but at the moment marriage is the furthest thing from our minds," she explains. "Besides, I don't want to get married just yet. I have my career to think about." Donald adds that it may take two years before he is "financially secure" enough to support a wife. When Ann's father suggests the couple date other people until they are ready for marriage, they give it a halfhearted attempt. Predictably, both are miserable in the new arrangement and recommit to monogamy by the end of the episode.

As they seal their renewed commitment with a kiss, Ann improvises mock wedding vows. "Do you promise to love, honor and cherish me as long as I love, honor and cherish you?" she asks as Donald nods his consent. "I now pronounce us boy and girl," she announces, her choice of wording both providing them a symbolic commitment and marking them as young people who will mature into marriage. However, Ann's insistence on postponing wedding plans echoes the attitudes of many young college graduates who chose to delay marriage to develop independence and pursue careers.

Actress Marlo Thomas's portrayal of Ann is at once relevant and retrograde, resembling Doris Day's image in several respects. Like Day,

Constant companion: That Girl *featured a chaste and committed relationship between Ann Marie (Marlo Thomas) and Don Hollinger (Ted Bessell). Courtesy of ABC/Photofest.*

Thomas plays a character younger than her years (scripts hint that Ann is in her very early twenties), is perpetually perky, and dons a fashionable wardrobe implausible on a struggling actress's salary. As in Day's early 1960s sex comedies, she is continually put in sexual situations but adheres to her principles. In one first-season episode, a snowstorm and overbooked hotel conspire to make Ann and Donald sleep in the same hotel suite. Ann, visibly unnerved, pulls her winter coat around her for protection; Donald mutters that he deserves a boy scout merit badge, and the two retire to separate beds. In such episodes the final punch lines are reserved for Ann's father, who learns that the couple is sharing a room and must be reassured of his daughter's chastity.[115]

While Ann's traditional parents expected that eight months of steady dating should lead to marriage plans, youthful audiences had expectations of their own. As *Look* Magazine wrote in 1967 about Marlo Thomas's portrayal of Ann:

In one episode of *That Girl*, boyfriend Ted took his shoes off, and Marlo squealed about what funny feet he had—as if she'd never seen them before. "Come *on*," wrote in one viewer (from Berkeley, no doubt), who questioned the credulity of a young actress going around with a boy for so long and not being more intimate with him. "Well, I just can't play it as if they're having an affair," says That Girl. "That's too thick."[116]

Look's article—which labels Thomas's character a "paper doll" and "Petunia Pure"—acknowledges the chasm between *That Girl* and the sexual mores of modern urban dwellers. However, by positioning the dissatisfied viewer as being "from Berkeley, no doubt," the article implies that only youthful, radical viewers would look to television for sexual realism. According to the article, the twenty-nine-year-old Thomas acknowledged "that no girl . . . [in] show business stays as bright and fresh and sweet as the character she plays." She defended her character by explaining the limitations of the medium: "But this is television, and it's comedy, and you have to keep it in the realm of hot air. What I do is just keep playing the character as if she is just beginning. That's what people want."[117]

The 1968 *That Girl* episode "Call of the Wild" both plays upon Ann's implausible purity and acknowledges her sexual impulses. Burned by a casting director's perception of her as "wholesome" and "fresh-scrubbed," Ann decides to cultivate a little sex appeal. The experiment begins innocently enough: standing in front of the mirror in her bathrobe, munching Eve-like on an apple, she extends one shapely gartered leg. She tosses the apple aside and performs an impromptu striptease as the soundtrack kicks up with bawdy music and wolf whistles. Just as she is putting her whole body into the dance, casting her robe off to reveal a lacy camisole, she gains an unexpected audience: Daddy, who has entered through the unlocked apartment door to check on his daughter. "Put that back on!" he shouts.[118]

The embarrassed Ann reflexively crosses her arms over her chest, then drapes her father's overcoat over her exposed body. Her father declares: "If this is what living in New York is coming to, I absolutely refuse to let it continue." Alarmed that Ann might "put on an exhibition like that for television," he orders her: "Pack your things, you're coming home."

When Ann explains she was merely trying to conjure up some "sex appeal," her father is only mildly comforted. "Sex appeal? That's fine talk, coming from a little girl from Brewster," he snorts, jokingly threatening to move next door to her to guard her chastity. While the conflict with her father is quickly diffused, this brief dialogue positions city life and sexualized media culture as a corrupting force on single women, capable of transforming innocent "little girls" into sexual sirens.

While the aired episode of "Call of the Wild" presents the striptease as a momentary impulse, the original script presents the scene as both more provocative and premeditated. In the original version, Ann studies herself in the mirror in her work clothes, adopting "various seductive poses." She then changes into a sexier outfit—high heels, a low-cut dress with jacket, and a feather boa—and "slithers into the room like a burlesque stripper coming on stage." As she performs with "*good-humored* abandonment that Gypsy Rose Lee in her best days might have envied," off-stage voices yell: "Take it off! Take it off!" Her father enters just as Ann is unbuttoning her jacket, then rushes to cover her with his overcoat. In this version, Ann reacts with a "mixture of half-embarrassment, half amusement."[119] This version of the script—in which Ann *plans* the striptease and is amused by her father's indignation—suggests that the writers did not always perceive her character as wholly "Petunia Pure."

In the aired version of "Call of the Wild," Ann recovers from her striptease fiasco and tests her budding sex appeal on her boyfriend. Relaxing with Donald in her apartment after a movie date, she surprises him with her forward approach. Leaning toward him in her leather minidress, she asks, "When we're alone together, and you look at me, like now, what happens? . . . Do you feel something so uncontrollable inside of you? Something along the lines of, say, animal passion? Visibly uncomfortable, Donald answers cautiously. "You could say animal passion, tempered with respect, of course." As he moves hastily toward the door, Ann embraces him in a passionate kiss, which he shrugs off. The phone rings, and Ann turns her attention to her father's call as her boyfriend makes a swift exit.

Although Donald refuses to take the bait, Ann's amorous middle-aged employer decides later in the episode that she does, indeed, have sex appeal worth pursuing. After a successful commercial shoot, he drives Ann home, invites himself into her apartment, and pins her to a wall. Donald, hearing Ann's protests through the apartment door, rushes in to pull the casting director off Ann and accidentally tears her

knit dress in the process. Ann's father arrives just as the couple is re-
pairing her torn dress and angrily accuses Donald of making a rough
sexual advance. As the original script describes the setting, "Don has
the two pieces of the strap of Ann's dress in his hand. It looks like he's
about to pull them apart."[120]

Embarrassed by his mistake, Lou admits he was just worried about
"Ann, living here all alone, a beautiful young girl with sex appeal." The
episode acknowledges that Ann's sexuality must be carefully controlled,
as it poses a threat both to the equilibrium of her relationship and her
own safety. (Ann, for her part, is delighted that the casting director and
her father finally recognize her sexual nature.) By stopping the striptease, ending the date early, and interrupting what appears to be sexual
assault, Ann's ever-present father and boyfriend save her not only from
sexual victimization but also the loss of her best judgment. Her father's
earlier comments about New York's corrupting influence on Ann and
the risks she takes "living here all alone" remind us that it's not just
overeager boyfriends and abusive employers that pose a threat to her
morals, but city life itself.

Although *That Girl* often presented its heroine as both pure and
compliant, scriptwriters clearly grappled with perceptions of city life
and showbiz as corrupting for their young heroine. In the third-season
episode "Sock It to Me," Ann receives a movie role opposite a Broad-
way star. The humor revolves around her refusal to slap her costar as
directed in the play. However, the original *That Girl* script suggests that
Ann makes other compromises when the director asks her to "stimu-
late" the scene by "show[ing] a little leg." Her male costar faces her
with a "lascivious sneer." Ann gulps, hesitates, then hikes up her skirt,
whispering "Sorry, Daddy," under her breath.[121] This scene—which
was firmly crossed out of the script—presents Ann's sexuality as a trait
she exploits to further her career, much like the wayward women in the
contemporaneous film *Valley of the Dolls*. However, it also reinforces her
need for her father's approval.

Scripts were edited to protect Ann's femininity as well as her purity. In the 1967 episode cleverly titled "There's Nothing to Be Afreud
of but Freud Himself," Ann and Donald meet with a psychologist. In
the original script, Donald accuses Ann of being "pretty aggressive at
times." However, this term was removed in subsequent script edits: "aggressive" was crossed out, replaced with the gentler terms "stubborn"

and "argumentative."[122] While this may seem a minor change, it does reveal scriptwriters' effort to use language that would not impugn the character's femininity. It also may have reflected Thomas's experiences behind the scenes. As Thomas reflects in a 2007 commentary: "As a female producer I was being told I wasn't feminine. That it was too assertive, it was too aggressive, which somehow were male words. . . . It wasn't feminine to be assertive, to take command, to seize power."[123] Much like the Vassar college student who defined femininity as "being aggressive without letting men know you're aggressive," Thomas tempered her assertion with compliance to gender norms. "In the softest, most luxurious way . . . [I got] what I needed for the character."[124]

Single Women and Race Relations

In addition to negotiating changing gender roles, *That Girl* occasionally commented on Ann Marie's racial identity. Thomas was of Lebanese heritage, and producers emphasized the dark-haired heroine's whiteness. Bespectacled, curly-haired actor Harold Gould, who played Ann's father in the series' unaired pilot, was deemed "too Jewish" and replaced with the more anglicized Lew Parker.[125] Additionally, as *That Girl* shifted to more "topical" plotlines in its third season, Ann Marie confronted her racial privilege. In a 1969 episode, Ann befriends an eight-year-old African American boy after he is caught shoplifting and tries to take him home. When the boy informs her he lives on Park Avenue, Ann urges him to tell the truth. He regales her with stories of a large family, an abusive father named "Joseph X," and life in a slum among "fat rats."[126]

Ann attempts to return the child to a tenement apartment, only to meet with hostility and indifference from the apartment manager. However, she soon learns the child really does live on Park Avenue and reunites him with his father, a wealthy, well-dressed, upstanding comedian. The experience forces her to reflect on her own prejudice. As she admits to Don: "If he weren't black, I wonder if I would have believed him so quickly." She and Don briefly discuss their responsibility to create change so that no child needs to live in abuse and poverty. While the intended message is progressive, the boy's stories do advance stereotypes of violent black men and neglectful parenting, consistent with the 1965 Monahan Report, which blamed African American poverty on familial dysfunction.[127] Although the boy does have a loving father, he is lacking a mother and tries to adopt Ann as a maternal figure. This aspect of the episode emphasizes the single girl's maternal qualities and suggests that this stranger is better suited to motherhood than the child's own family members. Also, the child only meets Ann after he has stolen a candy bar, cementing associations of black youth with criminality.

That Girl was not the only media narrative of the time to present problematic relationships between white women and people of color. In the TV film *Gidget Grows Up* (1969), college-aged Francis "Gidget" Lawrence—based on the earlier teen sitcom character—moves to New York to become a tour guide for the United Nations. The job brings her in contact with a diverse range of people, including her roommate Minnie Chan (Helen Funai). When Gidget (here played by Karen Valentine) initially assumes Minnie is from China and compliments her on her English, Minnie gently corrects her. "I *am* Chinese, American style," Minnie says, laughing. "I'm from Reading, Pennsylvania." Although this brief dialogue challenges stereotypes, and positions Minnie as assimilated, she serves primarily as Gidget's sidekick throughout the film and habitually offers words of ancient Chinese wisdom culled from the fortune cookies her family mass produces. According to a 1970 *New York Times* article, even the most assimilated Asian Americans battled perceptions of themselves as foreigners—a perception that Minnie deflects in her conversation with Gidget but supports through her fortune-cookie shtick.[128]

Gidget's relationships with men of color are far less positive. She is trailed by an Arab man who follows her around the United Nations and even stands menacingly outside her apartment window in hopes of recruiting her for his harem. He is dressed traditionally in a long robe and turban, and Middle Eastern music plays every time he appears. Gidget's voiceover refers to him as "one unidentified Arab" but later reveals he is a wealthy sheik named Abdul. Although his cultural difference is ultimately played up for comedy, Gidget's fears of this dark-skinned, foreign man parallel white women's stated fears of minority men in real life. The production of the film also reinforced racial boundaries in romance. Gidget was originally scripted to date a Latin American UN representative named Eduardo, but producers changed the character to be a decidedly white Australian.[129]

Minority characters also play menacing roles in the 1967 movie musical *Thoroughly Modern Millie*, a story of two flapper-era singles braving the big city. Unlike Ann Marie and Gidget's generic apartment buildings, the perky heroines of *Thoroughly Modern Millie*, set in 1922 New York, seek the protection of the Priscilla Hotel for Single Young Ladies—and face the graver threat of being sold into a "white slavery" operation in Chinatown. The hotel is guarded by a villainous, racially ambiguous housemother (Bea Lillie) and her bumbling Chinese henchmen, who drug and kidnap unsuspecting residents. The racist characterization of the captors plays upon silent-film formulas that positioned Asian men as the kidnappers and sexual oppressors of white women.[130] White slavery—or more specifically, the practice of kidnapping young women and selling them into prostitution—was a documented concern for single women, especially recent European immigrants, prior to 1920 and was dramatized in several early films.[131] Reviewers commented on *Millie*'s racial casting: One New York reviewer suggested that the Chinese male characters are silent in the film not because they are "inscrutable," but because they are embarrassed by the "rancid, insipid" script.[132] Another found the "Fu Manchu touches" comical, writing that apartment manager "Bea Lillie is such a droll villainess that her wiles and plots evoke guffaws instead of chills."[133]

Whether perceived as spoof or stereotype, the racialized themes of *Millie* and other media texts are important to understanding concerns about single women's safety in 1960s New York. Low-rent apartment complexes often placed young white women in close proximity to racial Others: One white woman interviewed for *The Girls in the Office* in the late 1960s freely complained about the dark-skinned men who threatened her sense of safety.[134] Urban race riots and the perceived militancy of civil-rights activism in the late 1960s fueled widespread fears of black men. Although Asian Americans were not as prominently represented in media culture, both the *New York Times* article and the film *Gidget Grows Up* indicate that even assimilated young Asian Americans were perceived as foreigners.[135]

The victims in *Thoroughly Modern Millie* are preyed upon as they sleep and disappear into white slavery operations without a trace—much like real-life 1960s women who were stealthfully assaulted and murdered in their urban apartments. Yet the film text sets up people of color as a convenient scapegoat. *Cosmopolitan* reported in 1967 that the increasing number of crimes committed against young white women in urban areas were largely committed by "lily-white" men and could not be blamed on racial conflict. Other newspaper articles confirmed that whites' fears of African Americans in the late 1960s were unfounded, as interracial assaults were uncommon.[136]

Aggressive Androgynes and Demure Damsels: *Millie*'s Gender Politics

While *Millie*'s dark undertones reflected the historical threats asso- ciated with women's move to the city, the musical largely served as a romantic farce about femininity and tradition. Both *That Girl* and *Thor- oughly Modern Millie* counter their heroines' independent spirit with feminine appearances and ambitions. *That Girl*'s heroine is marked as girlish, as she desires protection from the two men in her life. Thomas's trendsetting look—including short dresses adorned with huge bows, and heavy makeup that accentuates her large eyes and rosy cheeks— adds to the youthfulness and femininity of her character. In *Thoroughly Modern Millie*, the title character pairs a more androgynous look with an aggressive attitude and aspirations toward equality. However, mar- riage remains central to her immediate goals, marking her as more con- ventional than Ann.

Producer Ross Hunter, who had earlier produced *Pillow Talk*, claimed *Millie* offered a "clean" alternative to the trend toward sex, vio- lence, and perversity in film. Although it was set in the Roaring Twen- ties, critics noted parallels to modern "swingers," as *Millie* parodied an era when "young people looked and acted almost as funny as some of them look and act today."[137] One reviewer deemed Millie both an "equality-for-sexes flapper" and a "parallel to today's mini-mod" as she "swings . . . and lives exuberantly." Another called her a "symbol for the new woman of America."[138]

The film's opening musical sequence introduces us to Millie (Ju- lie Andrews), an ambitious newcomer to New York who looks to her contemporaries for cues on how to dress and behave. Millie marks her entrance into city life with a dramatic makeover: She sheds her luxuri- ous curls for a sleek bob, trades her flowing black dress for one with a short pleated skirt, and takes up cigarettes. Noticing that the new fashions are more flattering on flat-chested women, she is fitted with

97

Feminine flourish: In Thoroughly Modern Millie, *Trevor Graydon falls for the feminine Dorothy* (right) *as Millie looks on.* Left to right: *John Gavin, Julie Andrews, and Mary Tyler Moore. Courtesy of Universal Pictures/Photofest.*

constraining undergarments and admires her androgynous flapper figure. "Goodbye, good-goody girl," she sings. "Here comes thoroughly modern Millie now." However, the artificial constraints are not enough to contain her full bustline, which resurfaces at the end of the opening musical sequence, to Millie's dismay and embarrassment. Her attempts to contain her inner feminine, romantic nature and become "one of the boys" similarly fall flat.[139]

Millie walks back to the Priscilla Hotel just as wealthy, aspiring actress Miss Dorothy (Mary Tyler Moore) arrives in a cab. While Dorothy's pin curls, bonnetlike hat, soft voice, and shy demeanor mark her as wholly feminine, brash Millie has a different self-image. "Women today are free," she reminds Dorothy. "We can go out into the world and make a living for ourselves, and I fully intend to." That night Millie meets Jimmy—a lithe, flamboyant single man—at a dance, takes a death-defying drive with him to the hills, and aggressively makes out with him at length in the front seat of his red car. Between kissing sessions, she sits up straight and informs Jimmy that she cannot commit to anything long term, as she plans to secure a stenographer job and marry her wealthy boss. The idea of working only to achieve marriage—to a wealthy man, at that—seems somewhat retrograde, but Millie pairs this ambition with a modern attitude.

"I'm your equal," she insists, as she attempts to physically dominate Jimmy in the car's front seat. "I'm going to meet you men on your own terms. Cater to your craving for efficiency. Learn to talk sports, tell jokes, smoke, drink, and yes," she adds, as he nuzzles her neck, "if I have to, I'll even kiss you back." She takes Jimmy's head in her hands and kisses him firmly, as the two sink into the seat. "You see," she concludes, "love has nothing to do with it."

"Now's the time for fun! Especially for the New Woman," she declares. "The old rules are out, and they haven't made up new ones yet."

"Gee," says the smitten Jimmy. "I never met a modern before."

Millie's perceptions of modern dating—in which long-term love is no longer the primary goal, and rules of etiquette have been replaced by more forward behavior by young women—echo media reports on the 1960s singles scene. That she associates equality with adopting masculine mannerisms and interests corresponds with the popular concern that both career women and single swingers were at risk of losing their femininity.[140]

In the following scene, Millie goes job hunting. She chooses her prospects carefully, calling ahead to inquire about the marital status of the company president. When Millie meets her new boss, the classically dark and handsome Trevor Graydon, the film's soundtrack serenades them with a humorous medley of "The Hallelujah Chorus" and "Babyface." Spotting sports trophies on her boss's desk, Millie feigns interest in baseball and golf, and she earns the job by taking accurate dictation and producing a letter in record speed. To her chagrin, Trevor rewards her efficiency by granting her a male nickname: "John." While trying to get her boss's attention as a woman *and* an equal, she accepts a date with seemingly carefree, underemployed Jimmy.

Millie is a narrative of class mobility. The heroine seeks to improve her class status through refashioning herself and marrying up, just as

99

Helen Gurley Brown had long advised single women to do in her advice writings. Millie is inspired when she meets Muzzy (Carol Channing), a twangy-voiced former showgirl who married a millionaire and inherited his mansion. Muzzy invites Millie, Jimmy, and Dorothy to an overnight party at her estate, performing a magic trick en route. "Love is very, very near," she predicts with a wink, handing an ace of hearts card to Millie. At the party Millie is surrounded by slim figures in imported silk and is embarrassed to be visible as a working girl in her plaid dress. She is torn between her budding attraction to Jimmy and her commitment to marrying a man above her class status. She confides in Muzzy, who urges her to marry for love rather than money. Just as Millie opts to romance Jimmy instead, dressing herself in a flowing feminine nightgown, she happens upon him waving the demure Dorothy into his room. Back at the Priscilla Hotel, Millie lashes out at Dorothy, advising her to crop her curly hair for a more modern look.

"Starting tomorrow I'm going to be unspeakably fatal," Millie decides. Dressed in a severe, form-fitting black-and-white dress and a tight hat that nearly covers her eyes, she strides into her office in pursuit of her boss. "What is your opinion of [taking a woman] by brute force?" she growls, posing provocatively on his desk. Trevor, flustered by his stenographer's forward behavior, orders "John" to return to work instead and soon finds a more feminine companion. Standing outside with Millie during the lunch hour, Trevor's eyes meet with Dorothy's, and a romantic ballad cues up. He is horrified to learn of Dorothy's plans to cut her hair: "Bobbed? With your beauty?" The perturbed Millie looks on as Dorothy—dressed in delicate ruffles and an oversized Sunday hat—accepts a dinner date.

The aggressive Millie cannot compete with Dorothy, who only needs to lower her eyes and bat her eyelashes to attract the modern male. And—like the "new feminists" in the *Newsweek* article who paired their career ambitions with the need for a domineering mate—Millie's statements about wanting equality differ from what she truly desires in a relationship.[141] In one scene, Jimmy tries to win back Millie's affections by scaling ten stories to enter through her office window. As she opens the revolving window to let him in, Millie falls outside and dangles from a flagpole until she is rescued by Jimmy's strong arms. She is touched by this grand gesture and accepts a dinner date. When Dorothy is drugged and sold into white slavery, Jimmy cross-dresses as a flapper and goes undercover to find her, ultimately relying on Millie to rescue them both. However, this overt gender-role reversal is undermined in the film's final scenes.

By the end of the narrative, Millie learns that Jimmy is really a millionaire in disguise; Dorothy is his sister, and Muzzy his stepmother. By casting aside her materialistic ambitions for true love (and proving herself to be a "good, old-fashioned girl" in the eyes of Jimmy's butler) she has earned the prize of marriage and assumes an appropriately feminine role. "I don't want to be your equal anymore," she tells Jimmy. "I want to be a woman. A dandy little bundle for a fellow to cuddle." She promises to grow out her curls again as their kiss dissolves into a scene from their wedding.

Thoroughly Modern Millie highlights the advantages of assuming an aggressive front but suggests that success in romance ultimately requires, to use *Cosmopolitan*'s wording, "a new return to femininity and softness."[142] Millie's aggressiveness did help her survive the dangers of the city and advance in her secretarial career—in contrast to Dorothy, whose softness made her easy prey for abductors. Although Millie's modern nature also seemed to initially attract Jimmy, he recognized the "old-fashioned girl" underneath and seemed to welcome her return to a more traditional role. Millie's narrative resembles accounts of 1960s singles, who realized the aggressive approach that they used to navigate dating scenes was of little utility in maintaining a long-term romance. Like many of her 1960s contemporaries, Millie is both thoroughly modern and traditional as she eagerly surrenders her hardened exterior upon finding true love.[143]

Naive Women and Deceptive Men: *For Singles Only*

While most single heroines of the late 1960s either lived alone or in drab women's hotels, the 1968 B-movie *For Singles Only* dared to situate them within a coed swinging-singles complex. Like *Thoroughly Modern Millie*, the film contrasts different approaches to dating and gender expression, presenting the singles scene as simultaneously desirable and dangerous. Although the film is set in Los Angeles rather than Fort Lauderdale, and features career women rather than college students, *For Singles Only* seemed to borrow characters and plot conventions directly from the 1960 comedy *Where the Boys Are*.

The film glorifies the singles life as a commercial phenomenon. According to *Variety*, the film was "juiced exactly right for what is supposedly the biggest block of regular moviegoers." The film opens with aerial shots of singles socializing by a turquoise swimming pool, appealing to what *Variety* termed "the under-25 audience of pseudosophisticates who presumably would love to live like this."[144] The setting is an apartment complex called Sans Souci (a French term for "carefree"), and the upbeat theme song refers to a "new scene", and "mad way of living." Supporting character Nydia works for a computerized dating service, a reminder that singles are reinventing and modernizing romance. Additionally, posters for the film play up a sexualized perception of the singles life. "See how the single half lives!" trumpets the headline, beneath the poster's central image of a couple embracing behind an apartment door. The woman is wearing a swimsuit that exposes her back; the man looks over her shoulder with a sly expression. The press book promises "all the fun, fury and excitement of the boy-girl togetherness apartments . . . where it's party time 24 hours a day!"[145] The movie further emphasizes sex through close-ups of female residents in bikinis and a poolside pageant in which women display their painted legs and midriffs as works of art.[146]

Despite these provocative visual elements, marriage, rather than sexual freedom, is the key motivation of the women in this film. The *Hollywood Reporter* described the main narrative as "guys on the make and the chicks who suffer a rutty ride to the altar."[147] In the opening scenes, a wedding party leaves the apartment complex as new residents Anne and Helen walk in. At first glance the women seem remarkably similar—both are elegant, slim brunettes with long hair and dark eyes, and critics remarked on their resemblance—but the film continually contrasts their approaches to sex and dating.[148] Sensible Anne (portrayed by Mary Ann Mobley, a former Miss America), is a former Peace Corps volunteer who brags she knows how to say "no" to men in seven languages. In scene after scene, she talks back to and even slaps dates who dare to get fresh with her. Helen (portrayed by Lana Wood, younger sister of Natalie) is a librarian with a "genius-level" IQ of 155. Her intellectual clout, however, is paired with naïveté about dating.

When Helen first meets fellow apartment-dweller Gerald, she's spouting statistics about Los Angeles' climate. He claims to like "intelligent girls"; the two tour an art gallery together and bond over their

For Singles Only: *Apartment manager Milton Berle inducts newcomers Helen and Anne into a singles community.* Left to right: *Lana Wood, Ann Elder, and Mary Ann Mobley. Courtesy of Columbia Pictures/Photofest.*

love of history. As Gerald seems older than the other residents, dates more than one woman, and engages in shady business deals, viewers may suspect he has ulterior motives in romancing Helen. After the other singles shed articles of clothing to play a flirtatious game, Helen takes the game a bit further. "Let's play by ourselves," she tells Gerald, sitting on his bed. She first turns away from his kisses, but then yields to temptation. He pushes her against the bed, she wraps her bare legs around him, and her face reveals, as the script puts it, "at once the agony and the ecstasy of the first man."[149]

In contrasting scenes, Anne avoids such ecstasy, firmly saying good-night to her date at her apartment door and excusing herself from the room when a make-out session becomes too intense. Like many young women of the late 1960s, Anne encounters a heightened pressure to have sex. "What are you, one of those professional virgins?" one frustrated man asks when she deflects his advances. "No," Anne retorts, "but you sure are an amateur Don Juan!" The men in her apartment complex tastefully refer to Anne as "old Ironside" and joke that "not even a torpedo could penetrate her hull."

Even Helen chides Anne for her scruples: "You'd better make up your mind there's only one way to hold a man," she says, predicting her own sexual experimentation will lead to marriage. Helen's hopes are soon dashed upon learning from Gerald's *other* girlfriend that he is already married—and "on the make" for single girls. Suddenly hysterical, Helen jumps in her car and speeds down the highway to a dark, nearly deserted beach, where she walks numbly toward the ocean. Three men on the boardwalk are playing a carnival shooting game. They put down their guns and instead target the wayward woman. Saucy music plays as Helen, dressed in red, descends the wooden stairs to the beach. The men follow, grab her, and rip at her clothes as she screams. Although viewers are spared the full impact of her rape, eerie camera shots of a spinning Ferris wheel and bucking carnival horse leave little to the imagination.

Censors intervened in the scripting of this scene. Although the waning Production Code Administration approved the film as long as it was marketed for "mature audiences," censors cautioned that the rape scene should be staged carefully to "avoid a scene of unacceptably violent sex." Also, although the presence of the three men suggests a gang rape, censors urged filmmakers to "avoid the implication that a second man rapes Helen."[150] Perhaps due to censorship concerns, filmmakers removed a scripted scene of Helen after the assault, in which she is "out cold, her dress torn to shreds, her face bloody, her legs scratched. She is one horrible mess."[151]

Instead, we next see Helen at the hospital, talking to the friends gathered at her bedside. "Why did you do it?" asks Anne. "Why did you run out that way?" As in *Where the Boys Are*, the blame is placed on Helen's lack of caution, rather than the men's brutal act. Gerald's other girlfriend—whose revelation sparked Helen's hysteria—also visits Helen in the hospital, reassuring her that Gerald is a "low-life" and urging her to save heartbreak for "someone worthwhile." Helen is cheered by this affirmation of her own worth and then virtually vanishes from the narrative. When the concerned apartment manager asks about Helen, her friends breezily answer, "She'll be fine."

Helen's assault and recovery is jarringly juxtaposed with Anne's

Broken spirit: Helen (Lana Wood) recovers from sexual and emotional assault in For Singles Only. *Courtesy of Columbia Pictures/Photofest.*

romantic date on a houseboat. Anne's date, Bret, has learned to respect her sexual boundaries and arranges for them to sleep on different sides of the ship. Anne is wearing a white dress and white headscarf, and as Bret lifts her onto the top bunk to sleep, she resembles a bride being carried across the threshold. The movie ends with a poolside wedding for Anne, whom reviewers characterized as "the good girl who won't [have sex] and who consequently gets to be a bride instead of a broad."[152]

As with earlier melodramas, critics were torn in their response to the film. Although some critics called the story "spirited and interesting," others panned it as moralistic and clichéd. The *Hollywood Reporter* argued that Helen's madness over Gerald was "poorly motivated" and that her "brutal boost to maturity seems no more than a gratuitous piece of dramatic desperation."[153]

By setting up a dichotomy between Anne, who holds to her morals, and Helen, who relinquishes her virginity for a chance at marriage, the film echoes early 1960s film conventions as well as the conservative 1966 *Ladies' Home Journal* report on the Los Angeles swinging singles complex. Like the woman profiled in that article—whose femininity and innocence encouraged men to treat her with respect—Anne's moral stance serves as her protection.[154] Gerald matches the profile of the predatory male who preys on naive marriage-minded women, as well as documented cases of married men who sought to infiltrate the singles scene. While managers of singles resorts tried to weed out these married "gatecrashers," savvy single women developed detection systems of their own. "If you say—'You're married, aren't you?'—he almost always owns up," one woman told *Newsweek* in 1968.[155] Although the dialogue in *For Singles Only* gave no indication that Gerald was married and posing as single, critics noted that Gerald's "old-style hairdo and a certain uptight oiliness" indicated his outsider status.[156]

For Singles Only suggests that the responsibility rests on the single woman to distinguish genuine dating prospects from deceptive, self-serving men. The "genius-level" Helen might have known much about meteorology and modern art, but she knew little about the dangers of relinquishing her virtue or the need to distinguish a married predator from a single life partner. Her misguided experiment with premarital sex leads to her emotional instability and makes her easy prey for men's basest desires. Although Helen's rape occurred on a dark urban beach rather than a city street, the crime may also double as a warning about the dangers of city living for women. As *Where the Boys Are* conveyed eight years earlier, *For Singles Only* suggests that a woman who succumbs too easily to her sexual impulses is destined for deception, despair, and desecration. Yet the hospital scene in which Helen feels "visibly better" offers hope that this fallen woman can find redemption.

Ruin and Redemption in the *Valley of the Dolls*

Anne Wells, the "everygirl" heroine of *Valley of the Dolls*, learns similar lessons in her brushes with romance and fame in 1960s New York.[157] Unlike other media texts that emphasize the excitement and glamour of moving to the city, *Valley of the Dolls* portrays the journey with a more somber, melancholy tone. The film was adapted from Jacqueline Susann's best-selling 1966 novel, with a few strategic changes. Filmmakers set the story in the 1960s rather than the 1940s and centered the narrative on Anne's ruin and redemption, thus emphasizing the sexual and psychological dangers that faced contemporary single women in the big city. Anne's character in the film is also far more nostalgic for small-town life than in the novel and more traditional when it comes to marriage. Although the film was scripted by two women, Susann reportedly was unhappy with the changes and felt that "her novel had been taken from her."[158]

Twentieth Century Fox used the novel's sensationalism and popularity to promote the film. A studio pressbook bragged that Susann's book was the "fastest seller in the history of publishing," selling 6.5 million paperbacks in two months.[159] Director Mark Robson had promised that the adaptation would not sanitize the story, and early script notes indicate his desire to play up salacious elements. In one scripted scene, adulterous Neely (Patty Duke) waits for her lover dressed in "sexy at-home attire." Robson recommended she lie in bed naked instead. In a scene where her lover calls her an "oversexed little monster," Robson inquired in the margins of the script: "What happened to *tramp* and *bastard?*"[160] However, as *Valley* was produced in the last year of the Production Code's existence, its love scenes and language use were tempered by censorship. The Production Code Administration stipulated that the film would be approved only if advertised under the heading "SUGGESTED FOR MATURE AUDIENCES." Censors objected to multiple "profanities and vulgarities" in the original script and urged caution in filming scenes that called for nudity.[161]

The film's casting encouraged viewers to see its central characters as complex, capable of both purity and debauchery. Barbara Parkins, who had played the wayward Betty on TV's *Peyton Place,* starred as Anne, "the good girl with all the bad breaks," and former teen sweetheart Patty Duke played Neely O'Hara, the addiction-riddled, foul-mouthed singing sensation (or, as the film advertisements presented her: "nice kid—once!").[162] In a *Look* interview, Duke expressed relief at shedding her childhood TV role: "I'm not doing any more Patty Lanes," she declared, posing seductively with a cigarette. "Who'll want a 29-year-old teenager?"[163]

Much like the early 1960s "pregnancy melodramas," *Valley* presents a variety of female types but encourages viewers to identify with and root for Anne, "the well-bred New Englander who arrives in New York with bright-eyed innocence."[164] As Anne departs for New York on a somber train ride, her memories play like old home movies. We see romanticized images of all she left behind: that "wonderful old house," her worried aunt and mother, and her earnest boyfriend. "I'll never forget the night I told them I was going to New York," she narrates. "They said it was a dreadful place for a vacation. I announced I was going to work there."

At Anne's announcement, Aunt Amy looks up from her jigsaw puzzle with open-mouthed alarm; steady boyfriend Willie, however, takes the news more casually. As the two ice-skate hand in hand, Willie predicts that Anne will be back after a month, ready to "settle down" in Lawrenceville. But Anne, already "engaged to be engaged" to Willie, is not so sure. "I wanted a marriage like Mom and Dad's, but not yet," she reflects, as the train passes a graveyard. "First I wanted new experiences, new faces, new surroundings." The film's equation of "settling down" with death is countered by menacing images of New York: miles of graveyards, smokestacks, industrial bridges. Anne sits up, expectant but unsmiling, to take in the view as the theme song swells with emotion. "Gotta find out . . . need to find life on my own," Dionne Warwick sings. "How will I know what I'll be . . . if I don't go where I'm free?"

Anne's lust for new experiences, and her desire to delay marriage, mirror the attitudes of her generation. Jacqueline Susann's novel offers a more scathing critique of the dead-end life she had escaped, casting Anne's home life in a more negative light and explaining that Anne refuses to settle for a loveless marriage like her parents':

> She would never go back to Lawrenceville! She hadn't just left Lawrenceville—she had escaped. Escaped from marriage to some solid Lawrenceville boy, from the solid, orderly life of Lawrenceville. The same orderly life her mother had lived. And her mother's mother. In the same orderly kind of house. A house that a good New England family had lived in generation after generation, its inhabitants smothered with orderly, unused emotions, emotions stifled beneath the creaky iron armor called "manners."[165]

The film, in contrast, sentimentalizes Anne's feelings toward marriage, family, and small-town life. This strategic change presents Anne as traditional and marriage-minded at heart and provides her an alternative to the loneliness and despair she faces in New York.

Once in the city, Anne lands at the Martha Washington Hotel for

Women—its neon sign glowing like a beacon in the dreary winter weather—and promises the matronly desk clerk she will abide by the strict "no men upstairs" policy. Anne's aunt had stayed at the hotel, and she claimed "it was as safe as you could be in a city like New York." Wearing a formal brown coat that complements her dark eyes and pale skin, Anne applies for a secretarial job at a law firm that handles celebrity contracts. While the receptionist is charmed by Anne's elegant diction and Radcliffe credentials, her employer perceives her as a potential risk. "She's too good-looking," her older boss grumbles. "I'll just get her broken in, and some insurance agent will waltz up and marry her." Anne assures her boss that she's already engaged to her New England beau, "but I'm not going to marry him."

She is similarly noncommittal about marriage in an early conversation with Lyon, a young legal partner in the firm. The earlier grit and grime of the city gives way to a romantic midnight stroll, and the two stop to admire jewelry in shop windows. Anne explains that the piece of jewelry she does wear—Willie's fraternity pin—"can mean everything, or nothing," and smiles at Lyon's flirtations.

"I like career girls. We're compatible," Lyon says.

Anne counters, "There's a rumor they don't make very good wives," and she is slightly taken aback by his quick retort: "I'm not looking for a wife."

She admits she envies his resolve: "I don't know who I am, or what I want. I only know I have to find out."

Although she and Lyon soon have an affair, the scene was scripted to assuage censors' concerns about nudity. Anne undresses in Lyon's apartment, placing the fraternity pin she wears on the bedside table. She is wrapped in a towel that drops to her ankles as she joins Lyon, and the two become silhouettes caressing and kissing in the near dark. *Valley*'s scriptwriters described this as a "tasteful, delicate" love scene with "murmured words, soft whispers in the darkness—our imagination running riot." However, the scriptwriters also insist that Anne's act is motivated by love rather than lust. She leaves Lyon's apartment in the middle of the night, establishing that "she loves him enough to play the game, regardless of the rules."[166]

Although Anne has removed the fraternity pin symbolically tying her to her New England beau, she has not lost her hope for commitment. After Anne's mother dies suddenly, Lyon joins her in Lawrenceville.

Anne drives him home in the family station wagon, and the two walk up to a stately white house surrounded by fresh snow. "Everything is better here," Lyon proclaims, tossing a log onto the fireplace. As they kneel beside the hearth, he suggests they move to Lawrenceville together. "This wonderful old house and you beside me in that marvelous four-poster [bed] upstairs," he hints.

"It's a marriage bed, Lyon," she says flatly. "You were thinking of marriage?"

Suddenly serious, he responds: "You know how I feel about that."

"When you fall in love, you belong to someone else," Anne insists. Lyon, visibly annoyed, reminds Anne they have already had this conversation.

"How do you think I feel, sneaking out of your apartment at 4 o'clock in the morning?" Anne asks, her anger rising. "Don't tell me I knew what I was doing."

"But you did," he retorts. "You knew."

"But I loved you," Anne insists, pleading with her eyes.

Sensing her vulnerability, Lyon moves beside Anne. The two clasp hands and kiss, him ardently, her reluctantly. "Come on," he urges her.

"Do you think I could sleep with you here in this house?" she retorts, calling a taxi to take him to a motel.

According to the script, Ann is "devastated when she learns he is not thinking of marriage," believing that if Lyon really loved her, he'd want to marry her.[167] This scene is a reversal from the novel. In Susann's version, it is Anne who desires a fling on the four-poster bed and balks at Lyon's suggestion of marriage, fearing she will be tied down in her detested Lawrenceville.[168] By recasting Anne's sexual experimentation as unrequited love, the film both purifies her intentions and sets up a contrast between the adventurous single woman, who ultimately wants marriage, and the commitment-phobic bachelor, who seeks only to satisfy a momentary lust. Lyon's lack of commitment is demonstrated in the following scene of the film: He abruptly departs for England, leaving Anne a letter thanking her for the "moment of reckoning" and the "loveliest winter of my life."

While Anne grapples with the consequences of falling for the wrong man, her friends in the film serve as even stronger cautionary tales.

Warming up: Lyon (Paul Burke) and Anne (Barbara Parkins) discuss sex, marriage, and small-town life in Valley of the Dolls. *Courtesy of Twentieth Century Fox/Photofest.*

Both are subsumed by the loneliness of fame and a sexualized media culture that preys upon their youthful talents. Jennifer (Sharon Tate), a lanky model and pornographic actress, commits suicide upon learning she has breast cancer, rather than letting her perfect bustline be ravaged by disease. Neely (Patty Duke) is a young woman brimming with talent and childlike charm who transforms into a hardened, vindictive character by the movie's end. Neely repeatedly turns to drugs and promiscuity when her lovers and audience fail to grant her the adoration she craves. "I need a man to hold me!" she whines to Anne in one scene, as she downs pills with liquor. Sent to a mental institution to dry out, Neely momentarily reforms, but her addictions and adulterous impulses resurface. Although both characters warn against the damaging effects of fame, they also correspond with tales of 1960s single women who were driven to drugs and depression when the city failed to provide the career satisfaction and male companionship they craved.[169]

Much like melodramas of the early 1960s, the film also warns young women against developing into an unfeminine, bitter, loveless career woman. The one success story in this *Valley*, brassy middle-aged singing sensation Helen Lawson, has survived at the expense of her femininity. In an early scene she growls and curses at Anne, who has come to deliver a contract. Helen's auburn hair, red dress, and ruddy skin emphasize her fiery personality. Helen initially tries to thwart Neely in achieving stardom but later pities her youthful rival. "I'm a barracuda—I don't need pills like Neely," she smirks, tossing back a glass of champagne. After a memorable scene in which Neely tears off Helen's lustrous red wig, unmasking the gray, thinning hair of an aged woman underneath, the humbled Helen urges the bachelor Lyon not to repeat her mistakes. "Find yourself a good girl, have kids," she advises, "or one day you'll wind up alone, like me—and wonder what the hell happened."

In a 1967 documentary about the making of the film, novelist Jacqueline Susann commented on Helen's "emasculating" character. "She brought her loneliness on herself," Susann explained. "No man could relate to her as a woman anymore."[170] As actress Susan Hayward said of the character she played: "Helen's not typical. Most women are much more soft. Women are soft. They're only hard until they meet the right man and fall in love. Then it changes. Any woman would put true love before a career."[171]

The latter part of the film narrative, which spans several years, grants Anne a lucrative modeling contract, a new life in Los Angeles, and Lyon's returned affections, but it fails to grant her the happiness of true love. Upon learning that Lyon is having an affair with Neely, Anne slumps into despair and reaches for the bottle of red pills at her bedside. She stumbles disheveled, in her bathrobe, along the beach and falls face first into the sand as the waves wash over her and the plaintive theme song plays. This brief drug binge ends with Anne's return to beloved Lawrenceville, in a train ride that reverses her journey to New York. Back safe in New England, Anne runs into Aunt Amy's open arms. (Meanwhile, Anne's nemesis, Neely, cannot stay sober for her comeback musical, and she winds up drunk, despondent, and shrieking in a dark New York alley when her understudy steals the spotlight.)

In the film's final scene, clanging church bells announce a small miracle: Lyon follows Anne to Lawrenceville and finally proposes marriage. Anne swiftly declines the proposal. "So many years I've prayed

Fall from grace: Lovelorn Anne (Barbara Parkins) pops pills in Valley of the Dolls. *Courtesy of Twentieth Century Fox/Photofest.*

for this moment," she says, "now that it's come, I don't feel a thing." When Lyon urges her to reconsider, she walks out the door. "It wouldn't work," she says curtly. "Perhaps someday, Lyon, I don't know. Goodbye." She sets off into the woods, making fresh tracks and twirling in the newly fallen snow. The theme song pipes up, suddenly optimistic: "It was all here. Why was I blind to it then? . . . This is my world . . . this is where I'll start again." The scriptwriters describe the ending's emotional tone: "She takes a deep breath, flings out her arms in exultation, whirls around. At last she is free—free! . . . [Her face] is alive and glowing."[172]

By making rural, family-centered Lawrenceville the site of her salvation, the film recasts the big city as a ruinous environment for the single woman's morals and aspirations. However, by resisting the traditional film formula that would have paired Anne with Lyon or another suitor, *Valley of the Dolls* offers a somewhat empowering ending. (It certainly ends on a more enlightened note than the novel, which leaves Anne as an addicted, love-starved housewife who reaches for a tranquilizer to survive another New Year's Eve with Lyon.)

As they embarked on both literal and figurative journeys, single women in late 1960s TV and film offered inspiration for female viewers. *That Girl* reportedly yielded a large volume of viewer letters from women hoping to achieve independence and self-actualization, turning to Thomas for advice.[173] Despite their dark undertones, *Thoroughly Modern Millie* and *Valley of the Dolls* offered appealing class-mobility narratives in which single women achieved wealth and fame by daring to strike out on their own. *For Singles Only* alerted women to the presence of singles apartment complexes, even as it offered a problematic picture of what went on behind closed doors. Although many of these narratives ended with heroines wearing engagement rings and white wedding veils, they still provided alternatives to early marriage.

These popular media narratives capitalized on real-life singles cultures while downplaying their more controversial elements. Although young women interviewed in the popular press often expressed a desire to sever their ties to small-town communities, single women in media tended to maintain a close connection to home and family. Rather than attempting to meet a range of men, these characters centered their affections on monogamous, and often chaste, relationships. Furthermore, these narratives often featured isolated protagonists and—with the notable exception of *For Singles Only*—failed to represent the clubs, apartment complexes, mixers, and matchmaking services that comprised the collective urban singles scene. Thus, the singles life was presented as a journey taken by one relatable, conventional heroine rather than an entire generation of women rebelling against tradition. Sitcoms and melodramas were particularly conducive to this type of narrative, as these genres tend to emphasize the conflicts and choices faced by individual characters.

While they hesitated to represent the pleasures of singles scenes, these narratives certainly portrayed the challenges that many real-life singles faced. Even comical narratives grappled seriously with the threats urban life posed to women's safety and sanity. The single girl was presented as easy prey for kidnappers, stalkers, oversexed bosses and— particularly in *Valley of the Dolls*—a media industry that exploited youthful talent. She also struggled with her own psyche, evidenced in the addictions and emotional breakdowns that riddled these narratives.

Characters also reinforced dominant sexual values and power dynamics. Anne in *Valley of the Dolls* wanted marriage, while her boyfriend was content with having a sexual affair. In other stories, men assumed a predatory stance, deceiving and even forcing women into sex. As they told stories of white women negotiating urban life, these narratives also offered scarce and often stereotypical minority representations that reflected real-life race and class tensions. While *Millie* perpetuated cultural stereotypes of Asian Americans as foreigners, *That Girl* attempted to make a meaningful social argument about the necessity of ending poverty.

Yet perhaps the most radical elements of these narratives were their ambiguous endings. *Valley of the Dolls* closed with Anne Welles independent and contented—even with her virtue behind her, no man beside her, and no immediate marriage prospects—foreshadowing more actualized representations of single independence in media of the following decade. Also, although *That Girl* literally leapt to accept Don's marriage proposal in the series' last season, she resisted network and advertiser pressure to marry off her character, instead ending the season with the engaged couple heading to a feminist meeting. These rebellions against narrative closure presented singleness as more than a mere transitional phase for women.

Living Liberated

Single Women in Early 1970s Sitcoms and
Commercial Culture

In 1972 the National Organization for Women (NOW) waged a protest on the pages of the *New York Times Magazine*. The article's headline, "TV Commercials Insult Women," was bolstered by stills from two offending commercials. In an infamous Geritol ad, a "slavish wife" gazes upon her husband, who declares, "I think I'll keep her." In the still from a controversial National Airlines campaign, a sultry stewardess beckons, "Fly Me. I'm Debbie." National's campaign, in particular, was the target of concerted protest by feminists, who complained that the innuendo-laden campaign both contributed to harassment of female airline personnel and kept working women from being taken seriously.[1]

The following year Revlon introduced Charlie, a new advertising icon who was neither a slavish wife nor a sex object. The star of the successful perfume campaign was an independent working woman who commanded respect with her tailored pantsuit and confident stride. Among Charlie's counterparts in early 1970s television was Mary Tyler Moore, whose character modeled career ambition and contentment with being single in her thirties. The single women at the center of these representations enabled advertisers and networks to connect with young, urban consumers and to counter critiques of pervasive media sexism. They also reflected the broader influence of feminism and women's changing attitudes toward careers and relationships. While advertisers used the figure of the single woman to harness feminist ideals to consumer lifestyles, celebrated sitcoms such as *Mary Tyler Moore* framed feminist issues more as momentary interpersonal conflicts than matters of persistent collective discrimination. These representations also countered single women's ambitions and independence by emphasizing their femininity and situating them within figurative families.

In this chapter, I analyze feminists' advocacy for new images in media and the documented changes in women's roles and attitudes in the early 1970s. I then examine how advertising and television attempted to harness feminism for commercial ends. The single woman was often used as a symbol of women's liberation, and I argue that this media tendency had mixed ideological effects. On one hand, media identified a woman's decision to live alone and pursue a career as a political act, and sitcoms gently broached singles' struggles for equality in the workplace. On the other hand, mainstream media's overreliance on the successful white middle-class single woman as a symbol of feminism minimized the movement's relevance across lines of class, race, and marital status, and it suggested that women had "made it" in a male-dominated world. As these commercial images were designed to appeal to modern women and traditional audiences alike, characters were equally acquiescent and assertive and usually lacked the sexual sophistication of their real-life single counterparts.

Media Protest: From Fringe to Mainstream

Media representations had long been central to feminist activism: NOW founder Betty Friedan had both impugned print media in *The Feminine Mystique* and penned a 1964 series for *TV Guide* that criticized the tendency of television programming and advertising to represent women as ditsy, cleaning-obsessed housewives.[2] The founding protest of popular feminism in 1968 had positioned the movement in opposition to mainstream media as youthful protesters picketed the Miss America pageant and pitched their copies of *Ladies' Home Journal* and *Cosmopolitan* into "freedom trash cans"—along with those constraining undergarments. With the founding of NOW's Image of Women in Media task force in the late 1960s, media activism became more forceful and coordinated. Through sit-ins, strategically placed editorials, and government lobbying, NOW challenged the public's tendency to see stereotyped images of women as harmless or entertaining and inspired media industries to change their approach.[3]

   In one 1970 protest, a "strident voice of a young feminist" broke through the bureaucracy of a CBS stockholders' meeting, accusing the network of using and abusing women for profit. "You use our bodies to sell products!" she yelled, backed by members of the San Francisco Women's Liberation Front. Such tactics were commonly seen as extreme or even laughable. According to *TV Guide's* account of the

Working women: Rhoda (Valerie Harper) and Mary (Mary Tyler Moore) share a laugh on The Mary Tyler Moore Show. *Courtesy of CBS/Photofest.*

protest, the startled male executives insisted they were not misogynists, and the "little female assault was gleefully reported by broadcast journalists as an amusing aberration." However, *TV Guide* maintained that the protest was a symptom of women's wider discontent with media representations.[4] In the early 1970s both news and industry publications explored feminist complaints that commercial media—especially television and advertising—were out of touch with the roles and needs of the 1970s female consumer. While the *New York Times* and *Newsweek* quibbled over whether the tube was solely populated with "sex kittens" and "dingbats," *TV Guide* columnists asked the industry to be accountable to women with headlines such as "Is Television Making a Mockery of the American Woman?" and "What's Television Doing for 50.9% of Americans?"[5]

The most forceful arguments came from activists themselves: In the 1972 article mentioned at the beginning of this chapter, NOW members commanded several pages of the *New York Times Magazine*, accusing television networks and advertisers of perpetuating emotional abuse. "Watching commercials is like being blasted by some casually malevolent propaganda machine dedicated to the humiliation of women," they wrote. "For the millions of women painfully breaking out of their traditional roles, the persistent television stereotypes are like a knock on the head telling them to stay in line. The psychological damage is immeasurable." What's more, the authors emphasized, the stereotyped pattern was evident in all television programming, from patronizing news and sports coverage to entertainment television that revealed "a generalized contempt" for the female sex: "Women are domestic drudges and office ancillaries, dependent on men emotionally and economically, their extraordinary incompetence exceeded only by their monumental stupidity. Decision-making positions of power and leadership, authority and status in the community—these are the province of men only."[6]

The authors backed up their ideological arguments with statistical evidence. Of 1,200 commercials surveyed, women were largely portrayed as "involved in household tasks" (42.6 percent of commercials), "domestic adjuncts to men" (37.5 percent), or "sex objects" (16.7 percent). As the authors noted, "only 0.3 percent showed women as autonomous people, leading independent lives of their own."[7]

By identifying these patterns in representation, feminists hoped to address attitudes and practices that were less evident in everyday life. As historian Ruth Rosen notes, "the hidden injuries of sex" were difficult for feminists to document in the early 1970s: "There were no photographs of aggressive men, rapists, or scenes of domestic violence. Nor were there pictures of men excluding women from conversation, demanding that dinner be served on time, or denying women promotions."[8]

Media representations, in contrast, offered visible and quantifiable evidence of sexist attitudes and provided a common point of reference for audiences. *Time* noted in 1970 that in contrast to "oddball causes—from ban-the-bras to communal child rearing—that leave many women cold," feminists' stance against advertising was "quickly gaining wide support among women."[9] This sentiment was supported by reader surveys in other mainstream publications: In a 1971 survey, 40 percent of *Good Housekeeping* readers agreed "the modern woman is insulted" by commercials. In *Redbook*'s 1972 survey, 75 percent of respondents reported that media "downgrade women by portraying them as sex objects or mindless dolls."[10]

Divergent Visions

However, the means by which producers and advertisers should address these stereotypes was a matter of debate among feminists. An early NOW report initially recommended "a plethora of new images of women to supplement the aproned mother": "The vital career woman is one. There are many more. There are single women who are home-makers. There are women who work primarily because they are breadwinners, rather than because they have professional education or are seeking stimulations outside the family circle."[11] That media industries tended to simply replace images of housewives with images of single career women angered some feminists who desired more diverse responses.

The media protests were also a point of division and contention between white women and women of color within the feminist movement. White feminist platforms often made problematic comparisons by calling upon civil rights frameworks: NOW–New York, for example, pledged to use "all the forms of protest and pressure on networks, advertisers and editors which have been effective in abolishing the stereotyped images of Negroes and Jews."[12] Subsequent writings by white feminists compared women's representations to those of blacks—to the point of suggesting that African Americans were more fairly represented in media. "Drama regularly portrays blacks in roles that in life are reserved for whites, but women are almost always portrayed as conventional women, if not sex objects," wrote one feminist in a 1971 *TV Guide* article. "The writers aren't trying as hard for women as they are for blacks."[13] As sociologist Benita Roth notes, the common rhetorical strategy in seventies feminism to compare the struggles of women and blacks dated from white feminists' involvement in civil rights movements and revealed their opposition to racism. However, these comparisons often alienated women of color from the feminist movement and removed considerations of race from discussions about women's representation in media.[14]

When African American feminists and media critics contended with media representations in the 1970s, their complaints were often very different from those of white feminists. While white feminists desired more representations of working women to correspond with their entrance into the workforce, many African American viewers welcomed representations of black familial life that would counter negative stereotypes of domineering black women. As white feminists complained about the overexposure of white female bodies and sexuality to sell products, African American feminists complained about their lack of visibility.[15] As an African American feminist told the *Washington Post* in 1970, "We've had the greater sexual exploitation because we were ignored [by mass media]. We've not been seen. It's only been in the last couple of years that even the ads recognized the fact that we use toothpaste."[16] Furthermore, some women of color deemed the media protests frivolous and questioned their centrality to the white feminist agenda. As Linda LaRue wrote in her 1970 essay "The Black Movement and Women's Liberation," "'Common oppression' is fine for rhetoric, but it does not reflect the actual distance between the oppression of the black man and woman who are unemployed, and the 'oppression' of the American white woman who is 'sick and tired' of *Playboy* foldouts, or of Christian Dior lowering hemlines or adding ruffles, or of Miss Clairol telling her that blondes have more fun."[17]

When groups such as the National Black Feminist Organization (NBFO) staged media protests in the early 1970s, they advocated for redeeming the image of black men as well as women. In a 1974 protest statement, NBFO members complained that "few black women in TV programs are cast as professionals, para-professionals, or even working people"—paralleling complaints of white feminists weary of seeing women largely in domestic roles. But NBFO traced the problem to racism as well as sexism, noting that the relatively few black actors and actresses who were cast in white-collar roles "generally lack professionalism and give the impression that black people are incapable and inferior in such positions."[18] Citing the short-lived Norman Lear series *That's My Mama* as an example of "sex exploitation," the NBFO focused largely on the show's negative stereotypes of African American men as "hustlers" and "derelicts" who disrespect women.[19] This protest reveals African American feminists' reluctance to privilege gender concerns over racial ones, and their desire to recuperate healthy representations of African American families and relationships.

Changing Demographics and Lifestyle Feminism

While their specific demands differed, feminists and many female viewers in the early 1970s agreed that popular media failed to represent
their identities and interests. This complaint was strengthened by visible shifts in women's workforce participation and attitudes toward marriage. *U.S. News* reported in 1973 that young women were "moving into
a key role in the U.S. economy . . . entering the workforce faster than
men, [and] making up a greater proportion of it than ever before." The
article noted that 59 percent of women ages twenty to twenty-four—
"the prime child-bearing years"—were either working or looking for
work, and that the percentage of mothers of preschool-aged children
in the workforce had doubled since 1960.[20] Furthermore, news media
acknowledged that women workers were less likely to consider their careers a temporary pursuit, or to be working solely to supplement their
husbands' income.[21] While the change in work patterns was more dramatic for white women than for women of color, who had historically
been more present in the workforce, there were changes in the types of
careers that African American women assumed. Black women workers
began to move out of service and housekeeping jobs into white-collar
professions in the early 1970s. Between 1964 and 1974, the percentage
of employed African American women in white-collar jobs increased
from 23 to 42 percent, with the percentage in clerical jobs more than
doubling.[22]

The increasing availability and viability of long-term careers for
women corresponded with, and inspired, new approaches to marriage
and relationships. The average age of first marriage climbed steadily
during the seventies as young women delayed marriage—a trend that
demographers credited to new educational and employment opportunities and the disruptive effect of the Vietnam War.[23] Among white women,
36.7 percent of twenty- to twenty-four-year-olds were never married in
1973, a 9 percent increase from 1960. In contrast, nearly half of black
women in their early twenties were single/never married in 1973, a rise
of 12.1 percent from 1960.[24] A 1976 census report noted that the divorce
rate more than doubled between 1963 and 1975, and that most divorcées pursued divorce while in their twenties.[25]

The single working women profiled in popular magazines placed low priority on relationships, often claiming that romantic attachments conflicted with their careers. While *Harper's Bazaar* reassured readers that working women were far "too busy, too tired or too preoccupied for indoor sport," *Mademoiselle* found that many were "practicing, enforcing sex with a certain amount of detachment," pursuing career goals and self-actualization rather than commitment to a relationship.[26] The visible presence of unmarried, career-focused, and sexually self-directed women in the population was often cited as evidence of feminism and amplified the movement's perceived effect. However, these women were not necessarily feminists. As *Mademoiselle* characterized urban working women: "They don't speak in movement language. Their work is personal, and so, they feel, is their choice . . . of work as the center of their lives, their resistance to 'a relationship.'"[27] In a new *Redbook* series on single women, columnists made a similar distinction between their personal lifestyle and collective politics. One twenty-three-year-old columnist declared she "[didn't] want to live through a man" and asserted her right to remain single, even as she assured readers she "would never join a protest march for women's rights."[28]

Media scholar Bonnie Dow has used the term "lifestyle feminists" to refer to the young women who espoused access to the public sphere and freedom from traditional sexual mores without necessarily embracing the movement.[29] As early as 1973, marketing research identified "Life Stylers" as a promising audience.[30] In contrast to feminist radicals, who opposed consumerism as they challenged sexism, Life Stylers emerged as an ideal consumer group whose single status and upward mobility made them receptive to new marketing pitches.

Advertisers Target the "New Woman"

By the early to mid-1970s, advertisers were alert to the need to answer feminist critiques and address this new consumer group. Women within the advertising industry were among the most forceful advocates for change.[31] "Social critics who accuse advertisers of stereotyping women are not just a lot of far-out crazies," Rena Bartos, vice president of J. Walter Thompson Company, informed advertisers in 1974. "Career women who are extremely valuable customers of many products and services are acutely sensitive to sexist tonality."[32] Franchellie Cadwell, president of the Cadwell/Compton advertising firm, urged advertisers in a 1973 industry publication to reach out to a "female market who clutches an estimated 80% of the nation's spending power":

> Women's attitudes have been revolutionized, only advertising to women hasn't. Women no longer see themselves as slightly subservient, second-class citizens. They're conscious of being women and proud of it. They're no longer chained to unhappy marriages (57% of women obtain divorces). They work, in increasing numbers, at increasingly better jobs. They have money to spend. Education. Mobility. They're liberated alright. Just because they're not militant feminists on the march, don't think they haven't been through a revolution . . . they have.[33]

This distinction between savvy career women and militant feminists was also evident in a 1973 tobacco industry marketing report that strategized "how to harness the powerful social force" of feminism for marketing aims. Rather than trying to reach the "emotional bra-burning extremists" who were hostile to most advertising, the report identified Life Stylers, "a young group growing up with the lib movement," as the most promising target audience. "This group is reshaping a new life style, with new material values, a desire for freedom and mobility, and somewhat pitying toward the more old fashioned attitudes toward life style and lib," the report explained.[34] Another promising audience was the "Equal Recognition Seeker," who adhered to conventions of femininity and attractiveness "without undermining her convictions on her career."[35]

An earlier tobacco advertising campaign, of course, had successfully leveraged female independence and emergent feminism to sell a new cigarette for women. The campaign began as an appropriately feminine concept: A cigarette designed for a woman's "slimmer hands and lips," with a name that suggested "a feminine personality . . . moonlight, gentle breezes, and green hills."[36] According to creative director Hal Weinstein, the original ad copy for Virginia Slims appealed to traditional femininity: "Now there's a new thin cigarette especially for women because women are dainty and beautiful and sweet and generally different from men."[37] As Weinstein told advertisers in 1969, the slogan that would define the campaign came in a late-night brainstorming session.

Backed by the slogan "You've come a long way, Baby," the company contrasted the new woman—who owns, earns, and smokes where she pleases—with the repressed, kept woman of yesteryear. The ads strategically used bright colors to "point at the modern gal" and to contrast her with sepia-toned photographs of her foremothers.[38] By placing the introduction of Virginia Slims on a continuum that included past feminist gains such as voting and property rights, the ad text imbued smoking with political meaning. (As one print ad read: "In 1920 you got the vote and got out of the kitchen. But not until now could you feel comfortable with a cigarette in your hand.") As the "new woman" pictured in these advertisements was attractive and thin, no doubt aided by the appetite suppressant nature of the "slim" cigarette, the campaign equated a svelte figure with women's new freedoms.

By using distant, subdued images of 1920s suffragettes rather than picturing the protests of contemporary feminists, the campaign skillfully evoked the spirit of 1970s feminism without directly referencing that generation's agitation for equal rights. The company also sought to contain the broader implications of its liberating message: "Frankly, we weren't sure, with our theme 'You've come a long way, Baby'—that we could run this advertising in *Ebony*," Weinstein said. "But why not? As long as it still comes off as a cigarette ad, not a civil rights message."[39]

Suspecting the new woman might need a perfume to mask the telltale tobacco scent, Revlon founder Charles Revson began to conceptualize a fragrance to appeal to "the woman who is sort of liberated but who isn't a bra burner."[40] Although competitors scoffed at the concept, it was hardly a new idea: In the early 1900s, perfume companies "replaced weak lavenders with strong musks and marketed them to liberated New Women," writes Susan Faludi.[41] Revlon's marketing team dubbed the project "Cosmo" and developed the perfume in consultation with focus groups of young women, who insisted "they wanted a perfume that reflected the new self-image they had defined for themselves."[42] *Time* noted in 1975 that Revlon's "semi-lib market" proved to be profitable: U.S. sales of Charlie exceeded $10 million in the fragrance's first year, and by 1975 Charlie was the top-selling American fragrance.[43]

In contrast to Virginia Slims' new women, Charlie was more clearly identified as a single working woman. Although Revlon's copy described the fragrance—and by extension, the model—as "gorgeous" and "sexy-young," Charlie's androgynous name, tailored pantsuit, and confident stride identified her as an empowered subject rather than mere sex object. As the *Wall Street Journal* would later describe the campaign, "Her walk—a long stride, with arms swinging—bespoke independence, confidence and a touch of insouciance."[44] At a time when even Revlon forbade pants as professional female attire—and a woman wearing a pantsuit caused a commotion in court—the ad copy's appeal to femininity countered the threat posed by Charlie's dress.[45] The active role that Charlie took in TV commercials cemented her as a contented single woman for the seventies, according to the *Wall Street Journal* in 1982: "She went into bars unescorted, signed the check in restaurants and dressed in tuxedos at night. . . . Most of all, she didn't need a man. Charlie wore cologne not as part of some husband-hunting scheme but because she liked the stuff."[46]

The long-running campaign cemented Charlie as a symbol of popular feminism and apparently contributed to more active roles for women in advertisements: "Women in commercials were shown not only alone, but riding motorcycles over fiery chasms, piloting planes and giving executive orders from the backs of limousines."[47] Nor was the campaign distinct from television programming. A popular seventies program originally dubbed *Harry's Angels* reportedly changed its patriarch's name to Charlie as a nod to the popular perfume. Furthermore, Shelley Hack, the model who portrayed Revlon's Charlie, took a short-lived role as one of Charlie's Angels in 1979.[48]

New Women, New Markets: Feminists Respond

These campaigns clearly hit their target. Revlon's sales soared, and Virginia Slims apparently helped foster smoking habits among young women.[49] These successful campaigns proved that consumers would respond positively to nontraditional marketing pitches, and thus paved the way for scripted television programs featuring similarly liberated singles. By glamorizing independence and rebellion, these advertisements may have helped expand dominant cultural expressions of femininity. However, it is important to remember that these campaigns resulted from clever marketing strategies, not earnest political insights. Many feminists have criticized the use of women's liberation images in advertising campaigns, and it is important to acknowledge the strong tensions between commercial media and organized social movements during this era.

"Is it the New Woman, or the New Market?" asked NOW in a newsletter headline.[50] Journalist and Students for a Democratic Society member Susan Sutheim cynically observed that "the new image of an adventurous, assertive, non-homebound woman" served more to meet marketing demands than women's needs for liberation. "An active, curious, well-educated assertive woman is a much better consumer than a plain old passive woman," she explained. "An active woman develops all sorts of new tastes, new interests, new ways of fulfilling basic needs—and that means you can sell her all sorts of new products."[51] Writing toward the end of the 1970s, feminist critics Deirdre English and Barbara Ehrenreich similarly observed that marketing to singles was a financial strategy more than a feminist impulse: Given the "new, self-indulgent mood of young women," marketers realized that "one sybaritic single could outconsume a family of four."[52]

Some feminists argued that media's focus on individual, successful single women masked the collective discrimination that women still faced. In a televised conversation with Helen Gurley Brown in 1972, Gloria Steinem criticized texts such as *Cosmopolitan* for "saying that you can be whatever you wish without any changing of the structure."[53] In a *Mademoiselle* report on the "New Feminism," radical feminist Ellen Willis similarly argued that persistent sexism and class discrimination hindered most women from achieving the privileged, "emancipated" status of the new woman. "Most women—the millions of file clerks, factory workers, welfare mothers, working-class housewives, daughters of rigid patriarchal families—are not 'new women,' and have never pretended to be liberated," she wrote. "Citing the pseudo-emancipation of an educated minority as proof that women are free has been one of the crueler sports of postwar sociology and journalism."[54] These comments reveal feminists' rightful frustration with media's lack of diversity and its tendency to advocate self-empowerment rather than societal change.

Television Addresses the New Woman

Furthermore, feminists argued that the tendency of television, advertising, and other media to foreground the young, single "new woman" obscured the presence of other groups within the movement and workforce. As a feminist author wrote in *TV Guide* in 1971, "You'd never learn from television that . . . half the working women in America are older than 37, or that there is any satisfying life at all for women that age." Of single characters, she wrote: "None of these women is challenging the family system, demanding a new kind of sexual relationship or a new division of labor in the home."[55] While she centered her critique on the popular *Mary Tyler Moore Show*, her analysis addressed the increasing prominence of young, single working women in television of the late 1960s and early 1970s. Among the earliest programs were *Julia* (NBC, 1968–1971), featuring Diahann Carroll as an African American single working mother, and *That Girl* (ABC, 1966–1971). While *Julia* was widely criticized for its failure to address racial tensions and represent African American communal life, *That Girl*'s antics had begun to seem artificial and antiquated by the end of its run.[56] These programs were followed by a new generation of television singles, which I address in this chapter. Most prominent and successful among the series was *The Mary Tyler Moore Show* (CBS, 1970–1977), which featured Moore as a single woman working in a Minneapolis newsroom.[57]

These series were fueled by marketing imperatives and built upon advertising's association of single women with lifestyle feminism. Like the models in the Virginia Slims campaign, single characters served as models of individual progress, set against the backdrop of the feminist movement. Like Revlon's Charlie, they balanced their autonomy and mobility with youthful femininity. Television, however, faced distinct challenges in representing single women's ambitions and independence. While advertisers had the freedom to target specific consumer groups, these television series struggled to appeal to "new women" without alienating more traditional viewers. As a result, feminist issues were often framed as relational conflicts, and characters' professional clout was undercut by the supporting and often subservient roles they performed in the workplace. Also, despite claims that these characters intended to "make it on [their] own," they shared their daily lives with a pseudo-family of neighbors and coworkers.

These sitcoms reflected patterns of cultural change in the 1970s, as well as the need to reach new audiences. While television networks had traditionally measured a program's success in terms of ratings, or total number of viewers, "the crucial change that began to occur around 1970 was a de-emphasis on numbers and a greater emphasis on 'demographics,' i.e., directing television shows toward specific audience groups," writes Jane Feuer.[58] Young, urban adults—particularly women—were increasingly targeted as prime consumers. A close ratings war between CBS and NBC in the 1968–1969 season further inspired CBS to abandon programs with rural appeal—such as *Green Acres* and *The Beverly Hillbillies*—for representations more appealing to youthful, urban audiences. In addition to new demographic models, the late 1960s also marked a significant transition in television advertising, from a format in which programs were sponsored by a single advertiser to a "magazine-style" format in which advertisers competed for time slots. When the FCC banned television cigarette advertising in 1971, the networks compensated for a predicted revenue shortfall by lowering rates and offering shorter, thirty-second slots to prospective advertisers. New programs such as *Mary Tyler Moore*, then, provided a cost-effective, targeted means to reach a desirable demographic.[59] The fact that Sandy Duncan's debut sitcom *Funny Face* was "grabbed up by sponsors six months before it was due to air" indicates how marketable the single woman had become.[60]

These single characters typically appeared in situation comedies, and their politics, independence, and sexual expressions were shaped by established genre conventions. Sitcoms were a natural setting for the new working woman. As Bonnie Dow argues in *Prime-Time Feminism*, situation comedies are "the type of programming into which women are most often and most centrally represented and from which television's most resonant feminist representations have emerged."[61] The success of *That Girl* and screwball romance films of the 1960s had helped cement the association between single women and comedy. Furthermore, television producers believed that women could not carry a successful drama, a prejudice that endured into the mid-1970s prior to the rise of female action leads.[62] As networks experimented with new characters and themes, sitcoms provided a calculated economic risk. A staged thirty-minute situation comedy was less expensive to produce than an hour-long drama filmed on location, and the nonserial nature of sitcoms allowed for syndication.

Sitcoms' predictable format and reliance on humor enabled them to broach political issues, such as female autonomy and changing sexual mores, without alienating audiences. Social commentary had been a part of comedy from its beginnings, and the rise of Norman Lear's political seventies sitcoms, such as *All in the Family* (CBS, 1971–1979), primed viewers to accept greater realism and controversy in the genre. As Dow describes the typical sitcom, characters disrupt the social order, then quickly restore it, as they "learn from their mistakes and are reintegrated into the group." Sitcoms' tendency to resolve conflict and restore community "can lend guidance to a culture that faces adjustment to social change," she argues.[63] Although single-women series of the early 1970s represented a sharp departure from television's earlier focus on family life, these programs adjusted to changing social attitudes without fundamentally changing patterns of representation. As Dow argues about *The Mary Tyler Moore Show*, "The [sitcom] genre adjusted to a new location (the workplace) and a new kind of character (the careerist woman) and then proceeded to slot these elements into familiar structures (the family) and role expectations (the accessible, nurturing, submissive woman)."[64]

On another level, these sitcoms occasionally used comedy to challenge the social order. Ella Taylor notes that comedy offers more flexibility than drama, enabling writers to create "multiple, conflicting and oppositional realities within the safe confines of the joke."[65] Norman Lear, for example, cleverly addressed racism and generational tensions through his flawed comedic characters. Although single-women sitcoms were more measured and subtle in their political negotiations, they broached topics such as equal pay and sexual reputation through comedy in ways that appealed to both youthful feminists and more traditional viewers. As they built on established genre conventions, many of these series also worked to expand the boundaries of situation comedy. Given *Mary Tyler Moore*'s commitment to character development and subtle comedy, many scholars and critics have granted the sitcom the elevated status of "quality television."[66] *Shirley's World* (ABC, 1971–1972) also broke new ground, blending comedy and adventure drama by placing its photojournalist heroine (Shirley MacLaine) in a range of exotic global settings.

Mary Tyler Moore debuted in 1970, just as *That Girl* entered its final season. *Mary* was quickly followed by *Funny Face* (CBS, 1971–1972), featuring Sandy Duncan as a student teacher and aspiring model, and the series was later revamped as *The Sandy Duncan Show*. Other single-women series included *Diana* (NBC, 1973–1974), starring former *Avengers* star Diana Rigg as a British divorcée embarking on a new career in fashion design, and *Karen* (ABC, 1975), starring Karen Valentine as an advocate for a citizen lobbying group in Washington, D.C. Like *The Mary Tyler Moore Show*, nearly all these series were named after established actresses, a trend that may have been intended to boost the series' appeal to audiences. Although all these imitative series were short lived, I argue that they collectively shaped perceptions of single women on television, often through heroines whose identities and actions were more daring than those of Mary Richards. Thus, I feel it is important to examine the short-lived programs alongside the enduring *Mary Tyler Moore Show*.

The ubiquity of single working women on television made this character type more acceptable and marketable, and it paved the way for female-headed action and science fiction dramas later in the decade. Also, as I will discuss later in this chapter, many of the conversations these series sparked about workplace equality and the pleasures and struggles of living alone were taken up by mid-1970s series such as *Fay* and *One Day a Time*, which featured outspoken divorced heroines with children. *Mary Tyler Moore*'s spinoff series *Rhoda* and *Phyllis* also offered popular images of a divorcée and widow, respectively.

This chapter calls upon the strength of earlier scholarship on *The Mary Tyler Moore Show*, which has long epitomized single-woman representations and second-wave feminism in television. As Dow writes, *Mary Tyler Moore* is considered the "first popular and long-running television series clearly to feature the influence of feminism," and it was unique in its assertion that "work was not just a prelude to marriage, or a substitute for it, but could form the center of a satisfying life for a woman.[67] Susan Douglas argues that *Mary Tyler Moore*'s themes and timing made it a "lightning rod for feminist criticisms and aspirations."[68] However, this chapter expands scholarship on television of this time period by measuring *Mary Tyler Moore* alongside other programs that offered portrayals of unmarried women without children. As I write, all but one of these programs are relegated to archives but still maintain a strong fan following online, which demonstrates their resonance with 1970s audiences. By including these lesser-known series, this chapter provides a more comprehensive reflection on single women in early 1970s television and illustrates how Mary Richards inspired and played into broader patterns of representation.

A Tentative Take on Feminism

That Girl's last season overlapped with *Mary Tyler Moore*'s debut, and the series has often been credited for inspiring characters like Mary Richards. Off-stage, actress Marlo Thomas became involved in early feminist activism and brought her changing political consciousness to the series. Her character Ann Marie traded her mod style and flip hairdo for bohemian fashions and long hair, and she pondered weighty issues such as pollution and racial stereotyping. Ann became engaged to long-term boyfriend Donald at the start of the season, and Thomas recalls intense pressure from the network and the series' sponsor, Clairol, to seal her character's fate with a televised wedding. Feeling that a wedding would send the "wrong message," Thomas opted to end *That Girl* on a less conventional note.[69] In the last episode, titled "The Elevated Woman," Ann identifies herself as a feminist and drags Donald to a women's liberation meeting. The pair become stuck in an elevator on the way to the meeting and use the close quarters to argue about the sexual politics of their relationship as they reflect on key moments from *That Girl*'s five seasons. By the time the elevator is fixed, the other feminists have dispersed. Thus, Ann Marie remains decidedly single but relegates her feminist activism to her romantic relationship.[70]

However muted, That Girl's embrace of feminism and desire to reconcile it with her relationship contrasted with traditional sitcoms of the early 1970s, which tended to poke fun at feminists. Although programs such as *Green Acres* and *The Beverly Hillbillies* occasionally evoked feminism, these plotlines suggested that "feminism comes from outside the home, from initially persuasive but shallow propaganda that infects women and turns them into something they're not. There is no basis for feminism in women's everyday, lived experiences," writes Susan Douglas.[71]

While the producers of *Mary Tyler Moore* did not set out to make a feminist series, the series' concept and dialogue were significant in positioning feminism as lived experience rather than humorous plot device. As producer Grant Tinker told the *New York Times* in 1974: "If you're going to write about a woman now, there is only one way to write: She has to be in touch with the world we live in."[72] In interviews in the early 1980s, producers spoke more openly about the show's stance toward feminism: "She wasn't a woman's libber except in the larger sense,"

Tinker said. "She felt she had earned a place. Sometimes she would go in and ask for a raise or more responsibility or a better title, but it wasn't the major thrust of the show."[73] Producer James Brooks explains, "We did not espouse women's rights; we sought to show a woman from Mary Richards' background being in a world where women's rights were being talked about and it was having an impact."[74]

Bonnie Dow provides insight into the historical setting that surrounded *Mary Tyler Moore*'s debut. The year 1970, she notes, was a time of heightened and visible feminist activism. Feminists staged a Strike for Equality in August 1970—a daylong protest against women's oppression—that was heavily covered in mainstream news media. Popular media were beginning to distinguish among feminist groups, discrediting radicals but giving greater credence to reformist feminists who advocated workplace equality. News media also emphasized the desirability of "thirtyish, never married" feminist activist Gloria Steinem. Dow deftly compares Mary Richards with Steinem's approachable image, arguing that Mary similarly functioned as a "'transitional figure' that made feminism seem less frightening."[75]

Although heroines like Mary Richards occasionally engaged in overt activism, they more often epitomized a lifestyle feminism that prioritized personal choice over societal change. In *Mary Tyler Moore*, Dow argues, "feminism becomes a matter of lifestyle choice, not systematic oppression or social transformation. Even Mary's rejection of the possibility of marriage at the end of the first episode is a rejection of a *particular man* who has been inconsiderate and unreliable. Her decision is *individual* rather than political, in keeping with [the] sitcom's general individualistic philosophy."[76] Like the advertising campaigns described earlier in this chapter, *Mary Tyler Moore* equates liberation with an independent attitude, making its heroine merely a "libber in the larger sense." Consistent with the familial tone of situation comedy, the series centers on Mary's choices and personal relationships, rather than broader political implications.

Entering the Workplace

Much like their predecessors in late 1960s television and film, many of these sitcoms open with the heroine arriving in a new city and reveling in the pleasures of urban life. Mary's opening montage—in which she bids farewell to family and friends, drives alone to Minneapolis, and revels in her urban freedom—evoked *That Girl*. But while *That Girl*'s journey was marked by upbeat music and Marlo Thomas's broad smile, *Mary Tyler Moore* took a different tone. "How will you make it on your own?" intoned the somber theme song, cautiously concluding: "You might just make it after all." As Taylor notes, the opening theme song highlights Mary's independence and sets up the tone of the sitcom, namely "individuals negotiating troubles in a muddled way and surviving them with cheerful resignation."[77] As Moore had achieved fame as doting wife Laura Petrie on *The Dick Van Dyke Show* (CBS, 1961–1966), viewers could imagine Mary Richards as Petrie "dropped . . . into a new and confusing world without the security of [a] suburban home, husband and family."[78]

Yet the somber opening gives way to more classic scenes of playful celebration. Fashionable Mary strides through the city on her own, stopping at an urban intersection to toss her knit hat in the air. *Diana*, debuting three years later, offers a more glamorous journey as its heroine flies from London to New York, savoring the experience as she sips a glass of wine. *Shirley's World* and *Karen* also emphasize the single woman in motion, as jet-setting Shirley captures the world through her camera lens, and Karen—alternately dressed in loose T-shirts and fitted business attire—rides her bike across D.C., backed by political landmarks and patriotic flute music. Only *Funny Face* relies on traditional conceptions of womanhood, as a yellowed slideshow chronicles Sandy's childhood in small-town Illinois and the theme song emphasizes Sandy's status as the perfect date.

Several of these series begin with heroines applying for new careers, often battling implicit and overt sexism in their efforts to be taken seriously. That these young women established successful careers in traditionally male-dominated professions such as journalism and political organizing is a significant change over previous representations of single women, which often placed them as secretaries, schoolteachers, or itinerant models and actresses. Furthermore, the fact that these heroines were producing television news, designing fashions and photo spreads, and spearheading political action may have been a direct response to feminist activists who demanded greater involvement of women in media production and political organizing.

Mary Tyler Moore's pilot episode provides a particularly memorable interview. New to Minneapolis and newly separated from her long-term boyfriend, Mary Richards applies for a secretarial job at a television news station. Informed that the position is filled, but told that a producer job has become available, Mary spars with gruff older station manager Lou Grant (Ed Asner) to become hired. She initially bristles at, but then readily answers, illegal interview questions about her age and marital status.[79] That Mary recognizes Lou's discriminatory tactics but still eagerly accepts the position typifies her approach to feminism. As Dow argues, "she is a woman sophisticated enough to recognize sexism when she sees it, but is not necessarily assertive enough to do anything about it."[80] Similarly, Susan Douglas calls attention to Mary's voice and body language in this early scene, suggesting that the heroine's tendency to waiver, hedge, and display feminine emotions softens the statements she makes.[81] Furthermore, Mary settles for lower pay as the price of access to a male sphere — leaving a battle over equal pay for later seasons.[82] Thus, the first episode does display a feminist sensibility but offers mixed messages for viewers. As Dow reads the episode's message, "That Mary and others recognize that her gender does make a difference is meaningful; however, that Mary accepts this situation with good humor, and is grateful for the job, is equally meaningful."[83]

While the scene serves to temper Mary's activism, her interview and salary negotiations also resonated with single women's experiences in the workforce. Much like Lou Grant, many employers in 1970 openly stated their preference for hiring men, a trend that feminists perceived as symptomatic of widespread workforce discrimination.[84] Although Mary's rise from secretarial candidate to associate producer could be viewed as a desirable promotion, viewers learned that Mary was hired at ten dollars less a week than she would have earned as a secretary at WJM-TV. This differential "represented the price of 'making it' in a male-dominated profession" and paralleled a complaint in a 1970 feminist publication.[85] "I am paid less than a clerk, but given a title which is, I am told, worth more than money," wrote a single personnel manager. "I have my job because no man would work for my salary."[86] That Mary often functioned more as a secretary than a producer — taking dictation, scheduling appointments, running errands — undermined the significance of her position title for female viewers. While in concept Mary was one of the young women whom *U.S. News* predicted would eventually rise above the gender-segregated nature of 1970s employment, "she

Too tall? Divorcée Diana (Diana Rigg) conceals her height in an interview with a shorter male designer in Diana. *Courtesy of NBC/Photofest.*

hardly ever gets to write the news or report it on camera—even though she appears to be several times brighter than the men who do," complained one *New York Times* writer in 1973.[87]

A similar dynamic structures the debut episode of *Diana*, in which sophisticated British divorcée Diana Smythe interviews for an entry-level design job in New York. Critics noticed similarities between Diana and Mary Richards, caustically calling her series "The Mary Tyler Less Show."[88] In her initial interview with the firm, Diana fields questions about her advanced age, hints at her divorced status, and reassures her penny-pinching boss that despite her experience, she's "willing to accept minimum salary." Her figure factors prominently in the interview process. Upon learning her dress is hand-sewn, her prospective employer asks to examine the hem, his glasses steaming up at the sight of her lanky legs.[89]

In a subsequent interview with a short male designer who is known to discriminate against tall women, Diana conceals her stature by crouching down in her chair and agreeing to model a short dress. She ultimately rises to her full height, addresses the designer's prejudice head-on and is hired based on her merits—but only after a comical sequence in which she strips and struggles to squeeze into the too-small outfit. The interview thus entails the humbling and sexual objectification of this forceful single lead, diminishing the strength of her stance against workplace sexism. Much like Mary, she is sophisticated enough to recognize discrimination when it occurs, but she settles for lower pay as the price of access to a male-dominated design firm.

In contrast, Shirley MacLaine's character in *Shirley's World* both stands up to a chauvinistic employer and advocates equality in the series' first episode. The series' opening credits feature Shirley's photographs of student riots and thus associate her with youthful activism and idealism. In the pilot, this American photojournalist applies for a job on the staff of the British-based magazine *World Illustrated*, presenting editor Dennis Crandall (John Gregson) with a glowing reference letter. When Dennis doubts the letter's veracity and asks if Shirley is playing a practical joke, Shirley rises and confidently paces around the office, informing him that she is, in fact, as "ingenious" and "resourceful" as the letter promises.[90]

Impressed by Shirley's forcefulness and confidence, the editor gives her a test assignment to interview and photograph a politician who belongs to an exclusive club. Shirley dutifully enters the stately Berkeley Club to conduct the interview—only to be ushered out the door by an alarmed doorman. "You're the first female in 140 years" to enter the club, the doorman informs her, adding that even Queen Elizabeth was denied entry to this male preserve. "But that's medieval!" Shirley exclaims, trying not to laugh. Her amusement turns to indignation, however, when she learns her editor is a club member and has set her up for failure.

When she is rebuffed in her attempts to interview the politician outside the club, Shirley cooks up a more outrageous scheme. As bawdy music plays, she strolls to the seedy part of town and hires strippers for her cause. "How'd you like to help a fellow working girl?" she asks. She leads an army of erotic dancers back to the Berkeley Club, their stream of high heels clicking in time to marching music. Once inside, the women hand their coats to the surprised doorman—revealing miniskirts and heavy makeup underneath—and make a beeline for the club's senior members. One woman wraps her legs around a stately gentleman; others feed grapes to their charges or smother them with kisses. Shirley stands over the trysts, triumphant, snapping photos from every available angle.

After she develops the photos to use as blackmail, Shirley is granted an interview with her source. (The interview is conveniently covered by music, so viewers are not privy to her journalistic skills.) She hands her boss the finished article and threatens to quit. "You sent me on this ridiculous caper," she accuses, her voice rising. "I don't want to waste my time playing games." Her boss retorts that the job will entail "a lot of things you don't like," but admits he admires Shirley's ability to stand up to him. The episode ends peacefully, with the two sparring journalists on a dinner date.

Shirley's actions in this episode have resonance for feminist organizing. The militant stream of women into the club evokes the radical feminist sit-ins that were happening in media, corporate, and educational settings in the early 1970s—albeit with a sexualized twist. As historian Georgina Hickey notes, male-only restaurants, bars, and other public accommodations were common in the United States in the late 1960s and early 1970s, and these sex-segregated spaces were targets of concerted feminist protest. "Common assumptions that equated lone women with prostitution or at least questionable morality encouraged such [segregation] policies," Hickey writes.[91] Shirley, then, is not only infiltrating a male bastion but also taking a stand for the broader access of women to networks of power. The fact that she infiltrates the Berkeley Club with women of "questionable morality," however, supports the assumptions that were used to justify sex-segregated spaces.

Shirley's interview and tactics represent a marked difference from Mary and Diana's more acquiescent approaches; although she jumps through hoops to get the job, she does stand up to her boss's assumptions about her experience and his unethical assignment. Yet we could argue that she staged her stunt mostly to impress her boss—and she accepts a date with him by episode's end. It is never stated that the Berkeley Club is permanently open to women, aside from Shirley and her rebel crew.

Karen Valentine's character in *Karen* (airing in 1975, toward the end of *Mary Tyler Moore*'s run) is more politicized at her sitcom's outset, as she is employed as an organizer for Open America, a Common Cause–type lobbying group. Critics described Karen as "an intelligent single woman who views the world with insight and wit," as well as a "'now' character who isn't a woman's libber or a young housewife."[92] Although the series was created by the same minds who developed *M*A*S*H* (CBS, 1972–1983), the series soft-pedaled its political aspects, instead mining its heroine's life for interpersonal and relationship conflicts. Critics suggested the series had a difficult function to play, given Americans' sensitivity about political corruption after the Watergate scandal. While one female critic thought *Karen*'s scripts were "too cute" and needed more "wildly irreverent humor" in the style of *M*A*S*H*, another female critic derided the show as too "full of self-righteous political patter."[93] Ultimately, *Karen*'s conflicts tend to revolve less around national politics than whether she should date an employee of a corporate public relations firm that is antagonistic to Open America, or how she should deal with a friend's husband who works for the timber industry. Like the heroines before her, she voices her political principles but also tries to make peace with less enlightened men.

These heroines used their wisdom and charm—an intangible quality that Lou Grant calls "spunk"—to overcome discriminatory barriers and gain access to professional careers. (Sandy Duncan's character is an exception, as she works as a freelance model.) Once in the workplace, however, television's single women tended to function in "the

Behind the camera: Shirley (Shirley MacLaine) snaps pictures and stirs up controversy in Shirley's World. *Courtesy of ABC/Photofest.*

recognizable roles of idealized mother, wife and daughter," according to Dow.[94] For example, Mary produced programs less often than she sharpened pencils and made phone calls, and critics seized on the fact that this "glorified secretary" was still calling her boss "Mr. Grant" by the series' end.[95] Furthermore, a feminist *TV Guide* columnist complained that Mary's emotional nature made her "such a hazard on the job that she vindicates the gentleman's agreement that keeps women out of real-life television newsrooms."[96] Diana and Shirley often functioned less as artists than relationship counselors, mediating in colleagues' and clients' marital troubles. Karen and Sandy often prioritized relationships above their careers. In one episode, Sandy ditches a publicity date with a movie star—presumably her route to modeling fame—to soothe a friend's hurt feelings. Karen, who risks her political reputation and principles to date a desirable man from a rival PR firm, is most often seen answering phones and organizing paperwork for her curmudgeonly male boss.[97]

Thus, these series tended to emphasize women's entrance into male-dominated institutions, rather than their ability to change how workplaces operated. As these women functioned effectively within male-dominated workplaces, these series suggested that "access is the major problem for women; that is, given the same opportunities as a man, a woman's success or failure from that point on is solely a matter of individual choice and/or ability."[98] The characters' relational and supportive roles also reflected the tendency of sitcoms to prioritize relationships over individual ambition, as I address in the next section.

However, Ella Taylor argues that Mary's nurturing, supportive functions in the workplace also reflected historical realities in women's work. As greater numbers of women entered the professional workplace in the 1970s, the American workplace placed less emphasis on "individual performance and achievement" and more on "cooperation and caretaking." Furthermore, feminist researchers later in the decade revealed that workplaces assigned women to "subordinate and exploited roles to the extent that they reproduce their traditional family roles at work."[99]

Finding Community and Workplace "Families"

Traditionally, the domestic sitcom has focused on family relationships, and even as the genre stretched to encompass women as workers rather than wives and mothers, it retained its familial structure. In all of these sitcoms, the women's coworkers, neighbors, and roommates functioned as symbolic family members. Male bosses alternately served as father figures or romantic interests, and colleagues and neighbors lent protection and moral support. In *Prime-Time Families*, Taylor argues that the televised image of workplace families helped compensate for a sense of alienation from work that many Americans felt in the 1970s. As workplaces became more corporate and mechanized, televisual workplaces "assumed the warmth and solidarity, the emotional intensity and nourishment, and the protective functions of the families and communities we believe we once had, and have lost," argues Taylor.[100] As I have posited throughout this book, Americans tended to worry about the safety and social stability of single women on their own; thus, the ever-present friends and colleagues in these programs helped to normalize characters and ease viewers' anxieties.

In some cases, the presence of female friends and neighbors amplified the series' feminist resonance. Scholars and critics have argued that frequent conversations among Mary, her droll married landlord, Phyllis (Cloris Leachman), and her acerbic single neighbor Rhoda (Valerie Harper) functioned as a form of feminist consciousness-raising, in which the women debated changing notions of marriage, sex, and women's work. The influence of feminism was also evident in the show's authorship. Over its run, the series hired fifteen female writers, including Treva Silverman, the first woman to hold the position of senior story consultant at CBS.[101] Silverman frequently challenged scripts she considered sexist, and her writing evolved to reflect women's changing image. By the third season, she was no longer penning Rhoda's character as desperate for marriage, "because that wasn't how women felt about ourselves."[102] Rhoda was not the only character to change and evolve. Mary, too, gained greater assertion and consciousness over the course of the series, rather than playing to formulas like her predecessors in popular culture.

In addition to serving as political sounding boards, the coworkers, neighbors, friends, and family in these programs function in protective and even romantic roles. In *Funny Face* (later revamped as *The Sandy Duncan Show*), Sandy is a perky young woman from small-town Illinois attending college and working as a model in Los Angeles. Although an early *Funny Face* episode in which she obtains her own phone line emphasizes her solo apartment and ability to take charge of her own domestic concerns, the fact that the older telephone repairman takes a personal interest in Sandy's life and career reassures us that this is hardly a lonely woman adrift in the city.[103] Sandy's landlord and neighbors often drop in without knocking; among them are a sophisticated older married couple who even chaperone Sandy on a date. A writer for *The Sandy Duncan Show* explained that Sandy's neighbors doubled as family figures and confidantes, including a protective police officer, a "big brother" type who "knows how vulnerable she is." The series also featured frequent phone calls from her father to "establish that someone cares deeply about Sandy."[104]

Similarly, Karen's roommates share meals and talk openly about dating and sex. Karen's older coworker, Dena, also serves as a source of motherly romantic advice. In the episode "What Are Friends For?," Karen is home alone, battling loneliness and a cold virus. The episode presents Washington, D.C., as a dangerous place for lone women. Karen's roommate makes wisecracks about urban crime, and the evening news cheerily announces that the crime rate has risen only 7 percent in the last week. Hearing a creaking noise outside her bedroom door, Karen calls the police, only to discover that the intruder is a friend coming to check on her. Her empty apartment soon fills up with friends and coworkers sharing chicken soup and talking politics, and the police join the party when they finally arrive.[105]

The concept of neighbors as family is taken to an extreme in *Diana*. As *Newsweek* explained Diana's provocative dilemma: "Her rich archeologist brother has lent her his apartment while he is away. . . . But he has also given unending duplicate keys to male friends who keep dropping in unexpectedly." Living in her brother's apartment, continually surrounded by zany guest stars, Diana lacks the "good sense to change the lock," *Newsweek* noted.[106] In the pilot, a female neighbor enters with a Great Dane intended to protect Diana from the dangers of the city. Later in the episode, Diana climbs into the double bed only to discover her brother's drunken friend Gerald sleeping there. After clarifying the confusion, she merely tells him to scoot over. Although the script makes clear that Gerald was incapacitated ("You're the first girl I ever slept with that I *slept* with," he confesses), another of her brother's friends shows romantic interest in Diana, embracing her when she returns from her harrowing interview.

The tendency of these sitcoms to present coworkers and neighbors as ever-present family members situated the new woman within a web of relationships, sparking humorous conflicts and creating a cast of supporting characters in the process. For some critics, the supporting cast served mainly as a distraction or annoyance. *Newsweek* wondered why Mary and Diana were continually "surrounded by weird characters who insist on dragging them into their own hangups."[107] However, the concerted emphasis on relationships rather than personal autonomy also countered potential anxieties about women's independence and placed these singles in recognizable feminine roles: as confidantes, sisters, daughters, and love interests. To echo NOW's earlier complaint about women in media, it was near impossible to find truly "autonomous [women], leading independent lives of their own."[108]

The tendency of coworkers to function in familial roles both humanized the workplace and blurred the lines between home and work. In *Mary Tyler Moore, Diana,* and *Karen,* older male bosses drop by single women's apartments unannounced, often in states of inebriation and heartbreak. Karen's gruff boss even spends a few nights on her couch while he recovers from a fight with his wife.[109] While these situations create comedic tension, they also placed relationships between women and their male bosses in a more familiar register. During its seven-year run, *Mary Tyler Moore* offered multiple interpretations of Lou and Mary's relationship. While their age and generational differences would suggest a father-daughter relationship, the series also hints at latent romantic attraction. In the last season, Mary and the (now-divorced) Lou attempt a dinner date but burst into laughter at the awkwardness of their arrangement. In another episode, three of Mary's male coworkers fantasize about being married to her.[110]

While Karen dates men she meets through work, including a senator, *Shirley's World* featured a woman enamored with her more traditional, older boss. That Shirley seemed to be more occupied with capturing his heart than advancing her own career success irritated some critics. The *Saturday Review* lamented that Shirley ostensibly "carries the banner of Women's Liberation," but her acquiescence to her boss and reliance on his "superior masculine wisdom" prevent her from becoming a truly "emancipated female." As the critic complained: "The series pendulum, swinging back and forth between Shirley free and equal and

Shirley submissive and contented, is caught between the world of yesterday and today."[111]

That description could apply to Mary Richards, who enacts similar contradictions in her moments of assertion. As Dow notes, the episodes in which Mary is forced to be less than nice "are milked for the comedy of her extreme discomfort," and she "returns to her accommodating patterns by the end of the episode."[112] This pattern of comedic assertion and accommodation are evident in the third-season episode in which Mary makes an argument for equal pay.[113] *Mary Tyler Moore*'s third season represented an important shift, as the series raised the "occasional mild women's-lib theme" and scripted Mary as "aggressively feminine instead of passively feminine." As a producer told *TV Guide*, "Instead of just reacting shyly to everyone else, the Mary character now yells at people and fights back."[114] Yet, consistent with the familial nature of workplace sitcoms, these conflicts were framed more as family dramas than feminist activism.[115]

At the opening of season three, Mary is fretting over attending a meeting with WJM-TV's station manager. "It used to be I felt like I could be myself," Mary tells Rhoda. "Now I feel like I represent women everywhere." Her comment works on multiple levels, referencing the show's increasing resonance for feminism and her forthcoming battle with her boss. Gathering financial records for the meeting, Mary discovers that her predecessor, a man whom her coworkers describe as a "terrible" employee, made fifty dollars a week more than she. The widening pay gap between men and women was a collective concern at the time this episode aired. *U.S. News* reported that in 1972, "for every dollar a male worker earns, a working woman on the average earns only 58 cents—down from 64 cents in 1957." The magazine also provided statistical evidence that "women hold most of the lower-paying jobs," and "whatever the job, women earn less than men."[116]

Indignant, Mary marches into Lou's office without knocking, her rage masked by tears and incoherent speech. When her boss ignores her outburst, dismissing it as a "woman thing," Mary finds her voice. "I would like to know why the last associate producer before me made fifty dollars a week more than I do."

"Oh, because he's a man," answers Lou, later adding: "It has nothing to do with your work." Incredulous, Mary confronts his reasoning,

Holding her own: Mary's character became more assertive in The Mary Tyler Moore Show's *later seasons, battling with boss Lou (Ed Asner) about issues such as equal pay. Courtesy of CBS/Photofest.*

at one point towering over the seated Lou with the righteousness of her cause. (That she is wearing a red dress—characteristically a color that the more forthright Rhoda wears—underscores her militancy.)

"He had a family to support. You don't," Lou concludes. "Come back when you have an answer to that."

Speechless, Mary leaves, only to reenter a moment later. "A-ha!" she exclaims. "Because financial need has nothing to do with it. You would have to pay the man with three kids more than the man with two kids, the married man more than the bachelor. And you don't do that, do you, Mr. Grant?"

Mary's impassioned pitch for equal pay is undercut by the camera shots used in this scene. As she catches Lou in a contradiction, the camera focuses not on her triumph but on Lou's perplexed expression. However, viewers are again encouraged to identify with Mary when anchorman Ted Baxter enters to ask a trivial question. Lou welcomes the interruption and turns his attention to Ted. The men banter as Mary stands between them, quivering with the indignity of being ignored. The camera angles effectively foreground the relationship issues—Mary's frustration, Lou's conundrum—rather than the political implications of equal pay, a move consistent with situation comedy conventions.

In the next scene, Mary overrides Lou's opinion at the station manager's meeting. Taken aback by his employee's treachery, Lou seeks comfort in a tavern. Mary approaches him with a conciliatory gesture, saying, "Look, I'm not mad anymore." Lou, however, is unwilling to let go of his anger, insisting that Mary "sold [him] out for fifty bucks a week." Mary reassures him that personal relationships supersede her demands for equal pay. "I care about you," she says. "I love you."

When a disastrous newscast inspires Mary to insult anchorman Ted on live television, Lou grunts his approval and decides she *has* earned a raise—of twenty-five dollars a week. Mary seems less than thrilled by the offer, and Lou concedes: "That's not the point, huh? Okay, I'll try to find the rest." Although Mary returns to her earlier demand for equal pay, it is noteworthy that she is granted a raise based not on her production expertise or on principle, but for her "spunk." As in the earlier confrontation, interpersonal dynamics—the coworkers' shared distaste for the arrogant anchorman—supersede the feminist argument for equal pay. While this outcome blunts Mary's political stance, this episode also exemplifies the tendency of the sitcom to sublimate individual rights to the higher priority of family unity. Both Mary and Lou are presented sympathetically in this storyline, providing multiple points of identification for viewers—be they fiery feminists or beleaguered employers.

Diana Rigg's character also takes a personal approach when she addresses unfair hiring practices. Although she blithely accepts blatant age discrimination in her first interview, she is indignant to learn that her second interview will be with a feisty, short designer who balks at hiring taller women. Warned in advance about his height prejudice, she decides to minimize her stature in the interview. Her prospective boss is impressed by her artistic flair when she sits, concealing her height, but suddenly changes his mind when she stands. Diana catches him in a contradiction: "You liked my designs," she says. "What you don't like is my height." However, she addresses his distaste through self-deprecation and gentle humor.

"We have something in common," she tells him. "A height problem." She shares memories of an awkward childhood in which she "suffered" for her height.

"I was always taller than my dates," Diana laments.

"I couldn't reach mine," he admits, ultimately deciding to hire the tall, talented, and empathetic Diana. The solution suggests that the root of the problem is not discrimination in hiring, but the personal sensitivities of a vulnerable male.[117]

Sexual Stirrings and Committed Flings

In a 1971 *TV Guide* titled "TV and the Single Girl," a female reviewer celebrated Mary Richards for her independence and resourcefulness, comparing her favorably to earlier representations such as *That Girl*.[118] However, the critic complained about the series' cautious treatment of sex in its early seasons. "When it comes to sex, *The Mary Tyler Moore Show* glares with discomfort. Any woman who at the age of 30 becomes visibly unnerved by the presence of an attractive man is in mighty big trouble. There is a whisper of 'seduction' on that show, and it has the ring of 1956. No one expects to see Mary Tyler Moore romping in bed on CBS, but the subject could be handled more maturely."[119] Indeed, the series producers did struggle with network discomfort about Mary's sexuality and marital status. Mary Richards had originally been conceptualized as a divorced heroine, but producers were strongly warned that "the public will never accept a divorcee as a funny heroine, no matter how relevant."[120] As producer James Burns described the initial meeting with CBS executives, "It was strongly hinted that if we insisted on having Mary divorced, the show would go on at 1 in the morning."[121]

A 1970 *TV Guide* article summed up the compromise: "She's not divorced, only jilted. She's been going with this guy—well, actually they've been living together, but we don't talk about that."[122] Mary's stated age, coupled with her never-married status, in some ways raised more provocative questions than a divorced heroine would. Television critic Sally Bedell writes that the decision to cast Mary as "a woman who just ended an affair . . . sounded more promiscuous" than the original conception of her as a divorcée. "But the CBS management felt more comfortable with some ambiguity. They decided that viewers could either assume—correctly—that Mary had tossed away her virginal halo, or they could more innocently conclude that she had engaged in a platonic romance."[123] However, in the first season, Mary rarely did more than "peck a suitor on the cheek," supporting a more innocent reading of her character.[124] In contrast, Mary's neighbor Rhoda seems more sexually knowledgeable, and scriptwriters often used the Jewish, dark-haired, sarcastic character to emphasize Mary's more conservative and conventionally feminine qualities.

While Mary's workplace provided a setting to duel with traditional Lou on issues such as equal opportunity and pay equity, Mary's relationship with her parents—who moved to Minneapolis in season three—prompted discussions on changing sexual mores. Although the Mary Richards who emerged in season three was more sexually daring than ever before, script changes reveal that her exploits were carefully edited for the screen. In the 1972 episode "Just around the Corner," Mary leaves on an evening date to the opera and returns after 8 A.M. Mary's parents are aware of her absence and ask her where she was all night, but she refuses to disclose details. As Mary is only shown leaving and returning to the apartment, viewers are similarly left to their own assumptions.[125] In an earlier, unproduced version of the script, however, Mary gives Rhoda a play-by-play, explaining that she and her date talked until dawn:

> *Mary:* "Suddenly the sun was coming up, and then we went to breakfast."
> *Rhoda:* "In the romantic glow of sunrise, did he propose?"
> *Mary:* "Yes, but not marriage."[126]

While this earlier version offers a more innocent version of events (on Mary's part, if not her date's), Mary's refusal to explain her date to her parents or to confide in Rhoda in the episode that aired mirrors the scriptwriters' earlier decision to present Mary as a jilted woman who had just ended an affair. That is, viewers could presume innocence or assume that Mary engaged in premarital sex. As Moore told *TV Guide* in 1973, this discreet approach was also in line with the series' subtle nature: "Let's face it. 'All in the Family' has opened it up for all of us, and now Mary Richards in the show can tell her mother she was out all night and not explain where and with whom. That's as far as we want to go. We're not 'Maude.' I feel strongly that sex is a private thing not to be shared with an audience."[127]

A later episode, "You've Got a Friend," implies that Mary has a sex life but again omits the specific details. Seeking a closer friendship with her father, Mary invites him over to dinner. Her mother drops him off, and upon leaving the apartment she reminds him: "Don't forget to take your pill." In unison, Mary and her father answer: "I won't." The studio audience laughs uproariously. While her father wheels around with a shocked expression, Mary's darting eyes betray her embarrassment at having revealed too much.[128]

Despite this provocative joke, strategic changes in the episode reveal the scriptwriters' hesitance to grant Mary a sexual past. In the aired episode, Mary mentions she just ran into an old high school boyfriend, Bobby Morgan.

"You remember," she tells her father, "you and Mom came home early one night, you found Bobby and me with the lights out. . . ."

"I never trusted that kid," her father grumbles.

"He's a priest now," Mary informs him, to the audience's delighted laughter.

From there, the conversation quickly turns to Mary's hurt feelings that her father missed her high school graduation, a poignant scene in which her father conveys his love and respect for the woman she has become.

However, unpublished earlier drafts of the script implied that more went on between Mary and Bobby (who, in this earlier version, grew up not to be a celibate priest but a married man with children). In these drafts, Mary challenges her father's decision to ground her after catching Mary with her boyfriend in the dark.

"We weren't doing anything wrong," she insists.

"Then why were the lights out?" her father asks.

"You think I'd be foolish enough to do something in my own home?" responds the insolent Mary. She reminds her father that Bobby was quite a catch: "Every girl would give anything to go out with him."

"I don't want my daughter giving anything," her father grumbles and proceeds to grill her about her sexual past. As the script outline describes the dialogue: "[Her father] just wants to be assured that she never, uh . . . with him. Mary assures him that she didn't. He starts to question her about the next fellow after that and Mary wonders if he really wants to go on with this."[129]

By omitting this discussion from the final version, *Mary Tyler Moore* evaded the patronizing father/daughter dynamic that had animated earlier representations of single women such as *That Girl*. It also conveniently sidestepped the guarded topic of Mary's sexual past and emphasized Mary's mending of her relationship with her father above her sexual independence. In both versions of the script, Mary emerges a complex character—old enough to be on the Pill, yet still desiring her father's support and approval.

Although *Karen*, airing in 1975, could be more daring about sex, the series similarly created ambiguity about her sexual exploits. Instead, the series' sexual relevance was created through supporting characters and settings. As producers' original plan to pair Karen with a platonic male roommate concerned the network, the revamped sitcom had Karen sharing a divided house with an African American single woman and an oversexed white newlywed couple.[130] In one episode, Karen agrees to a secret meeting with a corporate whistleblower in a porn theater. Although we never see the film, Karen's facial expressions betray her deep discomfort with the sex acts depicted onscreen.[131] Although Karen, like Mary, occasionally had an overnight date, the series emphasized this was not typical behavior for Karen. Her worried friends stay up late awaiting her return in one episode, and in another they call the police to report her missing. Like Mary, Karen rarely disclosed the details of those all-night encounters, instead allowing viewers to draw their own conclusions.[132]

Her character also neatly sidesteps the issue of her sexual history. In one episode, she bristles when her senator boyfriend grills her on her sexual past, trying to ascertain if she will make a suitable political wife. "You're not asking, you're interrogating," she says, rejecting his marriage proposal.[133] In contrast, Karen's African American female roommate Cissy (Aldine King) is more promiscuous, prompting speculation when she returns early from a date. "Nothing happened," she sighs. "He doesn't *anything* on a first date."

When her roommate suggests "that means he respects you," Cissy admits, "I wasn't hoping to get *respected*." She wears a skintight red dress to increase her odds of romance on the next date. While Cissy's sexual urges lend cultural relevance to the sitcom, they do come at the expense of sexualizing this African American woman to a greater extent than Karen—similar to *Mary Tyler Moore*'s contrast between Mary and Rhoda on matters of sexual experience.[134]

Notably, when these sitcoms portray their lead characters engaging in sex, they frame their relationships as romances rather than casual affairs—a sharp departure from popular press reports of single women's "detached" approach to sex. Karen's all-night date with a senator (after which she tells her incredulous roommate that they "just talked" for eleven hours) ends with a marriage proposal. Similarly, Mary responds negatively to a date who proposes casual sex but willingly indulges in an affair with a former boyfriend in season three.[135]

In the 1973 *Mary Tyler Moore* episode, Mary agrees to a date with former boyfriend Tom. When he arrives at her apartment door, Mary is dressed for a night on the town. He suggests they stay in and takes her in an embrace despite her protestations. Mary softens to his kiss. "Okay, let's go out," Tom finally says, moving toward the door. It is Mary who makes the ultimate decision to stay in, telling Tom that she knows of a restaurant that delivers. *TV Guide* was still reeling from the scene three months later: "It was hard to believe. There was Mary Tyler Moore, national symbol of sweet chastity, being kissed passionately on the neck for all to see on the television screen."[136]

The article partly credited the change to character development. As writer Treva Silverman remarked about Mary: "We can't Little-Orphan-Annie it up anymore, with the little circles instead of eyes, and the kid never grows up after 50 years." However, the change was also influenced by the brazen tone of the relevant programming that surrounded Mary. The series' producers had "watched gleefully while Archie Bunker demolished all the old situation-comedy taboos" with "frank dialogue about menopause, premarital relations and the sexual enthusiasms of Archie's daughter and son-in-law." But they knew that *Mary Tyler Moore*'s "great leap forward into contemporaneity" would have limitations. After scriptwriters granted Phyllis a gay brother in an earlier episode, they were sternly warned by the network to "be careful that the show does not go outside the bounds of its natural perimeters."[137]

TV Guide conceded that, given Mary's earlier "goody-goody" image, "converting Mary Tyler Moore into an unrestrained swinger would be as unbelievable as parachuting Mary Poppins into a bawdy house."[138] Accordingly, the episode in which she sleeps with an ex-boyfriend clarified that this was not casual sex, but rather, as the episode title tells us, "Remembrance of Things Past." Rhoda's reference to Tom as "a guy you used to love," and Mary and Tom's profession of love for each other at the end of the episode, grounds their affections in romance. Nor does Mary seem content with a one-night stand, as she anxiously awaits Tom's call the next day and is driven to tears with frustration by his inability to commit. "We each want different things. Mary, you want a deeper relationship. You want to be wife, mistress, mother, sister, friend," Tom acknowledges, emphasizing the single woman's more traditional qualities. However, the episode ends on a more neutral note, as the couple concede their differences and gaze lovingly at each other.

Mary's contemporaries varied in their openness about sexual matters. The twenty-five-year-old Sandy Duncan, scripted in the model of *That Girl*, was presented as young and virtuous. Both *Funny Face* and *The Sandy Duncan Show* open with scrapbook of yellowed photographs— Sandy as a beaming baby and child ballerina, Sandy as a sprightly young woman flying a kite. The theme song lyrics, addressed to a male suitor, present Sandy as "a girl you slay dragons for" and "bring home to your folks." In the *Sandy Duncan Show* pilot, Sandy rushes to correct a telephone repairman's impression that she's part of an illicit profession because she accepts jobs over the phone. (She's merely an upstanding freelance model, she explains.) Later in the episode, Sandy goes to a hip club on a date but wears a traditional long dress, marking her as out of place with the more youthful styles surrounding her. By the end of the episode, she accepts a date from a nerdy, unpopular classmate, accompanying him to a college party and allowing him to place his letter jacket around her shoulders.[139] Constant visits by Sandy's friends and neighbors also kept her on the straight and narrow. In one 1972 *Sandy Duncan Show* episode, neighbors were worried about Sandy's boss visiting her apartment at night. As a critic described the episode: "Assuming that the boss could have one thing in mind and one thing only—hanky-panky—Sandy's neighbors popped in on her with a vengeance, separately and in combinations, every minute and on the minute, all grimly determined to protect her from any remotely fleshy encounter."[140]

Although Sandy seems content to be single, the series presents her as marriage material. In one episode of *Funny Face*, student teacher Sandy learns that one of her young students has chosen her as a suitable match for his single father. Sandy intervenes to help the child accept

Too traditional? In Funny Face *and* The Sandy Duncan Show, *Sandy Duncan was a perky, innocent single woman modeled after* That Girl. *Courtesy of CBS/ Photofest.*

his father's fiancé, but not until she tries on the engagement ring to see how it feels. (Tellingly, it sticks.) Ultimately, however, Sandy's traditionalism contributed to the series' demise. As the executive producer admitted: "It was awfully old fashioned in a year when *All in the Family* and *Mary Tyler Moore* were doing realistic comedy."[141]

In contrast, the producer of the contemporaneous series *Shirley's World* vowed it would be among the first television series to grant a single woman an "obviously healthy sex life."[142] *Shirley's World* was canceled before he could carry through on that promise, although an early episode did feature its sprightly lead posing as a geisha.

The series *Diana*—which debuted in 1973, following Mary Richards's maturation—also aimed for sexual relevance. Diana Smythe, as a divorcée, sports a sexual sophistication that the other never-married heroines lack. In the pilot episode Diana shares her bed with her brother's friend, and her apartment has a couch in the living room that often serves as the site of sexual advances. She is not offended when a friend falsely assumes she spent the night with a suitor, and she often makes wisecracks that hint at her casual attitudes toward sex. As she explains her mastery of American colloquialisms: "I've learned to tell my dates, 'Why don't you give me a call,' rather than 'Why don't you knock me up.'"[143] However, even Diana seems more motivated by relationships than casual affairs. An early episode reveals she is haunted by an old beau, played by Riggs's former *Avengers* costar Patrick Macnee.[144]

Although *Diana* failed to last beyond a single season, it numbered among several mid-1970s series about divorcées. This was in part a response to the rising divorce rate, but also a reflection of changes in television industry assumptions.[145] Dow suggests that *Mary Tyler Moore*'s occasional use of divorce as a plotline helped ease acceptance of its use in comedy. Furthermore, divorce added a "new twist to the single-woman formula." In fact, the spinoff series *Rhoda* granted its married heroine a separation and divorce in 1976 in order to *increase* its character's appeal.[146] While their status as single mothers places them outside the focus of this book, divorced characters such as Ann Romano in *One Day at a Time* (CBS, 1975–1984) and *Fay* (NBC, 1975–1976) enabled bolder and more-feminist identified heroines. The short-lived *Fay* featured a fortyish, sexually forthright woman who evaded social control. In the series' pilot, she defends her right to have casual affairs, much to her grown children's dismay.[147] Dow argues that Fay was a threatening character for mainstream television and "lacked the docility and 'good girl' persona of Mary Richards." In contrast, the thirty-four-year-old Ann of the long-running *One Day at a Time* offered a softer approach, yet was "more self-consciously liberated than Mary Richards." For example, she uses her maiden name, *Ms.* Romano; asserts her right to make parenting decisions; and explains her divorce as a quest for self-fulfillment. Her status as a mother of two teen daughters also grants her greater responsibility than childless single characters.[148] These sitcoms arguably spoke to the concerns of never-married women, as they stressed the importance of self-actualization, the need to rewrite the rules of femininity, and the preference for living alone over being unhappily partnered.

Early seventies sitcoms represented a step forward for single women representations. In contrast to earlier programs such as *That Girl*, they granted heroines more stable and realistic professions that related to viewers' real lives and focused more of their attention on the workplace. They gave visibility and viability to women entering male-dominated professions, and—in the case of Mary's equal-pay argument and Diana's interview—modeled responses to overt discrimination.

Although films of the late 1960s had offered memorable portrayals of single working women, they often ended with white weddings. In contrast, these sitcoms presented characters who were content to be perpetually single. *Mary Tyler Moore* ran for seven years on CBS, sparking multiple spinoffs in addition to the imitative programs I have described. Single characters' collective presence on the domestic medium of television made them a more accepted part of everyday life and captured a consumer demographic that would respond enthusiastically to action heroines in the late 1970s.

Arguably, these programs' political potential was blunted by the limitations of the sitcom genre and the desire to appeal to diverse audiences. As a "libber in the larger sense," Mary hit the right balance: She was a woman who could work in a male-dominated newsroom without upsetting gender roles, indulge in occasional affairs without becoming an unrestrained swinger, and acknowledge feminist issues such as equal pay without towing the political line too heavily.

Mary's adoption of "lifestyle feminism" countered the movement's perceived excesses while making causes such as equitable pay and sexual self-determination palatable to mainstream audiences. That middle-class white single woman were the foremost representatives of "lifestyle feminism" is significant, as these programs largely deflected attention from marital concerns and the multiple forms of discrimination that women of color faced. That these women could, indeed, "make it after all" with professional jobs and classy apartments masked the economic struggles that real single women endured. And the constant presence of coworkers, friends, and neighbors in these women's solo apartments diffused the radicalism of a character enjoying life on her own terms.

Perhaps these programs' real progress was in the arena of sex. In comparison to Ann on *That Girl*—who held poor Donald at bay for five seasons—these characters had both implied and overt affairs. A 1975 *TV Guide* column argued that the latter seasons of *Mary Tyler Moore* were more radical than Norman Lear's sitcoms. The Lear comedies "are monogamous to the hilt," primarily portraying affections between married couples, critic Edith Efron noted. While Lear offered the occasional gay or swinger character, Efron felt these were merely "comedic stick figures introduced for pedagogic purposes and have no emotional reality."[149] Efron instead located the "emotional challenge to the American puritan sexual tradition" in programs such as *M*A*S*H* and *Mary Tyler Moore*, "where beloved protagonists transgress against traditional moral codes without a stitch of dramatic punishment."[150]

The sitcoms' tentative acknowledgment of single women's sex lives and desires—and the lack of punishments for having sex—was significant evidence that media industries and societal attitudes were starting to change. As the script changes and casting decisions for *Mary Tyler Moore* and *Karen* reveal, however, producers in the mid-1970s were still uncomfortable with granting a grown woman a sexual past or a male roommate. That these heroines tended to conflate sex with love contradicted the liberated attitudes of the young women interviewed in the popular press, who seemed decidedly more cavalier about sex.

These programs primed Americans to accept even bolder representations of women's work ambitions and sex lives. By the mid-1970s, single women had infiltrated the masculine realm of television police drama, demonstrating greater assertion and using their bodies as well as their brains to assist them on the force. By the time Mary went off the air in 1977, embracing her coworkers in a platonic group hug, television was populated with sexualized singles and superheroes who took feminism in ever more daring directions.

Claiming Sexuality and Power

*Working Women and Wonder Women in 1970s
Action Series*

Popular media have often portrayed the single woman as vulnerable: to the vicissitudes of city life, to men's advances, or to her own baser impulses. But *Mary Tyler Moore* and her contemporaries in early 1970s situation comedy acknowledged women's ability to survive and even thrive as single urban professionals. Network television took single women a step further in the mid- to late 1970s, casting them as lead characters in police and science-fiction dramas. Like their predecessors, these characters possessed both professional and interpersonal skills, and they knew how to assuage male egos. Yet they also possessed exceptional beauty and strength and often strategically used their sexuality to achieve their goals.

By comparing long-running "single girl" sitcoms such as *That Girl* to mid-1970s action dramas, we can see marked differences in how single women approach sexuality in the workplace. In a 1969 episode of *That Girl*, aspiring actress Ann Marie (Marlo Thomas) accepts a gig as "Miss Chicken Big," the leggy, dancing mascot of a fast food chain. After a tap-dancing tour of upper New York, Ann, still costumed as a chicken, accepts a ride home from her boss, a leering older man who resembles Colonel Sanders. She becomes alarmed when he drives her far from her destination and indignant when he places his hand on her exposed leg. Ann raises herself to her full feathered height, threatens to call the ASPCA, and demands to be let out of the car. That she firmly resisted her employer's advances could be seen as progress for the series. In a 1968 episode, Ann was pinned to the wall by an amorous boss and merely pleaded: "Don't make me raise my voice." Yet the fact she raised objections under the guise of animal rather than women's rights softens her response with humor and hints at the lack of language to address her indignation.[1]

As women moved from comedic to dramatic roles in mid-1970s

television, they also moved from repelling to initiating advances. One such heroine was police officer Christie Love (Teresa Graves), who broke ground as one of the first African American female characters to command a title role in a network production. In *Get Christie Love,* the 1974 television movie that inspired the ABC series, Christie botches an investigation by throwing a criminal off a balcony—and nearly loses her post in the process. Wearing a conservative tweed coat, she appears before her boss and begs to remain on the case. "Give me three days. If I don't come up with anything by then, you win," she offers.[2]

"Win what?" asks her white police captain, exasperated.

"You name it, you got it," Christie retorts, jutting out her hip. The captain sighs, ordering Christie to report for a more routine assignment. She parts her coat to reveal a shapely leg and smiles saucily—using her body as bait. She succeeds in gaining more time to investigate the case.

In each series, representations of sex in the workplace served a strategic purpose. For *That Girl*'s Ann Marie, her bosses' amorous advances served both to mark her attractiveness and emphasize her vulnerability. Her resistance to advances reassured viewers that she was not *that* kind of girl. The prevalence of sexualized workplace interactions in other sixties representations of working women may also have served to alleviate anxieties about women newly entering the workforce by emphasizing characters' attractiveness above their professional competence. Series such as *Get Christie Love* challenged a network taboo against placing women in leading dramatic roles—and used sexual appeal to ease their acceptance. Furthermore, the increasingly sexualized nature of television in the 1970s allowed flirtations and innuendo that would have made That Girl blush.[3] While Christie's aggressive sexuality played into historical media stereotypes of African American women, she also shared much in common with white action heroines on 1970s television. The fact that she initiated the bet with her boss seemingly places her character in control while also speaking to emerging feminist complaints about women's objectification.

In this chapter, I argue that prime-time action series such as *Police Woman, Get Christie Love, Wonder Woman,* and *Charlie's Angels* answered feminists' call for more empowering images of working women while addressing critics' fears about the chilling effect that feminist ideals might have on workplace interactions. The action heroines' heightened

Partners in crime: Police officers Captain Reardon (Harry Guardino) and Christie (Teresa Graves) flirt and solve cases in the TV movie Get Christie Love, *which started the series. Courtesy of ABC/Photofest.*

femininity and sexuality countered the perceived feminist trend toward androgyny and eased concerns that workplace equality would erase differences between the sexes. These women's relative autonomy and strategic use of sexuality—to solve cases or elicit confessions for the protection of women and the greater good—identified their attractiveness as a source of power and leverage in the workplace, rather than merely a site of victimization or objectification.

The fact that most of these characters were single or divorced is significant. As I have explored, the single working woman was one image advertisers and programmers used to appease feminist protesters and reach new demographic groups from the early 1970s onward. The action heroines' unmarried status distinguished them from the domesticated housewives that dominated earlier TV and provided a point of identification for young female viewers, who were increasingly defining themselves in terms of careers. Singleness, however, also cast these women as sexually available and thus accessible to male viewers' fantasies.

Television and Titillation

Scholars have characterized the 1970s as a time of marked cultural change. The increased visibility of feminism, combined with the movement of more middle-class women into the workforce, both destabilized family structures and undermined earlier assumptions about gender roles. Given that the three major television networks captured up to 90 percent of the viewing audience prior to the rise of cable, television was a pervasive and influential medium that helped interpret those changes. In her study of sexuality in seventies TV, Elana Levine contends that "television's take on the sexual revolution was more widely consumed than any other."[4] Sherrie Inness further argues that television both responded to and shaped changes in women's work roles as its programming turned toward female-centric dramas in the mid-1970s. Inness writes:

> The popular media played a part in disseminating changing gender ideology. But the media did not only convey changing women's roles; they also altered these roles and created new ones. For example, the concept for *Charlie's Angels* stemmed, at least partially, from the increasing number of women in non-traditional jobs, including the police force; what emerged was a show that had its own impact on how women created and lived their lives. Thus, examining the popular media is vital for understanding social change in the 1970s.[5]

While Inness positions *Charlie's Angels* and similar series as important historical texts and potential sites of empowerment for women, other scholars and critics have characterized seventies television as ephemeral and exploitative. Many of the television programs that prominently featured women in nondomestic roles were branded "jiggle TV," a label that denies the programs any cultural significance beyond sexual objectification.[6]

While the meek Mary Richards has often been acknowledged as a symbol of popular feminism, the breakthrough action heroines that moved women from daytime comedy to nighttime drama are often seen as co-opting or antithetical to the movement. According to 1970s critics writing in popular magazines, action programs featuring nubile women appealed "less to women than to men and prepubescent boys" and offered "very little to please a woman whose consciousness has been raised even a degree or two by the [feminist] movement."⁷ While such critiques rightfully called the networks to account for their exploitative use of women's bodies, they also denied the experiences of female viewers who were inspired by seeing women in active roles.

Susan Douglas acknowledges the tensions within television programming, wryly referring to action heroines as "bionic bimbos" yet highlighting the significant differences among programs; for example, the repeated victimization of women in *Police Woman* is countered by the relative competence and solidarity of women in *Charlie's Angels*. Douglas and other scholars often draw from their own memories and experiences of the shows to counter negative critiques. While Whitney Womack remembers the Angels as "smart," "cool," empowered women who reflected feminist ideas, Douglas admits she found *Charlie's Angels* pleasurable viewing when she was in graduate school.⁸

Elana Levine situates TV's action heroines within the broader sexual culture of 1970s television, which conveyed changing sexual mores through provocative costumes and suggestive dialogue rather than explicit sexual relationships. However, she contends that action series offered more than just titillation. Characters who were both beautiful and powerful, forceful yet feminine, met the needs of diverse viewing audiences and reinforced perceptions of innate differences between men and women. Thus, these series both reflected feminist insights and played into the rhetorical strategies of antifeminists. "Because the question of sexual difference and its relationship to feminism was so hotly contested at the time," Levine writes, "it was possible in popular discourse to link [*Charlie's Angels*] to the movement in one instant and understand the program as the nadir of patriarchal oppression the next."⁹ Furthermore, these programs' tendency to focus on an exceptional woman—as the lone female member of a police force, or a superhero with unparalleled powers—was a nonthreatening means to address collective cultural change. As Levine argues, "Television's emphasis on idiosyncratic characters grappling with sexual change could make it seem as if the sexual revolution was not about challenging the heterosexual nuclear family, patriarchy or the capitalist system, but only about the choices of certain individuals."¹⁰

This chapter acknowledges the inspirational role that action series served for many women and girls in the seventies. However, it resists the tendency of some critics to either claim these series as empowering or disparage them as sheer sexist drivel. Instead, I consider how these narratives reflected broader understandings of feminism and sexuality in the workplace. I follow the lead of media scholars, including Douglas, Inness, and Levine, by examining key differences among the series and exploring how television skillfully negotiated tensions between feminism and antifeminism. However, I hope to offer new insights on these programs' creation and cultural influence through my analysis of archival production materials. I also consider the particular implications these series had for single women, many of whom were assuming new work roles and rethinking their relationships with men. Although the pending Equal Rights Amendment was foundational to debates about gender and the workplace, so were emerging discussions on everyday "flirting" and sexual harassment.

ERA: Equality at What Price?

From 1974, when *Police Woman* debuted, to 1977, when *Charlie's Angels* first aired, Americans were engaged in fierce debates over the Equal Rights Amendment and the concept of sexual harassment. These conversations reflected key questions about the implications of feminism and gender equality: Were men and women fundamentally different or essentially the same?[11] Were women as physically capable as men? How would the workplace function without sexual banter, so long an accepted dimension of gender relations? Did the behavior and attitudes feminists termed "sexual harassment" really constitute oppression, or even pose a problem, for women? These questions had particular implications for single women who were entering the workforce in greater numbers and who contended daily with sexual advances.

When the Equal Rights Amendment passed the Senate in March 1972, advancing to the states for ratification, advocates assumed its approval would be "quick and easy."[12] Simply stated, the amendment proposed that "equality of rights under the law shall not be denied or abridged by the United States or by any state on account of sex."[13] As historian Flora Davis notes, however, the prospect of removing differential treatment for women and placing them in unsuitable work positions fueled a social movement of its own. The state-based nature of ratification carried the conversation into the heartlands, and activist groups that formed in the mid-1970s kept the ERA in the national spotlight until its 1982 defeat.[14]

ERA opponents such as Phyllis Schlafly reframed the amendment as the sole concern of antifamily, unfeminine activists who would deny women their natural prerogative to be homemakers and mothers. In her 1974 newsletters, Schlafly characterized the feminist agenda as "a series of sharp-tongued, high-pitched whining complaints by unmarried women. They view the home as a prison and the wife and mother as a slave."[15] According to Schlafly, "women's libbers don't understand that most women want to be wife, mother and homemaker" and "would rather cuddle a baby than a typewriter."[16] She erroneously insisted that the ERA would force women to work—as men would no longer be required by law to provide for their families—and would deny women their right to motherhood in custody disputes.[17]

As Levine notes, many of the groups that rose up to oppose the ERA and the feminist movement used sexual difference as their rallying cry, evidenced in group names such as "Women Who Want to Be Women" and "Happiness of Womanhood." These groups "had a significant impact on many Americans, largely because their endorsement of a fundamental, irrevocable and beneficial sexual difference resonated with many people's heretofore unquestioned beliefs about sex and gender."[18]

While they may not have been anti-ERA activists, single women interviewed by U.S. News in 1975 expressed negative perceptions of feminism and tried to distinguish their professional accomplishments from a feminist political stance. A twenty-six-year-old Chicago trial lawyer told the magazine that she "avoids feminist groups": "I am not one of those professional women who want to shove other women out of their homes. I think the role of housewife should still be an option." Another interviewee posed the question: "If the women take over the men's jobs, what are the men going to do?"[19] While these opinions were not necessarily representative of single women nationally, their presence in a mainstream news magazine helped frame the ERA as extreme, even to the single working women it purported to serve.

ERA opponents also implied that the majority of working women found the amendment unnecessary and potentially hazardous to their well-being. As activist Naomi McDaniel argued in a brochure for

Schlafly's group, Stop ERA, the Federal Equal Opportunity Act of 1972 had already removed protective labor laws for women, "forcing women to do men's work that women are not physically able to do."[20] Were the ERA to be ratified, "all this injustice and nonsense will be locked forever into the U.S. Constitution," wrote McDaniel. Citing complaints from working-class and minority women suddenly forced to do "men's jobs"—from heavy lifting to cleaning urinals—the brochure characterizes ERA as a fraud "promoted by a handful of women who sit at comfortable desks and never have to lift anything heavier than a stack of papers."[21] (Although the brochure hints at the larger class- and race-based concerns fueling opposition to the ERA, elsewhere women of color and working-class women advocated for its ratification.)[22]

Opponents also used the prospect of a gender-neutral military draft to evoke fears about placing women in combat. "Foxholes are bad enough for men, but they certainly are not the place for women," Schlafly flatly stated.[23] However, as Flora Davis notes, surveys on the issue indicated that the public worried more about women's power than their safety: "One survey reported that 97 percent of those polled thought it was fine for a woman to be a nurse in a combat zone (where she could easily be killed), while only 59 percent believed women should be air defense missile gunners based in the United States. Apparently, many Americans had a gut reaction to any suggestion that women could be aggressive and powerful."[24]

Sexual Harassment and Postliberation Flirting

Just as the ERA was reframed as a narrow agenda rather than a collective concern, feminists tackling sexual harassment in the mid-1970s were accused of making a political issue out of harmless flirtations—or of denying the ability of individual women to deflect and resist sexual advances. Media coverage of a verbal harassment case in 1973 revealed the entrenched attitudes that activists would soon face in framing harassment as a feminist issue.

In the 1973 case, a group of working women in downtown Hartford asked police to protect them from the barrage of "obscene gestures and catcalls" they received from construction workers as they walked to lunch. The police intervened by declaring a "stretch of sidewalk . . .

off-limits" and threatening to arrest any man who dared make a harassing gesture.[25] According to the *New York Times*, the men defended their right to "girlwatch" ("You can't touch, but you can look," one said), and the women interviewed "seemed to find the whole thing silly."[26]

"If a man makes an obscene remark to me, I can take care of myself," one office worker said. "If they're just whistling, well, what's the harm?" A waitress who called the construction workers "good boys" surmised, "It was probably some old bag who never gets whistled at who complained."[27] A female reporter, who found herself "followed by whistles and calls" as she reported on the Hartford scene, concluded that "girl-watching will always be a favorite male sport—police notwithstanding."[28] Even before harassment debates were formally set into motion, these articles assumed the naturalness of "girlwatching," presented legal intervention as an unreasonable approach, and discredited the women who complained. The articles implied that women enjoyed or did not mind the attention—and had the innate capacity to protect themselves against obscene remarks.

When the term "sexual harassment" was coined in a 1975 lawsuit, feminist groups such as Working Women United and the Alliance Against Sexual Coercion quickly formed around the issue. As legal historian Carrie Baker explains, these groups drew from the rhetoric of the rape crisis movement, arguing that individual verbal and physical infractions supported a larger system of oppression that hindered women's full participation in the workplace. Unlike media coverage of the ERA, which gave credence to erroneous assumptions about the amendment's effects, Baker notes that much early news coverage of sexual harassment was both sympathetic and well informed. A 1975 article in the *New York Times* and 1976 *Redbook* survey on sexual harassment helped bring the issue to public attention and generated a "tidal wave of response" from women who had been harassed.[29]

However, other media accounts implied harassment was mostly a problem for women who were not smart or assertive enough to negotiate sexual advances and suggested new rules of etiquette rather than legal recourse. In several articles published in the late 1970s, "women were encouraged to dress modestly and be more assertive, including making eye contact, using authoritative body language, speaking with conviction, and not diluting the message by smiling," writes Baker. "As late as July 1979, *Working Woman* published an article that similarly assumed that assertiveness was an adequate solution to the problem of sexual harassment and even discouraged legal solutions."[30]

Editorial columns that appeared in the mid- to late 1970s further undermined feminist efforts by accusing them of exaggerating the issue and making a political case out of "flirting." As a female *Harper's* columnist quipped in 1976, "A lot of women would feel deprived without a reasonable quota of sexual harassment per week."[31] Amid calls for legal intervention on one end, and new etiquette rules on the other, several columnists advocated for the return of "flirting" in the workplace and daily life, both as a means to preserve gender difference and to diffuse sexual tension. According to *Newsweek*, feminists opposed flirting on broader grounds than the sexual harassment issue. As columnist Ann Taylor Fleming portrayed the feminist stance: "Women seeking their liberation cast a cold eye on flirting and found it to be sexist, divisive, demeaning, role-playing and otherwise ugly and useless. With men, they would be straight, demanding, fair, nonfrivolous—no games, no lowered lids, no blushing cheeks, no sleight of hand or eye. They would get their jobs, and their sex, on merit."[32]

In *Mademoiselle,* another female columnist who once took smug satisfaction in refusing to flirt likened her new love for the sport to "slowly waking up from the sexual coma, realizing I am not just a motorized head and enjoying . . . femininity."[33] Nor was this enlivening practice at odds with equality, columnists argued. Writing in 1977, Fleming posited a "post-liberation flirting" in which "the smiles are not so shy or the lids so lowered," and in which both sexes participate equally: "Women are sassier . . . the men . . . are becoming more coy, subtler, more 'female'—and better flirters. What a relief. We both—women and men—can flirt with immunity again because we have become at least somewhat liberated from the fear that we will have to 'come across' if we smile a little too saucily."[34]

Male columnists agreed that flirting is "adapting to the new era of sexual equality," as women "no longer play the passive role."[35] One columnist firmly distinguished the practice from harassment: "Wolf whistles and sexual innuendoes have as much to do with flirting as the hustle has to do with ballet," he quipped. "Flirting is appreciative, not possessive."[36] Although flirting promised "instant intimacy" and was "safer than sex," the fact that both sexes were actively participating meant the dangers were distributed more evenly.[37] Fleming wrote:

Some of my women friends have been pounced upon by men who mistook their bolder smiles, their wiser wisecracks, for definite come-ons. That's fair. Things between men and women haven't quite shaken down yet. A nurse I know flirted rather heavily for some months with a doctor, who one day backed her up against a medicine chest. It was the same old story except that . . . the nurse did not wax offended but admitted that she got exactly what she deserved.[38]

At a time when growing awareness of sexual harassment led some feminists to advocate for a "taboo on sex at work,"[39] these columnists more optimistically argued that sexual boundaries would sort themselves out without legal intervention. Even the threat of assault, they implied, should not stop women from expressing their attractions.

In summary, those against ratification of the Equal Rights Amendment often used women's physical inferiority, or weakness, as a reason for their opposition. According to their argument, innate gender differences best suited women for motherhood—not physical labor and certainly not military service. In contrast, those opposing sexual harassment laws used women's clout and capabilities to build their case. According to this argument, women were not only savvy enough to negotiate sexual advances, but they might also enjoy making advances of their own. Yet these columnists also emphasized the need to preserve gender differences in the workplace, rather than striving for a sexless equality.

As I will explore in the latter part of this chapter, 1970s action series were shaped by and participated in the larger dialogues about gender and sexuality that fueled the disputes about the ERA, sexual harassment, and "flirting." The flirtatious femininity of Farrah Fawcett and her colleagues visibly preserved gender difference in the workplace and distinguished the women of *Charlie's Angels* from unappealing "libbers." The inferior firepower and physical capabilities of Police Woman and the Bionic Woman played into the same stereotypes about women's weakness that stalled ERA ratification. As television's action heroines came to the aid of sexually victimized women and faced near-rape situations themselves, they underscored the need for police protection against sexual violence. Yet these heroines were not wholly oppressed by sexuality, as they were able to leverage sexual advances to their advantage.

168

Television's Action Heroines Arise

Television historically has tended to relegate complex representations of women to situation comedies and to "individual characters placed in male-dominated dramatic settings," writes scholar Amanda Lotz.[40] Accordingly, *That Girl* placed a zany spin on serious issues facing young women in the city, and *Mary Tyler Moore* used comedic dialogue to address workplace equality. The move toward female-centric dramas in the 1970s broke from this trend, particularly in series such as *Charlie's Angels*, which offered a team of crime-fighting heroines. Lotz notes that while action dramas may offer women "an atypical physically empowered status," they tend to undermine the characters' power through exploitative camera angles and stilted dialogue. "Because they share narrative time with the spectacle of chases and fight scenes, these series sometimes lack the textual complexity of other dramatic narrative forms," she writes. Furthermore, "many action dramas structure their narratives episodically, inhibiting long-term character and plot development." Additionally, the unrealistic aspects of many action dramas — such as *Wonder Woman*'s superpowers and fantasy settings — limit their applicability to real-life women.[41] Nevertheless, the movement of female characters into lead dramatic roles was a significant shift in the 1970s, one that reflected changes in industry and audience expectations.

Several factors spurred the rise of female dramatic heroines in mid- to late 1970s television. First, as Levine notes, new demographic models from the late 1960s identified women ages eighteen to forty-nine as the most desirable television audience because they held the most disposable income and made the majority of household buying decisions. To reach this audience, producers and advertisers were forced to acknowledge the broader effects of feminist activism.[42] Although radical feminists were most vocal in their opposition to television, surveys and marketing studies revealed that a broad spectrum of female viewers were troubled by the popular media's tendency to represent women as sex objects or helpless housewives.[43] Advertising approaches such as Revlon's highly successful 1973 Charlie perfume campaign, in which a confident single woman in a business suit strides the city, underscored the commercial advantages of representing working women.[44]

Secondly, demographic shifts were fueling the need for new images. The percentage of American women who worked, and the percentage who remained unmarried, increased dramatically during the decade. Although most women remained in traditionally female and low-paying career fields, there was a steady climb of women into professional occupations such as law and a slow but symbolic trickle of women into traditionally male realms such as police work and construction.[45] New laws such as the 1972 Equal Credit Opportunity Act enabled single women to apply for mortgages and credit cards in their own names, thus increasing women's economic clout.[46] According to the U.S. Department of Labor, the percentage of never-married women in the population increased "phenomenally" between 1968 and 1978: "Among women 20 to 24 years of age, the proportion who were single rose by one-third (from 35.9 to 47.6 percent), while the share of never married women in their late twenties posted a striking 75-percent gain (from 10.3 to 18.0 percent)."[47]

U.S. News reported on this "growing army" of single women in 1975, noting that among those in Chicago, "few seem greatly concerned about discrimination and sexual harassment — minor and isolated problems, many say, in comparison with dull jobs and career doubts that prompt some [women] to quit and head for home, or the altar, after a year or two."[48] Yet a female sociologist interviewed for the article characterized singles as "an increasingly important social force," arguing that "the increasing divorce rate is adding to the visible group of single women. And demographers believe many single women are making a conscious choice not to marry."[49]

In addition to appealing to new demographic groups, the female action heroine was a novel representation that helped producers navigate a period of heightened network competition in the late 1970s, spurred partly by the introduction of cable television and video recorders. Scholars who have researched the rise of single women representations on 1970s television argue that "increases in program experimentation symptomatic of network rivalry played a more immediate role . . . than any public or private advocacy concerns."[50] This desire for greater experimentation in programming is reflected in network and producers' correspondence. A 1973 report revealed NBC was "looking for dramatic shows in NEW areas" and wanted to "get away from 'cops and robbers' and other franchise forms." Action heroines provided a new twist, and producers were reportedly "intrigued and titillated by the concept of women performing in male roles."[51] The production company Screen

Gems reported it was "searching for an hour action adventure show which would star a female investigator and at the same time avoid . . . clichés and cuteness" by presenting her as credible and intelligent.[52]

Action heroines were also prompted by concerns about television violence. The Surgeon General had released a much-publicized report in 1972 connecting consumption of violent television to violent behavior, and advocacy groups warned that violent prime-time television might have a pernicious effect on children. Rather than face government censorship, the networks vowed to self-regulate and reduce violent content in programs.[53] A female action heroine promised a softer approach to crime-fighting that would still be appealing to audiences. As one producer wrote in a 1972 memo: "A show about a woman detective could present a lot of exciting crime and action—yet stay clear of the violence and physical confrontations that always occur in shows featuring a male detective. This could fit in with the networks' 'anti-violence' campaign."[54] As I will demonstrate later in this chapter, producers for series such as *Wonder Woman* and *Charlie's Angels* often curbed violent content within these programs to meet network standards.

Despite the impetus toward female action heroines, the networks still contended with deeper misgivings about placing women in leading roles. "Why Can't a Woman Be More Like a Man?" *TV Guide* asked in 1973, bemoaning women's marginal roles in nighttime drama.[55] The article explored a familiar paradox: Despite the fact that evening viewing audiences were majority female, producers doubted that women would want to watch women on television or that viewers of either sex would take female action characters seriously. As producer Douglas Cramer told a scriptwriter in 1972: "While daytime television is directed to the woman's audience, nighttime series must have a more general basis of appeal. Women's Lib notwithstanding, when the husband head-of-the-household comes home at night he strongly influences which programs are tuned in."[56] (Cramer later created *Wonder Woman* to appeal across gender lines.) *TV Guide* credited assumptions about husbands' preferences for the shelving of producer Aaron Spelling's *The Bait*, an ABC "policewoman" movie that failed to become a series despite high ratings and critical acclaim. "Maybe for men there's something threatening about watching women in lead roles," acknowledged Spelling, who would later create *Charlie's Angels*.[57]

"Television Lib," a cartoon in a 1972 *TV Guide* issue, further explored

anxieties about upsetting television's gender balance. In the cartoonist's
dystopic vision of "liberated" television, a burly man sells laundry de-
tergent, and a female reporter enters a locker room blindfolded to conduct a postgame interview. In another panel, a female viewer watches a
familiar sitcom with her husband and gloats: "I love how Edith calls Archie a dingbat!" The illustrations imply that representing women's liberation on television would mean ridiculous gender-role reversals—and
that men would suffer as a result.[58] Producer Norman Lear imagined
such a role reversal in "All that Glitters," a short-lived 1977 sitcom in
which chauvinistic female executives ogled powerless males. In a 1976
production meeting, Lear argued that giving women greater power
would not address gender inequality: "The women would be playing
the same games, and the men would be playing the same games women
[now] play."[59]

The rise of prominent action heroines starting in the 1974–1975
television season countered television's tendency to portray women as
mere "professional auxiliaries" or "amusing idiots," as *TV Guide* put
it.[60] However, as Levine notes, these programs skillfully "balance[d] the
promise of women's liberation with the security of immutable sexual
difference."[61] Single women took starring roles in three police dramas:
NBC's *Amy Prentiss* and *Police Woman* and ABC's *Get Christie Love*, creating what one Chicago reviewer deemed a glutted market: "One thing
about television, it believes that if a thing is worth doing, it's worth
overdoing."[62] The series were based on successful experiments: *Amy
Prentiss* and *Police Woman* were spin-offs of existing police shows *Ironside* and *Police Story*, respectively; the *Christie Love* series was adapted
from a television movie.[63] The overt feminization and sexualization of
these characters may have heightened the programs' appeal and eased
anxieties that moving women into nontraditional roles would emascu-
late men. As actress Angie Dickinson described *Police Woman:* "It's
really the story of a woman who can stand up to men without being
resented by them."[64]

Get Christie Love and *Police Woman:* Femininity and Race on the Force

Police dramas were a familiar and accessible programming format for
audiences, and their popularity helped ease acceptance of women in

nontraditional roles. For example, Dickinson credits *Police Woman*'s early success to its basis in *Police Story* and its initial placement after *The Rockford Files* in NBC's Friday-night lineup.[65] However, Julie D'Acci argues this genre had historically bolstered traditional notions of male authority, as male actors ruled televisual police units, pursued criminals, and enforced the social order. Thus, as women entered police programs, they were often paired with more authoritative male leads and played up their sexuality to placate the patriarchal order.[66]

Police programs also reflected women's symbolic gains in the work world. In the 1970s, women constituted only a tiny percentage of sworn police officers, rising from 1.5 percent in 1972 to 3.38 percent in 1979.[67] Yet their very presence was the result of concerted legal struggle to be admitted to and promoted within male-dominated departments, thus representing a gain for feminism. As *Newsweek* noted in 1977, however, the small number of women working as "fire fighters, truck drivers, auto mechanics, jockeys and bartenders" tended to obscure the fact that "very little has changed" for the majority of working women: "Most of them still work in the traditional women's jobs—as domestic and social workers, teachers, secretaries and nurses. Only 2.7 per cent of the directors of major corporations are women. . . . Only 16 percent of working women are professional—most of them in teaching and nursing. . . . On the average a woman's salary is 62 per cent of a man's, the same gap that existed ten years ago."[68]

"It is so novel to see women where we have not seen them before that it obscures the massive nature of the problem," Equal Opportunity Commission head Eleanor Holmes Norton told *Newsweek*. "The great problems of sex discrimination have not been addressed, and though there has been a change in people's minds, in most areas where women are included they are still in the break-through phase."[69] For feminist critic Marjorie Rosen, the police programs followed the pattern of highlighting symbolic gains without acknowledging the pervasive nature of sexism: "With all these women functioning in a tough, formerly all-male environment, lip service can be paid to the notion of women doing liberated tasks. What's really going on, however, is subtle machismo," she argued.[70] A female TV executive agreed that police programs were headed in the wrong direction by merely placing women in men's roles rather than showing "what women really do" in most workplaces.[71]

The actresses themselves seemed hesitant to identify their roles with feminist gains. Jessica Walter, who portrayed a widowed police chief on NBC's short-lived *Amy Prentiss,* acknowledged that her part was a breakthrough: "Most parts for women are coat holders, assistants, secretaries. . . . All of a sudden shows for women are happening."[72] According to *Ms.* magazine, the series pilot "made a pretty good stab at consciousness-raising," as "closet feminist" Amy fights for and wins the position of chief over the objections of her less-qualified male colleagues.[73] However, Walter denied the show was a "women's lib thing": "I don't know many women's libbers and we didn't get much mail on that because we didn't push it in the show. As a matter of fact, it's a source of irritation to the character, Amy."[74] In the pilot, Amy bristles when a reporter addresses her as "Ms. Prentiss," reminding him that she prefers to be known as a "Mrs."[75] *Police Woman*'s Angie Dickinson also sought distance from feminism: "The idea of feeling a responsibility to the women's cause is terrifying," she told *Ms.* "I'd rather not feel that responsibility because I don't like crusading. I didn't take this show to prove anything."[76]

However, the fact that *Ms.* magazine provided a generally positive review of the police programs indicates their appeal to "women's libbers" and single viewers who took pride in being a "Ms." While noting that *Amy Prentiss* represented television's highest-ranking woman in blue, the article also celebrated *Police Woman* and *Get Christie Love.* The accompanying photos portray *Police Woman*'s Angie Dickinson and *Christie Love*'s Teresa Graves side by side. While Dickinson poses demurely, gazing off-camera, Graves confronts viewers with a close-angle karate chop. Racial differences are further reinforced in the language used to describe the characters: *Police Woman*'s Pepper Anderson is described as "a sensible, good-looking girl with a sense of humor . . . attractive to men and appealing to women," while Christie Love is characterized as the tough crime-fighter you would not want to meet in a dark alley — particularly if you are a serial-killing john.[77]

Studies of police women in the late 1970s and early 1980s found that fierce sexual harassment served as a barrier to their full participation on the force. "Women on the police force have complained that they cannot hang out with their co-workers after work and have a beer for fear that their behavior will be defined as 'loose,'" reported Working Women International in a 1981 report.[78] The report also described a "nightmarish" 1978 case in which "a police woman who dated one of her fellow police officers was barraged with phone calls from men on the force who assumed . . . she was the sexual property of all of them."[79] While real-life police women treaded carefully, their television counterparts enjoyed playing with fire—and often found their sexual appeal to be a useful asset.

The television movie *Get Christie Love* was based on blaxploitation films of the 1970s, which tended to represent African American women as equally beautiful and powerful, violent and victimized. As scholar Stephanie Dunn reflects on the raced and gendered contradictions of Pam Grier's character in *Foxy Brown* (1974):

> On one hand, the movie offers an image of a tough woman as action hero who wins out over the bad guys, a significant change in Hollywood film. . . . The film is further unique because its heroine is a black woman, depicted as feminine, beautiful and desirable. This dynamic marks it as very special, since Hollywood very rarely invests in this particular image of black women. On the other hand, the film's potential for being truly radical is limited because it does not ultimately upset the sexist and racist white patriarchal iconography of the black female.[80]

Black women most often appeared in early 1970s television in the role of prostitute, and even the powerful Foxy Brown masqueraded as a "high-priced" hooker for political ends.[81] Accordingly, Christie Love's first appearance in the movie is under the cover of night as she struts Central Park in a fur coat, mini skirt, and flowing wig, inviting catcalls and racial slurs from would-be johns. She accepts an invitation from an earnest white man who leads her to a dark corner of the park, pulls a switchblade, and demands she strip. "Don't hurt me; I've got two babies," Christie squeals, making helpless gestures as the man corners his apparent victim. Suddenly she turns the tables, using a karate chop to knock him to the ground, and calls for police backup. Although her stunt leads to the arrest of a serial killer who preys on prostitutes, Christie must answer to police captain Casey Reardon (Harry Guardino) for her failure to follow protocol.

The elongated scenes in which Christie struggles (later in the movie, she is again cornered in a dark garage, at knifepoint) may have appealed to viewers who found voyeuristic pleasure in women's victimization. However, Christie's demonstrated ability to physically defend herself against rapists and drug smugglers may also have provided a point of empowerment for female viewers, albeit at the expense of characterizing African American women as inherently aggressive. The racial markers of Christie's afro and street slang (her catch phrase was "You're under arrest, sugah!") signaled a certain "street credibility" to viewers that *Police Woman*'s more delicate Pepper Anderson lacked.[82] Also, unlike Pepper, who used a gun to defend herself and often depended on male colleagues to rescue her from danger, Christie's trained body serves as a weapon, and she appears to act independently from her male colleagues.

In her interactions with the older white police captain, Christie plays into other "controlling images" that have historically limited African American women's representations in media. She assumes the role of both insatiable jezebel and combative Sapphire,[83] directly challenging Captain Reardon's orders and using her sexuality as bait to get what she wants. She bristles at her boss's willingness to use her as a decoy for serial killers and insinuates that if she were truly appreciated, she'd be taken to a nice restaurant rather than a diner for a business dinner. Although Christie's complaints seem reasonable, her complaints fuel a common media stereotype. As Kimberly Springer describes contemporary images of angry black women, they are "always already angry, carrying a chip on their collective shoulders and ready to go off at the least personal slight." Although Christie's devaluation on the force may be due to her race and gender status, her grievances are presented as "personal—not structural or institutional."[84]

Christie's demand to be treated like a lady emphasizes the way that her race and appearance (short hair, slinky bell bottoms) work to position her outside normative femininity. However, her desire to be a feminine subject and romantic interest also counters the threat that her physical and professional power might pose to viewers. As Levine notes, actress Teresa Graves entered the series as an established sex symbol, stemming from her role on the racy variety show *Laugh-In*, and press coverage of *Get Christie Love* often played up the star's sex appeal.[85]

Much of the movie centers on the police captain's efforts to rein in Christie's unconventional tactics. When he tries to take Christie off a drug-smuggling case for blowing her cover, Christie counters with a bet: either she solves the case in three days, or he can have access to her body. Although the captain seems taken aback by her brazenness, he

Looking good: As Christie Love, Teresa Graves paired strength with fashionable femininity. Courtesy of ABC/Photofest.

does appear entranced with Christie. In one scene, the two investigate a suspect's swinging apartment, and Christie marvels at the mood music and lighting wired into the bedroom. "Turn you on?" she asks her boss flirtatiously, gyrating to the beat and pulsating lights.

"Turn you on?" he asks.

"You're a regular Don Juan, aren't you?" Christie teases.

"This isn't child's play," says the captain, referring to the investigation.

"Neither is this," says Christie, grabbing him by the collar.

In the end, Christie successfully manipulates a female source to uncover the members of a drug-smuggling ring. That evening Christie's boss follows her to her apartment door, suggesting they share a nightcap. "If you remember, I won the bet?" she teases, then relents: "Only one. That's my limit." The apartment door closes on their ill-fated relationship, Christie seemingly holding the upper hand.

When the film was translated into a weekly television series, Christie's character became more subdued. In an interview, Graves reassured viewers that her character was not going to be the "female Superfly" they saw in the pilot. "She was too tough for me. We want her to be believable. . . . She won't try her karate on 9-foot guys."[86] Echoed producer Paul Mason, "We will resort to karate only in realistic situations; what I am not taking out is the irrepressible personality of Christie."[87] The television series did curb Christie's abilities. In one episode, she stops to catch her breath while chasing a suspect, threatening to charge him with "MMT"—"Making Me Tired."[88] According to *Ebony* magazine, the actress's religious conversion also tempered Christie's provocative personality. The magazine reported that Graves became a devout Jehovah's Witness before the series began and negotiated a few conditions in her contract: "She never kills anybody on the show, never tells a direct lie (although she may assume undercover identities) and there is no profanity in the scripts." Levine asserts that Graves's newfound spirituality was prominently reported in the press, and the image of the actress as a religious woman made her nontraditional character more palatable to audiences.[89]

The series also softened and feminized Christie's appearance compared to the film. In the opening credits, she strolls through the city in a red dress, wears hair extensions, and dances in an elegant club. In the episode "Market to Murder," Christie—initially wearing a conservative blazer with long skirt and carrying a briefcase—uses her knowledge of fashion and jewelry to solve a case. Her boss, played by a different actor than in the film, maintains a strictly professional relationship. He says of Christie: "She's one of my best men."[90] While this line may indicate confidence in Christie's abilities, Levine argues that the incongruity between *she* and *men* underscores Christie's "unescapable sexual difference."[91] Accordingly, Christie engages in typically feminine behavior throughout the episode, modeling a suspect's fur coat for the admiring male officers and demanding compensation for a dress that was torn in the line of duty. "I can only go for a repair bill like my other men get," her chief says flatly.

Christie threatens to keep the fur coat they have seized from a suspect. "Do we negotiate?" she asks, playfully.

"I knew you'd kick up a storm," her boss sighs, acknowledging her difference from the other "men."

Christie's race served to set her apart from her white male colleagues and from most other television heroines. To some people, the fact that the series was based on the blaxploitation genre, and developed with the advisement of an experienced black female police detective from New York, promised a higher level of "awareness." As producer Mason told *Ms.*, "You just can't have your lead be a young, black woman who grew up in the streets, and not be aware of what she represents. I want to show a positive moral effect, not only from the woman's point of view, but from the black point of view. How great it will be for young black women to see one of their sisters up there in Christie's position on the right side of the law each week."[92]

Ebony reported that among the series' directors was Mark Warren, "the first black director on national TV," who had earlier worked with Graves on *Laugh-In*.[93] Despite these details, Teresa Graves told the *Chicago Daily News* that she did not want the show to "make a big thing out of her being black," expressing her distaste for shows such as *Good Times.* "I see that on television now, and that's garbage. I don't see making a big thing out of your upbringing or your background or your color or your religious beliefs. That's not important." Graves claimed she "never, never, never had any problems because of race," emphasizing instead the disrespect she faced as a twenty-six-year-old single woman: "I'm a grown lady and [family members] treat me like I'm 12."[94]

Accordingly, while some episodes referenced Christie's race, they also emphasized her refusal to consider it a limitation. In one episode a suspect suggests Christie faces heightened pressure as a "double minority" and asks her if she feels like "the female Jackie Robinson of the LAPD." Christie laughs. "No, I do not—because I'm not," she says, rattling off a list of other female police officers who preceded her. "The opportunity's there—and that's what I'm interested in." When the suspect reminds Christie of past discrimination that women and minorities have faced, she says flatly: "This is *now*."[95]

In the same episode, the suspect—who happens to be a light-skinned, red-haired African American man posing as a white man—is killed. He gasps to Christie as he dies: "Where I come from, black was not particularly beautiful, so I passed for white. With your help, I think I might have [made it]." The camera closes in on Christie's tears, underscoring the tragedy of his case and her more successful attitude.

In another episode, Christie travels to a rural jail to rescue Mexican American migrant workers framed for murdering a policeman. The rural white sheriff, upon meeting Christie, elbows his buddy and says: "Is she really a cop, Earl? They sure do package 'em nice in the big city." Christie is later surrounded by a motorcycle gang who warn: "It's real dangerous for a city girl to be running around down here." Although these encounters do not directly reference race, the repeated references to Christie as a "city girl" mark her as Other in a town where local authorities harbor hostility toward minorities. (The powers that be would prefer to see Mexicans "hanging from a tree," according the dialogue.)[96]

While Graves herself downplayed the series' racial significance, a television executive offered an alternate perspective on why Christie Love's aggression was curbed for the series and why the show only lasted one season. "The black woman heroine may be OK for urban movie audiences, but it won't play in Heartland, U.S.A.," Richard Pinkham told the *Washington Post* in a series about blacks on television. "You have to draw a sharp line of difference between a great black comedy and a black hero. Even though there is a large component of blacks in the audience, they are only 22 percent of the audience. Never underestimate the fundamental bigotry of the American heartland."[97] Other critics blamed the series' failure on its low budget and conventional plot structure, not to mention ABC's decision to air the show opposite NBC's popular *Police Woman*.[98]

Dubbed the "miracle of Friday night," *Police Woman* in its second season helped cement NBC's dominance and placed first in the Nielsen ratings more than once. Male critics puzzled over *Police Woman's* success, calling the series "mediocre" and formulaic, largely crediting its appeal to star Angie Dickinson and her supporting cast.[99] As Dickinson recalls, "We were much lighter than *Police Story,* not as legitimate."[100] While Christie Love sometimes struggled to be recognized as a love interest, divorcée Pepper Anderson in *Police Woman* was instantly recognizable as a romantic heroine. In contrast to Christie's initially more androgynous image, Pepper portrayed a cultivated femininity: She fought crime in a powder-blue pantsuit, with false eyelashes and hoop earrings accentuating her sexual difference.[101] Dickinson changed costumes numerous times in every episode, and she wore hair extensions to heighten her beauty.[102] Marked as more feminine than Christie, Pepper "used her sensuality to outsmart criminals,"[103] and her emotive nature and sensitivity served as both asset and barrier on the job. "It seems to me she got her job by playing up to the boss," one feminist critic complained. "She certainly is a flirt."[104] A male reviewer described Pepper as "naughty" and suggested an evening watching *Police Woman* could double as a date: "At the fantasy level, where TV is most effective, she promises a lot. A night with the divorced Pepper, even if she's questioning you about a police case, might be most enjoyable."[105] Dickinson recalls that *Police Woman* intended Pepper and her male boss Lieutenant Bill Crowley (Earl Holliman) to seem like they could be "boyfriend and girlfriend."[106]

However, other critics read Pepper as a more complex character. As *Time* described Dickinson's persona: "She [is] very feminine but very much a man's woman . . . and as good as a man with a gun or a deck of cards."[107] Furthermore, the series' producer claimed Dickinson was "no threat to women," instead functioning as a relatable "kid sister." "People who think Angie is a sexpot are misled. She's a cheerleader, she tags along, the kid sister the guys are fond of. They use her to play shortstop when they're short a man. She's a tomboy and a lot of fun. . . . [Women believe] if they just lose a few pounds and touch up their hair, they could do what she does."[108] Although Dickinson claimed that the series was "not playing up sex and glamour," she told *TV Guide* that she was "very happy being a sex symbol" and intended to use her assets.[109]

The first-season episode "Requiem for Bored Wives" demonstrates

The man behind the woman: Police Woman's *Pepper Anderson (Angie Dickinson) was often rescued by Captain Crowley (Earl Holliman). Courtesy of NBC/Photofest.*

the conflicting perceptions of Pepper as either sex symbol or scrappy "kid sister." The male scriptwriter who penned the episode claimed to like strong, independent characters who were "colorful, exciting, and hopefully sexy."[110] The original story began with Pepper rescuing a man and being invited to discuss her heroism on a radio program. However, her radio appearance was later changed to a call-in show that emphasizes Pepper's politics and sexuality. In the aired episode, Pepper enters her apartment after a long day at work, sighs, and begins to undress. She peels off her wrap skirt, turns on the radio, and goes upstairs, the stairwell accentuating her legs. By the time she has stripped down to a slip, dark hose, and heels—her figure framed by a wicker chair—radio host Larry Brooks is at the height of a sexist screed against "lady cops" and the notion that women can be as strong as men. The host tells listeners he's not for "women's lib," explaining, "I love women in their place—or mine—whichever happens to be handier." (His male cohost chuckles in the background, fueling Pepper's indignation.)[111]

Brooks dares police women to call in; Pepper visibly wrestles with the impulse. Dressed in a soft pink robe and gold earrings, she removes her robe for a second, revealing her back to the camera, then reties it and phones in. "I can't believe a grown man could really believe the nonsense you've been spouting, especially about police women," she says, with floral wallpaper as her backdrop. "And if you think it's funny, I think you'd better get a new joke book."

"Come on," Brooks replies, "where's your sense of humor? I'm the first to admit that women are not only equal to men, they're superior in many ways. But coping with violent criminals isn't one of them."

"It certainly is," Pepper seethes, her teeth clenched. "How much time do I have?"

When Brooks nicknames her "Sergeant Pepper" and calls her "cute," she replies: "Not as cute as what I'm going to tell you." The scene ends, and we next see Pepper at work the next morning, again dressed in cheerful pink, surrounded by male colleagues who congratulate her for "telling off that creep."

These opening scenes establish a feminist advocacy role for Pepper, even if we never actually hear her defend her profession. Yet she backtracks, agreeing to meet the radio host for lunch. He apologizes and Pepper concedes, "I made a fool of myself. . . . I'm not usually that obnoxious." The two exchange flirtatious banter, and Pepper informs her boss that beneath the radio host's bravado is a "real guy."

Also, the fact that Pepper stripped before picking up the phone to defend feminism and women's strength was strategically planned. As the scriptwriter described Pepper in the opening scene, "she had removed most of her clothes before picking up the phone, bringing her down to the minimum permitted by the U.S. Supreme Court and the National Broadcasting Company."[112] In other words, *Police Woman* would show as much of her body as obscenity laws and NBC's standards would allow. The original script also had Pepper cuffing an intruder while on the phone with the radio host. "I'm a burglar, not a rapist," said the intruder, admiring the undressed, gun-toting Pepper, "but I'm willing to switch."[113] Although the scene was cut from the produced episode, it does reveal the scriptwriter's efforts to blend empowerment, action, and sexuality.

Pepper frequently assumed sexualized roles in the show, posing as a stripper or masseuse to get close to a suspect. Also, at a time when feminists were just beginning to address rape as a political issue, *Police*

Woman used sexual violence against women for voyeuristic appeal. Voyeurism and violence structure the series' opening credits, which feature images of Pepper being grabbed and gagged and fetishistic shots of her legs and breasts.[114] Cases in the first few episodes involved a woman who "claimed she was raped just to get attention," "hitchhiking teenage girls who are raped," and women seduced by a "blackmailer" who films them during sex.[115] These plotlines sometimes emphasize Pepper's humanity and sensitivity, as she comforts rape victims treated callously by male investigators. However, Susan Douglas argues that the show's presentation of sexual violence often implied the victims were at fault: They were "young and single, and their occupational choices usually meant they were 'asking for it.'"[116]

Critic Marjorie Rosen notes that rape plots factored prominently in television at a time when networks used sex rather than violence to sell programs. "Sexual violence, television is telling us, can be separated from machine-gun violence," Rosen wrote in 1977. "It's all right to show the psychological trauma; just don't give us gaping wounds."[117] For Rosen and Douglas, this trend in cop shows also served as a form of antifeminist backlash. "At the very time when feminists were beginning to attack rape laws and the way victims were treated by police and the legal system, shows like this, under the guise of feminism, reinforced every negative stereotype about rape that perpetuated the system," Douglas writes.[118]

That Pepper herself often faced the prospect of rape, only to be saved in the nick of time by a male colleague, enabled the audience to "fantasize briefly about a woman who dared to do a 'man's job' getting her just desserts," writes Douglas.[119] The frequent rescue of Pepper by her male colleagues fueled other fantasies as well, according to *Police Woman*'s producer. "A man can play out *his* fantasies of being the protector while a woman can play out *her* fantasy of being so desired and loved that a man will risk his life to save her," he explained in a 1977 *Redbook* article. However, feminist critic Marjorie Rosen argued that this plot device "seems only to remind women of their vulnerability, their helplessness and—even in these liberated times—their inability to function, or even survive, solo."[120]

Although the episode "Requiem for Bored Wives" directly references feminist arguments about women's capabilities, even this story was changed to incorporate a dramatic rescue scene. As the episode develops, Pepper determines that radio host Larry Brooks is guilty of murdering his unfaithful wife, and she arranges a restaurant date with him to elicit a confession. He confesses to the crime, then kidnaps Pepper at gunpoint. The two speed away from the dock in his private boat.

In the original version of the script, Pepper privately meets with Brooks, who compliments her on her investigative skills. "Never underestimate the brain-power of a woman," he grumbles. When he kidnaps her, she orchestrates her own escape. She wrestles with Brooks, who punches her in the jaw; gains control of the speeding boat; and steers it into a rock wall before leaping to safety. She then swims ashore, brimming with confidence, and meets her surprised boss on the dock. In this version, Crowley marvels at her achievement, remarking to himself: "And to think they said women can't handle police work the way men can. And you know something? They were right!" The episode ends with Pepper back at her apartment, turning on the radio to hear another sexist call-in show—then firmly tossing the radio in the trashcan.[121]

The aired version both removes the references to women's abilities and restages the kidnapping scene. In this version, Pepper's colleagues accompany her to the restaurant, witness the kidnapping, and immediately chase after the pair in a police boat. Pepper does not attempt to change the boat's course, but she does dive off the side and wait for rescue as Brooks's boat hits the wall. The final scenes emphasize Pepper's femininity as, wrapped in a towel, she walks away from the dock with Crowley and frets about her appearance. "I look a mess," she laments.

"You look great to me," he says, then teases her for "cutting it a little close."

The script drafts themselves do not indicate why these scenes were changed. As networks were closely monitoring violence in 1970s programming, perhaps the fight scene on the boat deck was eliminated to reduce violent incidents in the episode.[122] Perhaps producers doubted that Pepper would be sent in alone to question a known killer. Perhaps the men's comments affirming women as smart and competent were seen as too heavy-handed and redundant after Pepper's earlier argument on the radio show. Whatever the reasoning, the ending ultimately presents Pepper as a hostage to be rescued, rather than an independent investigator steering her own ship, and undermines her feminist stance at the beginning.

Wonder Woman's Cooperative Power

Police women like Pepper were often criticized for their tendency to wait for rescue. Conversely, some critics perceived Christie Love as "cartoonish," arguing her toughness and killer karate chops placed her outside the realm of mere mortals. Seventies feminists on one hand demanded portrayals that resonated with real women's lives, but on the other sought solace in a superhero. Wonder Woman, an icon of women's clout in World War II, experienced a revival in the early seventies among white feminists who claimed her as a political symbol.

Some feminists considered Wonder Woman symbolic of women's multifaceted roles and capabilities. For example, when 2,000 feminists strode the boardwalk of Atlantic City in 1974, hoping to again "upstage" the Miss America pageant, they were headed by twenty Wonder Women wearing gold headbands, star-spangled navy skirts, and black boots—along with National Organization for Women (NOW) T-shirts. A NOW leader told the press that Wonder Woman represented "woman as a full human being—a provider, creator and thinker," in contrast to the objectified "bathing-suit clad Miss America."[123] She bragged that NOW's Wonder Women came in all ages, shapes, and sizes, unlike the narrowly defined Miss America. However, she took pains to support the women participating in the pageant: "After all, they are our sisters."[124]

For *Ms.* editor Gloria Steinem, Wonder Woman held even more powerful possibilities. Wonder Woman graced the cover of *Ms.* magazine's 1972 inaugural issue, framed by the banners "Wonder Woman for President" and "Peace and Justice in '72." Steinem further encouraged the heroine's revival by producing a reprint of creator William Marton's original comics, and she also penned a movie script of her own in the early 1970s that posited Wonder Woman as a radical feminist crusader.[125] In the unpublished film script, Wonder Woman looks through "fresh eyes" at "timid scurrying secretaries taking orders from male executives" and "wealthy women in heels too high to move."[126] She saves a distraught divorcée from jumping off the World Trade Center, smiling when the woman promises, "I'll never be a man-junkie again." Between unionizing prostitutes and cleaning up an oil spill, Steinem's Wonder Woman takes down the multinational pornography company Sex and Violence Unlimited.

In Steinem's script, Wonder Woman masks her contempt for men,

serving as assistant to Major Steve Trevor only to achieve greater political ends. Steinem describes Wonder Woman's first meeting with
Trevor: "She is in uniform, hair pulled back, glasses, and is clearly
trying to walk uncertainly, not stride, and generally look as 'feminine'
and deferential as she has seen other American females do: in short
to 'Uncle Tom.' WONDER WOMAN's effort to behave 'like a woman' as DI-
ANA PRINCE is a running sight gag of the film."[127] In Steinem's vision,
Wonder Woman represented radical feminism in the flesh and served
as a metaphor for young women confined by economic necessity to exploitative jobs.

Naturally, television's Wonder Woman lacked the militancy of
Steinem's heroine and resembled a beauty queen more than an everyday
activist. Yet, the medium offered more than one interpretation of this
comic book heroine. The networks experimented with different tones
and time periods, first casting tennis champ Cathie Lee Crosby as Wonder Woman in a 1974 TV movie. Crosby, described as a "spectacular
blonde beauty" and "extraordinarily feminine and single," considered
her character a sophisticated counterpart to James Bond, yet decidedly
female. "I want Wonder Woman to be stylish and feminine. She's not
aggressive," Crosby said. "And she should be catlike in her movements,
not muscular."[128] In the film, Crosby's Wonder Woman leaves the mul-
ticultural Paradise Island for the 1970s United States. She officially
serves as a personal assistant to intelligence officer Steve Trevor, but
he is aware of her dual mission. Diana tracks an international spy ring
and engages in flirtatious banter with criminals and colleagues alike,
smartly deflecting their sexual advances and showing some hostility to
amorous men.[129]

Crosby's Wonder Woman costume resembles an athletic suit more
than a superhero getup—she wears a long-sleeved jersey with an eagle
emblem, and blue tights that completely cover her legs. Likewise, her
powers demonstrate athleticism more than magic. She uses martial
arts to fend off attackers, battles a fellow Amazon with a kendo stick,
and uses a rope that extends from her belt to hoist herself over a wall.
(The actress performed most of her own stunts to enhance the film's
realism.) As one reviewer noted: "She totes weapons in her belt, yet
refrains from soaring around like the Flying Nun."[130] Although Crosby
had expected the movie to become a series, she and ABC parted ways
over their vision for Wonder Woman. As one reporter later explained:

"Cathy Lee wanted to play her in the James Bond 007 image, but the network opted for a comic strip character."[131]

The new *Wonder Woman* series resembled a comic book more than Crosby's "sophisticated camp," but it still engaged with some serious gender politics. As actress Lynda Carter told *Time*, Wonder Woman demonstrated that "women don't have to be unattractive to be independent."[132] The series epitomized cultural ambivalence toward feminism and female power. As Levine notes, Wonder Woman's bodily difference from men was the source of her strength, and she often battled androgynous villains.[133] Susan Douglas laments that Wonder Woman's strength relied on bullet-proof bracelets and campy special effects rather than true female capabilities. Furthermore, Douglas notes that this superhero's powers had limits, as she "never used her own powers to advance her own interests, and she never spoke of her own goals and ambitions."[134]

Although the 1975 pilot closely followed the plotline of the original comic—even situating Wonder Woman in the 1940s—Diana's decision to leave an Amazonian paradise to become the assistant to and protector of men seemed to posit antimale feminist separatism against a friendlier, more cooperative vision of equality. In the pilot, U.S. Major Steve Trevor (Lyle Waggoner) tumbles from a parachute onto the covert, all-female Paradise Island. As princess Diana (Lynda Carter) tends to his injuries, she falls for him. "There is something missing, Mother," she tells the queen, begging for an opportunity to return with Steve to the United States and "observe the male species."[135] As Douglas interprets her character, "she wasn't supposed to like or need men, but then she met one and kinda lost her resolve."[136]

Sounding like a radical separatist, the queen (Cloris Leachman) counters Diana's infatuation with a history lesson. "I named this island Paradise for an excellent reason: there are no men on it. It is free of their barbaric, masculine behavior," she says, contorting her face and biting her fist at the mere mention of men. Under male rule, "we women were slaves in Rome and Greece," she reminds her daughter.

"Thousands of years have passed," Diana suggests. "Perhaps men are now different?" Throughout the series she engages with men as more than oppressors: "They're like children, they're like gods, they're like geniuses and fools. They are all things," she tells her sister, dreamy-eyed. As Wonder Woman values men for their essential "maleness," she openly embraces sexual difference, Levine argues.[137] The character's romantic nature irritated some 1970s viewers. "Her only motivation to right wrongs appears to be to save her beloved Major Trevor from harm," one feminist critic complained.[138]

Both the series' theme song, which refers to Wonder Woman "fighting for [her] rights," and the opening sequence in which the superhero breaks free from her chains, had resonance for women's liberation. The pilot episode posits Diana against Martha, a deceptive Nazi judo champion, and enables her to assert American superiority through the lens of gender equality. "Any civilization that does not recognize the female is doomed to destruction," she tells Martha. "Women are the wave of the future, and sisterhood is stronger than anything." Punching out a Nazi pilot in the same episode, she tells him: "You obviously have little regard for womanhood. You must learn respect."

Levine observes that these overt feminist references were subdued over the course of the series—the theme song lyric was changed to the collective "fighting for *our rights*" in the second season, and by season three the lyrics were dropped altogether. Carter's costumes became lower cut and more revealing each season, and the dialogue offered fewer explicit feminist references. As Carter reflects in a 2005 interview: "The one thing that I regret in the [latter seasons of] *Wonder Woman* was that they lost some of the feminism. I think the networks were afraid that we would lose viewers if we were too feminist. I really wish that they had . . . trusted me enough to know that Wonder Woman could say feminist things and still be for women and not against men."[139]

While villains in the first season refer to Wonder Woman as "very attractive, quite strong and unfemininely pushy," her deferent alter ego, Diana Prince, a smart secretary garbed in huge glasses and a prim uniform, is described as "duller than a fat lapdog after dinner." Diana's boss, Steve, often teases her for being "all business" and fails to see her as a sexual object, even when she auditions for a beauty pageant in heels and a low-cut dress. Diana's transformation into Wonder Woman places the two on more equal footing, and Steve's attraction to her resembles flirtation between equals more than harassment of an underling. As Steve hails Wonder Woman's arrival in one episode: "Here comes help, and it's never arrived in a more beautiful package!"[140]

The slow-motion striptease that transformed the bespectacled Diana into the breathtaking Wonder Woman hinted at the hidden capacity

Plain Jane: As secretary Diana, Wonder Woman masks her power and her sexuality. (Lynda Carter and Lyle Waggoner.) Courtesy of ABC/Photofest.

within each woman. Statuesque actress Lynda Carter, who fought crime in a gold-plated bustier, star-spangled shorts, and thigh-high boots, bridged the divide between ability and beauty that NOW had drawn at the 1974 Miss America protest. Carter herself was a former beauty contestant who posed for Playboy between *Wonder Woman*'s first and second seasons, and critics marveled at her ability to embody both wholesomeness and sexuality.[141] (Or at least, as *Time* put it, to appeal to the "one, true least common denominator.")[142]

In the series' third episode, entitled "Beauty on Parade," Wonder Woman's alter ego, Diana, delights in joining a beauty pageant to investigate an assassination plot. The episode highlights Diana's versatile and multifaceted identity, as she is equally comfortable taking dictation and dancing provocatively for the show's talent competition. With a twirl, she transforms from a swimsuit-clad contestant to an Amazonian avenger, saving both General Dwight Eisenhower and a fellow contestant from certain death. Having proven her strength, she returns to the stage as Wonder Woman to claim her prize: the title of "Miss G.I.

Dream Girl 1942." The audience, equally women and men, rise to their feet as she accepts the crown. She shares her roses—and implicitly, the glory—with her fellow contestants, embodying the nonhierarchical notion of beauty that NOW's march espoused.

Wonder Woman's second season catapulted the comic into the 1970s, a decision that allowed scriptwriters the freedom to incorporate new technologies and broach contemporary issues.[143] However, script changes reveal the program still placed limits on how forceful Wonder Woman could be. The story begins in much the same way: a plane carrying U.S. security official Steve Trevor Jr. (also played by Lyle Waggoner) crashes on Paradise Island. Diana, recognizing Steve as the son of her former colleague, begs her mother for permission to return to the States and fight terrorism. The other Amazons agree to send someone from Paradise Island, and Diana's cousin Evadne challenges her to a duel to determine who will be the emissary.[144]

In the original script, this duel was a spirited fencing match. As the script describes the scene, "they slam together, BLADES RINGING, bodies striving. Diana hurls Evadne back, but slips—and Evadne whirls, slashes," cutting "a blood-red slash" across Diana's robe. The audience shouts and cheers until the athletic Diana emerges victorious.[145] In the aired version, the scene is a civilized competition of "Bullets and Bracelets," set to Olympic-style music. The queen asks, "Are you wearing your protective bracelets of feminum? Good. Then since neither of you can be harmed, the contest can begin." The women fire small pistols at each other and deflect the bullets in model-like poses, barely breaking a sweat. The onlookers, in multihued sheer dresses, clap and cheer quietly. Eventually, Diana's bullet hits the stone target behind Evadne. "Look, she's won the contest," an onlooker says calmly. Although the sport and sense of danger may have been subdued to curb violence in the program, the change in this sequence does credit Diana's victory more to magical accessories than physical prowess. (Likewise, a subsequent scene in which Wonder Woman is skillfully flying an invisible plane was changed to allow the plane to fly *itself*, emphasizing the capability of the plane rather than the woman.)[146] As Douglas argues, this superheroine's power tends to rely on gadgets and special effects.

Wonder Woman evolved somewhat in the latter seasons: for one, she becomes a much better communicator. When she appears out of nowhere in the second-season opener to rescue Steve Trevor Jr., she stays

The body beautiful: As Wonder Woman, Lynda Carter modeled female strength—and wore revealing attire. Courtesy of ABC/Photofest.

to talk with him afterward, fielding questions about her ageless beauty (we learn she is more than 2,500 years old) and previous working relationship with his father. In the original script, Steve Jr. considers Wonder Woman his savior and respects her right to evade questions about her identity. "You rescued me," he says. "So I won't push it; you've earned the right to do things your own way."[147] The aired version of the episode takes a more patriarchal tone, instead complimenting Wonder Woman on being "gorgeous" and "in great shape for [her] age" and telling her: "You helped me out, and I appreciate it." These script changes are significant, as they refocus attention on Wonder Woman's physical attractiveness and reframe her as helper rather than rescuer.

Script changes also curtailed Diana's powers when faced with an unwanted sexual advance. Later in the same episode, Steve Jr. has been kidnapped by terrorists and replaced by a clone that looks just like him. The clone, however, lacks Steve's sense of propriety, and Diana realizes something is wrong when the Steve lookalike makes a pass at her in her conference hotel room. She "smiles sweetly, seductively" to distract the clone, then makes her countermove. The original versions of the script granted Diana some muscle. In one version, she "throws him over one shoulder into a sofa." In another version, Diana throws a coffee table at the false Steve, "lifts him like a child [and] slams him down" when he tries to punch her.[148] In the aired version, Diana runs out the door, using the coffee table as a barrier to block his path. She transforms outside and returns as Wonder Woman, yelling, "Leave the girl alone!" She then blocks the impostor's punch, flips him, and ties him with her golden lasso to elicit a truthful confession.

Although the aired episode grants Diana sexual power over the false Steve—as she is able to distract him with her sweet, seductive smile—it denies her the power to physically defend herself. Apparently, a firm self-defense strategy required magic bracelets and a superhero costume.

The Bionic Woman: Equality and Deference

The Bionic Woman debuted in 1976, building on the successes of the earlier series. Douglas argues that, compared to Wonder Woman and the contemporaneous Charlie's Angels, "she was the least kitschy of them all. She didn't have a costume, was not constantly seen in bikinis or wet T-shirts, and didn't giggle all the time."[149] Actress Lindsay Wagner also differentiated her character from the others, describing the Bionic Woman as more independent than Pepper in *Police Woman*, as Pepper is "surrounded by an entourage of men who help her get out of trouble. I play a schoolteacher who is called upon by the government for dangerous assignments."[150] While reviewers joked that the Bionic Woman was merely Wonder Woman living under an assumed name, the show's producer claimed she was "not a comic-book-style heroine":

> She's very human, really. We established very definite parameters for her. She can jump to the second story of a building, but not the third story. She can turn over a car but not a truck. She can lift a ton, but not a ton and a half. . . . She's never aggressive when she's on the attack . . . unlike Wonder Woman, she doesn't go up to a guy and sock him in the puss. She's more clever than that. She'll pull out the rug from under him, and that's a lot funnier.[151]

The Bionic Woman thus provided a more subtle and less sexualized display of emerging female power than did *Wonder Woman*. While Inness remembers the character as a more independent and attainable ideal, Rosen's 1977 *Redbook* column castigated her artificiality: "The Bionic Woman does not breathe and does not bleed. Sterile and clean, when she falters in any way you can send her to the shop for repairs. How handy."[152]

The Bionic Woman was introduced as the fiancée of Steve Austin (Lee Majors) in his *Six Million Dollar Man* series, and her power came at the expense of her romantic life. "Steve and Jamie were planning to get married—then something went wrong," the voiceover informs us.[153] After a life-threatening accident requires doctors to replace Jaime Sommers's injured arm, leg, and ear with bionic parts, being near fiancé Steve only causes flashbacks of physical pain. Jaime is delighted with her new powers—"I feel like a kid with a new toy!" she exclaims—but puzzled by the pain that Steve causes her. "What I need is to get to know myself before I can be good for anyone else," she tells her doctor. Her necessary separation from Steve paved the way for a separate *Bionic Woman* series and another single action heroine.

The press widely reported on Wagner's successful salary demands. *The Six Million Dollar Man*'s ratings "soared out of sight" when Wagner guest-starred, and her agent used her popularity to negotiate a salary for the *Bionic Woman* series "that would make Howard Hughes envious."[154] Wagner's character, however, took a more humble approach. Like Wonder Woman, whose dual identity enabled her to model female subservience as well as strength, the Bionic Woman tempered her bodily powers with deference. The show's creator told *Time* he modeled the character after "an ideal date he had in mind, someone 'truthful, witty and eminently attractive.'"[155] A tennis player before the accident, Jaime worked in the feminine profession of elementary school teaching, maintaining her dual identity for the sake of national security. Douglas argues that the abrupt transition of her character from athletic tennis champ to the "more femininely appropriate role of schoolteacher" may have made her powerful role more palatable to audiences.[156]

As a *Newsweek* columnist argued in 1976, *The Bionic Woman* supported notions of women as physically weaker than men: As the "Eve-like offshoot of the Six Million Dollar Man," she "miraculously manages to be weaker than he even though they have the same machines in their mechanical legs."[157] When Jaime first tests her bionic capabilities, noticeable differences assure viewers that her powers will not outshine Steve's: He swims faster than she does, and he effortlessly pivots over the high jump while she barely clears the bar. Jaime and Steve also have a distinctly different relationship with their boss, Oscar Goldman: "The Bionic Man and Goldman treat each other as equals; for her, though, the relationship is like father and daughter, the knowing elder and the child-woman," Rosen observes.[158]

In the first-season episode "Angel of Mercy," for example, Goldman calls Jaime "sweetheart" and kisses her on the cheek as she embarks on a mission in war-torn Costa Brava, a fictional Central American nation. Posing as a nurse, Jaime accompanies gruff retired military pilot Starkey (Andy Griffith) to save a U.S. ambassador trapped in a bombed building. Upon meeting the delicate-looking Jaime, Starkey, sounding a lot like Phyllis Schlafly, remarks, "Is this a joke? No offense, but a jungle war is the last place a woman oughta be."

Jaime curtly responds, "It seems to me a jungle war's the last place anyone oughta be," but her behavior undermines her apparent bid for equality. In one scene, she enables Starkey to think he lifted a log, masking the fact she nudged it with her bionic foot. She pairs strength with nurturance, carrying a rescued child on her shoulders as she pulls the rubble off the trapped ambassador. In the end, the successful mission

Proving her worth: Starkey (Andy Griffith) is impressed by Jaime's (Lindsay Wagner) bionic strength and quick thinking in The Bionic Woman. *Courtesy of ABC/Photofest.*

is credited in the press to Starkey, "with a little help from lady luck" — preserving Jaime's confidentiality, but also denying her credit for her accomplishments. At the same time, viewers are well aware of Jaime's physical superiority and may find humor in her ability to placate men while performing her job.[159]

The two-part episode "Jaime's Shield" again places the Bionic Woman in male territory, as she poses as a police cadet to root out an enemy agent.[160] Like the detectives in *Charlie's Angels,* Jaime frequently went undercover in roles ranging from nun to lady wrestler, a plot device that enabled her to play with different feminine identities.[161] When Jaime is informed that the force is training women to be street officers rather than file clerks, she says: "I can get behind that."

"You'll look great in a uniform," her boss quips.

The script for "Jaime's Shield" pits the cadets against the "blatant male chauvinism" of male officers who whistle at the six women in uniform and doubt their physical capabilities. "Some of you ladies might want to do half the [obstacle] course. Don't be embarrassed," the chief tells them. Spurred on by sexism, the women struggle and stumble across the finish line; Jaime uses her bionic powers to perform effortlessly. When a police officer tests the cadets' reflexes by posing as a gunman, Jaime and one other cadet, Arleen, hit the floor, while the other women panic. Aside from our bionic superhero, Arleen "is the only one who seems comfortable with a weapon in her hand." The episode makes women's strength suspect, as viewers are encouraged to believe that "intense" Arleen is the enemy agent. (We later learn she is the police commissioner's daughter, rebelling against her father's efforts to feminize her.) Although this episode offers a more realistic view of the harassment and sexism that police women battled than either *Police Woman* or *Get Christie Love*, it again presents women as innately weaker than men.[162]

Charlie's Angels: Empowerment and Objectification

By promoting "three little girls" from safe desk jobs to perilous detective work, *Charlie's Angels* would present more enduring images of police women. The ABC series was inspired by earlier police programs, mimicking *Police Woman* more than *Christie Love*. Actress Farrah Fawcett told the *Washington Post*: "There are things I cannot do, and one of them is play Christie Love with guns blazing. God made men stronger. . . . He gave women femininity and intuition."[163] Early writers' guidelines described the show as *Police Woman*'s "Angie Dickinson times three."[164] The ensemble format enabled fuller representation of women's capabilities on the force—and ensured that the Angels were rescued by other women more often than by men. However, the fact that these detectives followed orders given by an unseen male authority and frequently wore revealing costumes complicated feminist readings of the series.

Much scholarship on seventies television has focused on this iconic series and the tensions it set up between empowerment and objectification. In *Tough Girls*, Inness categorizes the show as "semi-tough," noting that the Angels' independence, professional status, and comfort using weapons and motorcycles "represented a step forward" and "helped establish a precedent for the much tougher women" to come.[165] Douglas argues that the image of three women collaborating to solve cases and protect vulnerable women against chauvinistic men offered legitimate pleasures for female viewers. She writes that the Angels' tendency to go undercover—assuming diverse female roles and occasionally wearing men's clothing in the process—emphasized the constructed nature of gender roles.[166]

However, in most seventies critics' view, the series' innuendo, revealing costumes, and degrading plot devices deprived the show of any feminist significance. While Rosen called the Angels "braless, mindless, walking-talking sex-and-violence fantasies," journalist Judith Coburn described the series as the "misogynist" tale of "a pimp and his girls": "Charlie dispatches his streetwise girls to use their sexual wiles on the world while he reaps the profits."[167] By placing its shapely stars in bikinis, *Charlie's Angels* strategically "keep[s] males in a state of gape-jawed passivity and expectation," *Time* reported.[168] The fact that *Charlie's Angels* was originally conceptualized as *The Alley Cats*, a slang term for promiscuous women, further indicates the centrality of sexuality to the series.[169]

Levine acknowledges that the popular press often perceived the Angels as mere "sex symbols" and found their detective exploits unrealistic. However, she argues that the Angels intervened in more integral debates about sexual difference: their status as women gave them access to female-only spaces, and they succeeded as professionals while maintaining their difference from men.[170] Scholar Whitney Womack notes the Angels strategically used their sexuality to capture and punish sexist criminals, and that the detectives wore conservative business attire as often as they did bikinis.[171] In the following analysis, I highlight the tensions between empowerment and objectification that other scholars have identified in the series. However, I also draw from archival documents that address the series' characters and conventions. In contrast to some critics' perception of the Angels as "braless, mindless" sex symbols, producers sought to create characters who were smart, believable, and sexually respectable.

The tension between empowerment and objectification is central in the first-season episode "Blue Angels," in which the Angels uncover police ties to illicit massage parlors. At the beginning of the episode, Charlie (voiced by John Forsythe) assigns Sabrina (Kate Jackson) to investigate police corruption as a new detective in an all-male department: "Another bastion of male chauvinism crumbles," he announces. The women smile as Kelly (Jaclyn Smith) responds, "I like the sound

Almost angels: Creators of the hit series Charlie's Angels *capitalized on their leads' sexual appeal but guarded their morality in scripts. Left to right: Jaclyn Smith, Kate Jackson, and Farrah Fawcett. Courtesy of ABC/Photofest.*

of that!" Throughout the episode, Sabrina proves herself capable as a detective, and Kelly, posing as a police cadet, earns accolades for her marksmanship. Jill (Farrah Fawcett), meanwhile, flashes her smile in a massage parlor. Facing near death in a junkyard, the three women outwit murderous criminals with good timing and sharpshooting.[172]

The episode almost ends on an empowering note: Charlie commends the Angels on their investigation, adding that even the traditional police chief was pleased. "Why doesn't he thank us himself?" Kelly asks. Unlike earlier superheroes, these Angels ask to be recognized. However, the women's accomplishments are countered by visuals that suggest that boys will be boys. Coworker Lieutenant Bosley (David Doyle) is on the floor, succumbing to Jill's massage skills. Meanwhile, Charlie crudely jokes about the shapely woman plumber who has been "cleaning [his] pipes all week"—the presence of women in the trades providing further proof, he says, that bastions of chauvinism are crumbling. "You should see my electrician!" he jokes. The Angels laugh uproariously, humoring the sexism that hinders men like Charlie and the police chief from treating women as equals. Thus they prove their competence while preserving the status quo.

The Angels took distinct roles in this and other episodes, allowing female viewers to identify with different members of the ensemble cast. Sabrina, described by scholars as resourceful, smart, and androgynous, provided a point of identification for many female viewers and complemented Jill's role as sex symbol. As a production memo described the formula, "Sabrina tends to solve the cases and end up in jeopardy. Jill tends to be sexy and dumb." Kelly, the producers observed, most often played the friendly confidante and tended to fade into the background. While producers hoped to "break the pattern" a bit, they claimed they had "little choice with the JILL roles so far. She is the obvious one for the 'wide-eyed sexy' impersonations in most of the stories. . . . She can hardly complain either because she has, in almost every story, some good, funny scenes."[173] These memos reveal that Fawcett provided comic relief for the series, and that she was merely "impersonating" the sexy roles. As I will discuss later, producers carefully edited dialogue that suggested Jill had loose morals.

The contrast between Sabrina and Jill was reinforced by the actresses' images off the set. Jackson was an ERA supporter who reportedly declined to wear skimpy costumes; she cited her frustration with the "T and A" as one reason she left the series in 1979. Fawcett, in contrast, capitalized on her sex-symbol status and reportedly left the series after the first season to spend more time with her husband. As producers had dictated that "any replacement for Farrah should be comedy oriented," they replaced her with Cheryl Ladd, who played a similar character, Kris, Jill's blonde, perky younger sister.[174]

While Jill and Kris might have assumed "dumb" undercover roles, producers purported to represent the Angels as smart, competent detectives. In correspondence about a 1977 episode, a producer urged the scriptwriter to strengthen the Angels' investigative skills. "The Angels must do more and be smarter," producer Ron Austin wrote. "The Angels seem to be winging it (no puns please). They should be on top of the situation."[175] Similarly, when an early script featured unintelligent criminals, Austin instructed the scriptwriters: "Keep your 'heavies' smart! Unless the Angels themselves have 'worthy adversaries' they themselves tend to be ineffectual and are usually in jeopardy due to their own ineptitude. A smart heavy create[s] challenges for the heroines to overcome."[176]

Although *Charlie's Angels* has been often blamed for inaugurating the era of "jiggle TV," it presented its heroines as smarter than the well-endowed heroines on contemporaneous series such as *Three's Company*. At the beginning of season four, the Angels await Sabrina's replacement. A platinum blonde (who strongly resembles Suzanne Somers) enters the office wearing a tight T-shirt that accentuates her breasts; she engages Kris and Kelly in an inane conversation, asking questions in a little-girl voice. The Angels are relieved to learn she's just a maid and that Sabrina's real replacement is the suave Tiffany (played by Shelley Hack, the model famous for her role as a confident single woman in ads for Revlon's Charlie perfume). Although Hack lasted only a season, her androgynous suits, deep voice, and confident air helped distinguish the Angels from other "mindless, braless" television heroines.[177]

Yet even as they fought to make their Angels smart, producers seized opportunities to display female bodies. In the two-part episode "Angels in Paradise," for example, Charlie is kidnapped and the Angels are dispatched to Hawaii to rescue him. Producer Ron Austin instructed the scriptwriter to make the most of the island setting. "To give our audience a kick . . . why not open [with] dancing (with grass skirt) hula girls?" he wrote. He also suggested a scene in which a "dancer singles [the Angels] out for a sensuous, Hawaiian dance."[178] Accordingly, the aired episode features extended close-ups of hula dancers' swiveling torsos. In one scene, Sabrina watches the dancers from her window and tries to imitate their moves, shaking her hips as Kelly laughs. The humorous scene suggests that the Angels fall short of the natural sensuality of the island natives. By episode's end, the Angels are invited onstage to join a hula troupe. The dance is secretly filmed by Charlie himself, and Bosley practically salivates upon watching the film reel, heightening the voyeurism.[179]

Sometimes, however, producers opted for a more conservative approach. While they willingly exploited the bodies of hula dancers in the "Paradise" episodes, they did question a scripted massage parlor scene featuring "five braless GIRLS, more accustomed to evening work than day." In staging the scene, "please use restraint and good taste," producers instructed in a memo. "Also, please see to it that [the women] are of mixed racial origin."[180] In the aired scene, there are no close-ups of the masseuses' bodies, and at least one of the "girls" is a light-skinned blonde—allowing the series to evade charges of racial stereotyping. In notes on another script, producers recommended that the Angels wear evening gowns rather than swimsuits in a fashion-show sequence. "Oddly enough, I think we should have them model something other than bikinis. This show is up to its eyeballs in bikinis," Austin wrote.[181]

Sometimes the scripts called for more revealing camera shots, as when Kris infiltrates a nude beach in the "Paradise" episodes to get the information she needs to rescue Charlie. The scriptwriter claimed the beach scene was not intended to be "titillating" or pornographic, but merely to reflect a real-life setting. With the reminder that not every bather on such a beach goes nude, the network censors approved the scene but recommended the "use of a lot of towels."[182] The aired scene is a cautious compromise. When Kris is informed by the security guard that only nude bathers are allowed on the beach, she shrugs, casts her eyes heavenward, and unbuttons her bustier-type blouse as saucy music plays. Once on the beach, bathers in body stockings are filmed at a distance, and Kris beckons to her contact while hiding bashfully behind a large palm frond. She gains key information on Charlie's whereabouts and scurries away, hunched over. Upon hearing her story, the other Angels later laugh uproariously at her predicament.[183] The scene provides comic relief and suggests that stripping is not something Kris does eagerly or easily. As Levine argues, "When the characters did wear revealing attire, it was usually with a sort of eye-rolling acquiescence to the temporary absurdities their job demanded."[184]

As the beach scene reveals, producers did carefully monitor dialogue and licentious situations to preserve the angelic reputation of their leads. "Angel on Fire," a third-season episode in which Jill briefly returns to the series with her fiancé in tow, was determined to be "too strong and sexually overt." Producers nixed a line in which Jill proposes living with her fiancé before marriage, and the scriptwriter was also urged to "pull way back" on a scene in which Kris tests Jill's fiancé by trying to seduce him.[185] In the aired episode, Jill makes no mention of cohabitation before her wedding, and Kris innocently spies on the fiancé rather than attempting seduction.[186] In another episode, producers objected to a line comparing Bosley to a "gigolo"—perhaps refuting more salacious interpretations of the series.[187] Network censors also fretted about the Angels' drinking habits, asking that their alcohol consumption be "reduced and not glamorized" when reviewing scripts.[188] In the "Paradise" episodes the Angels do toast with tropical drinks, but they later vow to "never drink a mai-tai again," as the alcohol frees them to hula dance unashamedly.[189] A fourth-season episode, set at a college, was edited for alcohol and sexual-related content. In the original script, Kris masquerades as a college student and attends a drunken "orgy" where frat boys drench partygoers with beer. "I don't know this world or these people," Austin wrote on the script, "but it seems too broad?" The scene was ultimately cut from the aired episode.[190]

Comparing these script changes and production correspondence to the aired episodes of *Charlie's Angels* illuminates the tensions within the series. While the Angels were scripted to be smart and competent, the camera often zeroed in on their bodies or those of series extras to emphasize women's physical assets. The Angels frequently used their sexuality and flirting skills to advance their investigations; yet producers' reluctance to portray Jill in a committed sexual relationship prior to marriage, or to even show the Angels imbibing alcohol, indicates that these characters were held to traditional moral standards. These production details complicate popular notions of the Angels as merely "sex symbols" and demonstrate how sexuality and strength intersected in this iconic series about single female sleuths.

Working Women's Emerging Solidarity

The networks' approach to portraying action heroines apparently resonated with viewers: *Time* reported in 1976 that *The Bionic Woman* consistently rated among the top ten programs, far exceeding the popularity of its parent series *The Six Million Dollar Man*. Meanwhile, the wildly successful *Charlie's Angels* drew 23 million weekly viewers in its debut season, on par with the World Series. In 1976 the series sold ad spots for $100,000 a minute.[191] By early 1978 the success of *Charlie's Angels* and the sexy ABC comedy *Three's Company* had inspired a new trend on television. In dozens of proposed TV movies and series pilots, "pompon girls, roller derby queens, reckless coeds, bronzed beachgoers . . . wriggle in and out of fun, trouble and temptation," one reviewer observed.[192] As a Fox writer quipped: "This is supposed to be a time of women's projects on TV, but somehow all these women are good-looking, well-endowed and running toward the camera."[193] Television's "time of titillation" was short-lived, however: by the fall season of 1978, complaints from conservative groups, critics, advertisers, and industry insiders encouraged the networks to clean up their act.[194] Risqué shows such as *Soap* returned with less sex, and roles for women improved, according to *U.S. News:*

> One of the biggest changes in programming for all three networks involves the treatment of women, who have often been portrayed as sexual objects—frequently wearing as few garments as network censors permitted. In new series . . . women will be shown as capable, intelligent and caring—and in bikinis only when the stories really demand it. Some programs . . . were modified in mid-production to de-emphasize the sex as the result of pressure from network executives and actors and actresses who objected to sexism in scripts.[195]

NBC reportedly canceled its series *Coastocoast*—a *Three's Company*–inspired portrayal of airline flight attendants—after the Screen Actors' Guild held a panel discussion on the image of women. "Women are desperately disheartened to be faced in 1978 with the disgraceful trash . . . being transmitted in the guise that this is the American woman," Screen Actors' Guild president Kathleen Nolan told the panel.[196]

The shift in representation may also have been inspired by the release of the U.S. Commission on Civil Rights' 1977 report *Window Dressing on the Set: Women and Minorities in Television,* which called on the FCC to "begin a public dialogue on the role of women and minorities" and to better regulate network employment practices.[197] Drawing from new academic research and popular criticism on television, the report noted that female characters tended to be much younger and less powerful than their male counterparts.[198] (A 1979 update cited the reductive nature of "jiggle" shows such as *Charlie's Angels* as further examples of gender stereotyping.)[199] *Window Dressing* also documented the virtual invisibility of minority women on television and the tendency for African American women to be portrayed as either prostitutes or victims of violence. By summarizing numerous studies, the report gave a collective voice to media critiques and offered an analysis that took both gender and race into account. By suggesting that television stereotypes were linked to discriminatory employment and production policies—in other words, that "television offers a white male-dominated view of the world because white males dominate its decision-making structure"[200]—the commission outlined a plan of action. However, the commission's call for FCC intervention smacked of censorship, and some reviewers questioned the report's implications. As a *Washington Post* reporter wrote: "The wider, more provocative issue raised by the report is whether television programming should reflect the world as it is or offer viewers a lovely world-that-should be; whether any character who is a member of any . . . minority must be required to serve as a representative of the whole group. It sounds like a recipe for a universe of faultless ciphers."[201]

While *Charlie's Angels* has been credited for its influence on other exploitative programs, its ensemble format may also have inspired new images of working women's solidarity. While far from a "faultless cipher," the single working woman who would emerge in early 1980s television and film was smart and sassy and drew more definitive lines between her professional and sexual roles, reflecting changing attitudes toward sexuality in the workplace. In 1980, the same year that the comedy film *9 to 5* was released, *Newsweek* ran a lengthy article on sexual harassment. The article documented the growth of court cases, counseling centers, and lobbying efforts to counter the problem and explained that harassment encompassed "sexual innuendo and jokes," as well as physical advances.[202] According to attorneys interviewed in the article, "Men are learning that women are not going to take this kind of behavior," and "what women are learning is how to fight back."[203] However, given the difficulty of bringing a case to trial, *Newsweek* suggested that "for the moment, a woman's best response remains a firm, polite, nonthreatening 'no.' That is particularly true for verbal harassment. . . . Even sensitive men, women say, often will engage in this kind of banter unaware that they are offensive."[204] *Newsweek* also noted that "some feminists" endorse the approach of a Colorado woman who, "tired of being patted on her rump . . . wheeled around and purposefully grabbed her harasser by his genitals. He didn't bother her anymore."[205]

Fictional media in the early 1980s were replete with representations of women facing harassment and fighting back. In the dark comedy film *9 to 5*, which later inspired a television series, a trio of secretaries are fed up with constant verbal and physical harassment (including the indignity of being called "girls"). They kidnap and hog-tie their lecherous male boss, creating a more feminist-friendly workplace in his absence. The television comedy *It's a Living* (ABC, 1980–1982) featured "five spunky [waitresses] trying to keep a sense of humor as they fend off lecherous customers."[206] In the pilot, a waitress chases a group of rowdy men out of the restaurant when they refuse to respect her physical boundaries. Like *Newsweek*'s coverage, these representations emphasized individual women's strength and eschewed political solutions as a means to deal with harassment.

In the realm of television action drama, the police series *Cagney and Lacey* (CBS, 1982–1988) featured a crime-fighting duo with more feminist resonance. Julie D'Acci notes that *Cagney and Lacey* was first developed in 1974 by two female scriptwriters who had spent time observing New York female cops. "Unlike Angie Dickinson, who'd powder her nose before she set out to make a bust, these were women who took themselves seriously as police officers," co-creator Barbara Avedon recalled.[207] Hollywood producers passed on the idea, fearing the two leads were not "soft" or feminine enough. The series was revised in 1981 as a TV movie and series pilot. *Ms.* magazine, sensing the series' rarity, started a letter-writing campaign to keep it on the air.[208] Although the series featured sexualized scenarios—such as episodes in which the women went undercover to investigate an escort service—it also addressed feminist issues head-on. In the first season, the women dialogued with a Phyllis Schlafly–type activist. Later seasons featured a continuing plotline in which the single officer Christine Cagney sued her boss for sexual harassment. Feminist scholars have hailed the show for its gritty, less glamorized realism and willingness to tackle once-taboo topics such as abortion and domestic violence. As Aniko Bodroughkozy argues, "The show didn't contort its themes, narratives, and visual style to the degree that its forerunners did in order to 'soften' its representation of new womanhood."[209] However, D'Acci's research reveals the series was still shaped by concerns about sexual difference. Actress Meg Foster, originally cast as Cagney, was replaced with the more traditionally feminine and middle-class Sharon Gless to broaden the show's appeal and deflect perceptions of lesbianism. Also, Cagney tended to be more politically conservative than her married colleague Mary Beth Lacey, allowing different viewpoints on women's roles and women's liberation to emerge.[210]

Action heroines of the 1970s challenged the existing barrier against placing women in leading prime-time dramatic roles. These series provided a greater range of roles for actresses and diversified the genre in terms of gender and race. Although these programs were often far from realistic, they did show women competently carrying out police and military missions, and as protagonists went undercover, they encountered women in even more nontraditional roles, including female truck drivers and professional wrestlers. These representations may have also inspired viewers to pursue nontraditional careers. As Dickinson remarks about *Police Woman:* "We were responsible for a lot of women wanting to be cops."[211]

As I have demonstrated, plotlines and dialogue often directly addressed race and gender discrimination, albeit in limited ways. These heroines often gave lip service to feminism, countering negative perceptions of the movement circulating in society. Wonder Woman voiced the idea that "sisterhood is powerful," and the heroines of *Charlie's Angels* put this saying into practice by protecting vulnerable women against predatory men.[212] Pepper Anderson and Jaime Sommers directly confronted assumptions about women's inherent weakness through their investigations and rescue missions. And although Teresa Graves eschewed the role of racial advocate, her series was significant for placing people of color in more central and powerful roles than many of the earlier single-woman narratives.

Action series were particularly appealing and relevant to unmarried women, who desired images of women as more than wives or mothers. Whether they were divorced like Pepper Anderson or newly separated like Jaime Sommers, these heroines modeled female independence and the necessity of making a fresh start. Even Diana Prince's journey from the protected Paradise Island to dangerous Washington, D.C., functioned as a metaphor for leaving one's home, taking risks, and discovering one's true powers. These heroines' single status, of course, also made them more accessible to viewers' fantasies—viewers could dream of a date with Pepper, take a singles cruise with the shapely Angels, or imagine a wondrous romance between Diana and Steve.

The physical beauty and flirtatious femininity that made these heroines so appealing to audiences also marked them as distinct from men, thus supporting political ideologies that called for the preservation of sexual difference. Also, the fact that these heroines succeeded professionally despite being lone women on police forces and military missions suggested that worthy individuals would rise through their own merits—that there was no need for collective organizing, such as the pro-ERA movement, to enforce equality. That these heroines not only enjoyed workplace flirtations but also often initiated them suggested that women were already on equal footing in the workplace, and that sexuality functioned as a form of power for the single woman.

Courting Danger

Single Women and Sexual Aggression in 1970s Film

As 1973 dawned, New Yorkers were captivated by the story of Rose-ann Quinn, a single schoolteacher murdered on New Year's Eve by a man she picked up at a singles bar. Her death spurred discussion of the increasing dangers that young women faced in the city and the risks inherent in their quest for sexual freedom. Although Quinn initially surfaced in reports as an idealistic schoolteacher whose fatal flaw was being overly "friendly," news reports soon revealed a darker side of Quinn—a volatile woman who prowled singles bars by night and rev-eled in violent encounters with strange men.[1]

In *Looking for Mr. Goodbar,* Judith Rossner's novel based on the crime, Quinn transformed into the fictional Theresa Dunn, a single woman whose escalating sexual lusts culminated in her murder. The-resa was not the only oversexed, self-destructive single heroine of her day. In the popular novel *Sheila Levine Is Dead and Living in New York,* a weary single woman pursued casual sex while planning her suicide in intimate detail.[2] Both books were translated to film, countering the era's more celebratory cinematic images of single and divorced women and reinforcing historic perceptions of urban single women as lonely, desperate, or dangerous.

These were far from the first accounts to associate the singles scene with violence. While the plots of *Where the Boys Are* (1960) and *For Singles Only* (1968) had revolved around date rape and sexual assault by strangers, magazines and newspapers of the late 1960s were rife with reports of sordid singles bars and "career girl" murders. In crime re-ports of the 1960s, women were often portrayed as victims of random violence visited upon them as they walked to their apartments or even as they slept. In contrast, the victims in 1970s crime reports seemed to contribute to their own destruction by initiating interactions with their attackers and actively seeking casual sex with near-strangers. The bold risks taken by these crime victims corresponded with a broader shift in women's sexual attitudes and practices. As news media reported in the 1970s, "liberated" women were becoming increasingly aggressive in their quest for sexual gratification. This selfish quest reportedly left women emotionally damaged, made men emasculated and resentful, and strained already fragile relationships between the sexes.

Popular films and novels embodied these anxieties by linking female sexuality with danger, dysfunction, and self-destruction. In these narratives, single women's aggressive pursuit of sex served less as a source of freedom than a threat to men and a danger to themselves. However, the sensuous nature of these single heroines resonated with female viewers, even as their self-destruction signaled the dangers of taking sexual liberation too far.

This chapter begins by examining popular press accounts that blamed sexually aggressive single women for broken relationships and a crisis in male confidence. As I have argued throughout this book, the single woman was often used to symbolize feminist gains, and thus singles' changing sexual behavior was credited to feminism's perceived excesses. Popular press accounts pathologized single women and emphasized the dangers of their sexual drives, often insinuating that women were to blame for sexual assault and violence. Popular dramatic films and novels also highlighted women's self-destructive tendencies, and I compare these fictional texts to factual news reports and advice literature of the 1970s.

Adding Impotence to Injury: The "Sexual Confusion"

In 1972 two psychological studies made headline news and inspired a chilling *Mademoiselle* feature on relationships. One study reported that the suicide rate among women under thirty in Los Angeles County had more than quadrupled since the early 1960s, increasing at a much greater rate than among men. Psychologists attributed the increase to "growing conflict over what the woman's role is in society." Meanwhile, another study documented an "extraordinary" climb in sexual impotence among young men under thirty, tracing the problem to the "'reversal of [sex] roles' which has permitted women to be sexually aggressive."[3] These studies, *Mademoiselle* suggested, were interrelated and part of a greater problem the magazine termed "The Sexual Confusion." Wrote *Mademoiselle* columnist Karen Durbin:

The same kinds of messages have been coming through for many months now from friends and acquaintances of both sexes. They haven't been so drastic; I don't know anyone who has committed suicide, thank God, and I haven't had the awkward experience of going to bed with a man who was impotent. But I do know women who feel emotionally dead right now and men who feel emotionally impotent. A common theme runs through our conversations: distrust, confusion and fear about the other sex and our sexual identities and, most of all, an absence of any sense of the possibilities of men and women together.[4]

Although the author herself had participated in feminist causes, she suggested the movement was the source of these psychological problems and strained relationships. According to her article, the nascent women's movement had already "shake[n] the foundation of traditional male-female relationships," caused a "blurring" of sex roles, and "brought to the surface much of the hidden resentment women had for men."[5]

This concept of a "sexual confusion" was not unique to *Mademoiselle*. Many media reports argued that relationships between the sexes were damaged by a climate of sexual liberation that made women self-destructive and aggressive and made men impotent and resentful. Nor was *Mademoiselle* unique in suggesting that the "sexual confusion" largely stemmed from the influence of popular feminism. These generalized assumptions were reflected in African American publications, which documented a "crisis in the relationships between Black women and Black men" that was fueled by a historical legacy of racism. When asked by *Ebony* to compare this "crisis" to tensions within white relationships, an African American psychologist explained: "There is much more sensitivity and touchiness on the part of the Black male about issues of manlihood and more sensitivity on the part of the Black female about issues of womanhood and respect. . . . [Black women] are much more concerned than white women whether the Black male is exploiting them sexually or what they are getting in return."[6]

Singles grew in numbers and influence in the 1970s, and their sexual habits commanded media attention. As the *New York Times* reported in 1974, the decade witnessed dramatic growth in the singles population, partly due to "later marriages, a spiraling divorce rate and a marked trend against early remarriage after divorce."[7] According to popular reports, this growing demographic group took an increasingly casual approach to sex. In a 1973 *Mademoiselle* article, single women who prioritized work ambitions or feared being "controlled" or "tied down" by men were "practicing, enforcing sex with a certain amount of detachment." As one woman declared, "Sex is random now. It's with whomever I enjoy it with most *now.*" Another woman claimed to enjoy sex without "complications like commitment and vulnerability," saying of her current partner: "I like the safety of knowing he's not going to turn on me with hungry eyes and say he loves me."[8] *Mademoiselle* noted that these individual women were not necessarily feminists, nor did they speak in "movement language."[9] Yet their attitude toward sex was commonly blamed on the wider effect of the women's liberation movement. Feminism, according to popular media, both encouraged women to pursue selfish pleasures and heightened their expectations of men.

There was, of course, a diversity of viewpoints on sex within the feminist movement. As I have argued in this book, many feminists were initially critical of the sexual revolution as exploitative of women. Yet a new cadre of feminist-influenced authors and experts in the early 1970s encouraged women to follow their desires and demand sexual satisfaction. Historian Jane Gerhard argues that "many feminists emphasized women's capacity for orgasm and enjoyment of sex" to liberate women from conceptions that they were "naturally maternal rather than sexual." Gerhard writes, "Feminists who claimed sexual pleasure for feminism insisted that women could transform society by claiming full sexual entitlement and agency."[10]

Accordingly, Erica Jong's best-selling novel *Fear of Flying* (1973) acknowledged the allure of the anonymous, noncommittal "zipless fuck" for women as well as men and positioned sexual assertion as one means to self-actualization. *Fear of Flying* was one of many female-authored sex novels of the early 1970s that "introduced many nonactivist women to an emergent perspective loosely labeled 'feminist' by publishers and reviewers alike," according to Gerhard.[11] *The Hite Report*, published in 1976, both lamented women's lack of orgasms and urged the female reader to "'take charge' of getting them for herself during sex," just as men do.[12] Through these and other feminist-influenced texts, women challenged biological and social assumptions that deemed their sex drives and sexual needs as inferior to men's and "turned women's right to good sex into a political issue."[13] This challenge was apt to be criticized as well as praised: While Jong's book was castigated by some critics as a hostile objectification of men, *The Hite Report* was viewed by some as flawed, biased science.[14]

These explicit articulations of female sexual desire came at a time when Americans were questioning the merits of the second-wave feminist movement more broadly. As I have argued in previous chapters, proponents of the Equal Rights Amendment were often characterized as unfeminine and extremist in their efforts to eradicate sexual discrimination, and feminist efforts such as sexual harassment laws were thought to eliminate friendly flirtations between the sexes. The legalization of abortion in 1973 sparked a fierce countermovement in which opponents contended that abortion enabled women to evade the consequences of casual sex and deny their natural capacity to be mothers.[15] In line with these common critiques of feminist causes, "liberated" women who pursued or advocated casual sex were accused of ignoring innate gender differences, potentially harming themselves and their male partners in a selfish quest for satisfaction. The association of feminism with promiscuous sex also served the purposes of conservative critics such as Phyllis Schlafly, who, according to Beth Bailey, "purposely conflated women's liberation with the sexual revolution to brand the women's movement as radical, immoral and antifamily."[16]

According to critics, women who insisted on immediate sexual pleasure over long-term commitment denied their natural capacity for love and need for affection. As one female columnist admitted in *Vogue*: "When I say I want sex, I often mean I just want to be held. And I always mean I am looking for romantic love."[17] A 1975 *Harper's Bazaar* article entitled "One Lover or Many?" acknowledged that promiscuous sex can be satisfying "sometimes, for some women," but argued that "for most people, sex with the one you love in a secure relationship rather than a casual one is a better human experience." The author, a psychologist and sex therapist, also warned that noncommittal relationships could be a sign of psychological damage: "If you can let him leave without being deserted, it's either a sign of complete self-confidence and glowingly good mental health—or it could be a sign of neurosis in a woman who's isolated herself and cut herself off from feeling."[18]

Beneath the facade of the glamorized swinging single, these media reports emphasized, was a lonely and emotionally damaged woman.

Singles may "speak the language of liberation," *Mademoiselle* warned, "but continue to believe, deep down, that one plus zero equals zero. . . . Saturday night, for them, can still be the loneliest night of the week. And a holiday—almost any holiday—for a single swinging it alone can be deadly."[19] *Harper's Bazaar*'s 1975 themed issue on "America's Single Woman" included a lengthy article on "Coping with Loneliness, Drugs, Alcohol and Anxiety"—acknowledging single readers' propensity for emotional lows and addictive highs.[20] The *New York Times* in 1974 devoted a half page to the "hundreds of thousands of lonely women" in the city, acknowledging that for some singles, "even behavior that involves dark risks or defeats is better than feeling lonely."[21]

But women were not the only ones supposedly shortchanged by a climate of sexual freedom. Just as the feminist movement was often perceived as advancing women at men's expense, reports on swinging singles cited women's feelings of hostility and aggression toward men. "Where Are the Men Worthy of Us?" demanded the headline for a 1978 *New York Times* feature in which single women over thirty characterized bachelors as "bores, emotionally retarded little boys, cads, or men who fancy women younger than they . . . [or] sexually disappointing or incompatible."[22] Another woman interviewed in *Mademoiselle* flatly described her habit of engaging in casual sex with unworthy men. "I haven't slept with a man I really like in nearly a year," she complained.[23]

These women often found that their sexual overtures were perceived as a form of attack against the men they dated. One thirty-seven-year-old New Yorker complained that men were "polite to contemptuous, but never pleased" when she called to initiate getting together. "I've found a lot of fear of my own sexuality," she said.[24] Anticipating this reaction, advice columns warned women against calling men for dates, let alone calling the shots in bed. One woman interviewed in *Mademoiselle* urged women to clarify their intentions in pursuing men: "There was something hostile about the way I used to pursue a man I was interested in," she admits. "I didn't trust men even though I wanted them, and I was trying to control every new situation I found myself in. It was revenge, too, for all the years when men had had that kind of control—they had the right to call you, and you just had to sit there."[25] The sex therapist writing in *Harper's Bazaar* reminded readers that "[sexual] activity is not synonymous with aggression," contending that "aggressive, demanding women often are more interested in castrating and humiliating men than in sexual pleasure."[26]

The resentment, it seemed, was mutual. Single men, for their part, expressed feeling emasculated and defensive as their role as active partner in a sex relationship was usurped. Bachelors interviewed in a 1974 *New York Times* article expressed "dismay" at the fact that most women they met seemed interested only in one-night stands, and disdain for the women who operated within the predatory realm of singles bars.[27] A man writing for *Mademoiselle* admitted that being asked out on a date was more anxiety-producing than flattering: "Men aren't supposed to wonder if they'll come up to par," he wrote. "To feel this is to have some portion of your masculinity drained."[28]

Popular columnists and experts alike blamed women's increasing sexual demands—and women's increasing clout in society more broadly—for diminishing men's sexual pleasure and performance. While *Vogue* queried whether "women's lib" was ruining men's orgasms, other reports blamed feminism for a rise in male sexual impotence.[29] As one young research subject explained his sexual dysfunction: "When you get one of those liberated women in bed, you damn well better perform the way they want, or that'll be the end of the relationship."[30] A feminist sociologist interviewed by *U.S. News* in 1975 agreed that "'women's liberation' is increasing sexual anxieties among men" but offered a more nuanced and hopeful interpretation:

It is for some [men]. For them sex has become work. This is because in the past women were passive and just waited to have love made to them. We never knew then how many times men would be impotent, because they only had sex relations when they wanted them. But now that men are being tested when women happen to want sexual relations, they become aware of it and become more anxious about it. But I think the more we learn about sexuality, male and female, the less anxiety there will be.[31]

Some shared the sociologist's hopeful tone, perceiving the "sexual confusion" as a productive opportunity to begin to redefine male and female roles within relationships. The male columnist who balked at being asked out on dates began to reconsider "some of [his] old, worn-out ideas of what a man is, and just what makes a man different from a woman."[32] A female *Mademoiselle* columnist expressed optimism that, with time and understanding, "love between men and women may begin to look more like friendship and less like a lunatic torture system."[33] Yet when sexual liberation seemed to leave women emotionally damaged and men resentful and displaced, critics wondered whether the new sexual freedoms suited either sex. In the pages of the *New York Times*, single women claimed they did not want to be "female Don Juans, unfeeling sexual adventurers," and bachelors yearned for "sensitive and vulnerable" women who could be "equal without being unfeminine, honest without being abrasive."[34]

A pair of *Mademoiselle* headlines in 1976 perhaps best summed up the growing feelings of dissatisfaction among men and women. While the headline for a woman's column complained that "The Thrill of the Cheap Thrill Has Faded," the corresponding male columnist's headline asked, "Just What the Hell Does She Want from Me, Anyway?"[35]

Voracious Victims: New Perceptions of Murder and Sexual Assault

Male impotence was not the only, or even the greatest, social ill blamed on women's sexual assertion. A wave of violence against young single women in early 1970s New York was partly blamed on single women's risky, aggressive sexual behavior and self-destructive nature.

News reports had long emphasized the dangers that urban singles life posed to young, independent women. Feminists in the mid-1970s were still memorializing Kitty Genovese, a New York woman assaulted and murdered outside her apartment building in 1963 by a stranger who followed her home. According to reports, Genovese's neighbors witnessed the lengthy attack but failed to intervene or call police. Another high-profile 1963 case, covered well into the late 1960s, concerned the gruesome rape and murder of two career women in their luxury New York apartment by an intruder. One victim was the niece of author Philip Wylie, whose writings had demonized ambitious career women in the early 1960s. Media reports on these cases emphasized the virtue of the victims: Genovese was the "dying girl that no one helped," a "decent, pretty young woman of 28," according to *Life*'s report.[36] Janice Wylie, who hailed from an influential and respected family, was characterized as ambitious and idealistic. She had planned to join the first

Civil Rights march in Washington the very day she was killed.[37] Other reports warned of random violence that befell unsuspecting women as they slept or sat at their vanity tables.[38]

While most single women took precautions, others perceived the violence as inevitable. "Phyllis," a depressed single woman profiled in the book *The Girls in the Office* (1971), admitted she chose carelessness over suicide:

> *Eventually I'll be murdered.* . . . Some mornings I wake up and find out I've been sleeping in an unlocked apartment all night. And I do such dumb things. Some nights I'll come in and open my door, leave the door open and then turn on the lights. That's one of the stupidest things you can do in a jungle like New York. That's how a girl on Seventy-second Street got murdered. . . . Something like that will happen to me: I'm almost counting on it. Then it'll all be over, and I can rest.[39]

While few women were as careless as Phyllis, the single women murdered in early 1970s New York were not viewed as unwitting victims of random violence. Rather, they were increasingly seen as inviting the violence that befell them. In several prominently reported cases, single women were assaulted and murdered after they invited men they had just met up to their apartments or followed them to hotel rooms.[40] Police blamed the crimes partly on the women's lack of discrimination: "Young, sophisticated females who are liberated feel they can judge a guy's character after talking for a few hours," one sergeant lamented.[41]

These were far from individual cases, but endemic to a singles scene that was "swinging in some dangerous directions," according to the *Times*. According to a late 1974 report, "hundreds of young women from respectable, middle-class families [were] 'making it with street people' in a world defined by sex and drugs." The single swinger who seemed innocent on the surface was sordid underneath: "Sweet little Mary who spends her weekends in the suburbs may be the wildest thing on the streets of New York City," a police sergeant remarked. "It's absolutely amazing to see the Jekyll and Hyde personality they develop."[42]

When one such "sweet little Mary," Roseann Quinn, was murdered in 1973, she was initially characterized as too trusting and loose with her affections. A police officer told the *Times* that "a death like hers should be expected": 'If you live on the West Side . . . and you're friendly, affable, mix with all kinds of people and have a lot of night life, go to small bars . . . well, a lot's open to you. A lot."[43] However, a book by *New York Times* reporter Lacey Forsburgh revealed not only that Quinn was "friendly" toward the wrong people but that she was emotionally unstable, hostile toward men, and enjoyed violent sex.[44] Forsburgh's account also conveyed sympathy for the killer, a bisexual drifter who was spurned by Quinn for his failure to perform sexually, and who committed suicide after his arrest. "Perhaps *he's* the one who shouldn't have gone home with *her*," Forsburgh said.[45]

These crimes, and the ways in which they were reported, inspired feminist activism on sexual violence and influenced how women interpreted their own sexual behavior. Single women told the *Times* that they too had taken the risk of inviting men back to their apartments—and that they often failed to report assaults when they happened, as they considered themselves partly to blame. One woman, assaulted in her apartment by a stranger she brought home, survived by summoning neighbors to her aid. "I didn't report [the assault]," she said, after her neighbor, Carol Hoffmann, was murdered under similar circumstances in 1973. "What was I going to report? That I brought a man home with me?"[46]

Her reluctance was likely influenced by legal indifference toward rape. Until the mid-1970s, the rape statutes in many states, including New York, made sexual violence "nearly impossible to prosecute" and too often placed a victim's sexual history on trial.[47] In the relatively few cases that were tried, juries were unlikely to convict if it could be demonstrated that the female accuser had a promiscuous past or had "allowed herself to be picked up."[48] Through lobbying and awareness campaigns, feminists emphasized the prevalence of sexual violence and advocated for laws that focused on the prevalence of the crime rather than the character of the victim. As they worked for legal and institutional reform, some feminists also protested the eroticization of violence in film, advertising, and pornography.[49]

Feminists also used publicized rape and murder cases to illustrate the dangers of equating women's liberation with sexual freedom. The murders of "swinging singles" supported the radical feminist argument that "many women experienced sex not as an arena of pleasure but as 'brutalization, rape, submission, [and] someone having power over them.'"[50] As a radical feminist commented on the murder of Brigitte

Albrecht, a single stewardess and model murdered by her date in a hotel room in 1974: "Young women are destroyed by seeing liberation strictly in terms of sexual freedom."[51] While these accounts of slain single women spurred useful discussions of sexual violence in the mid-1970s, they also helped cement the link between aggressive sexuality and self-destruction.

Empowered and Erotic: Women in 1970s Film

Female journeys toward sexual liberation, and troubled relationships between the sexes, were major themes in popular films of the mid- to late 1970s. Scholars and critics documented a shift away from the dominant "male buddy movie" format toward films featuring independent and ambitious women. In "women's films" such as *An Unmarried Woman* (1978) and *Alice Doesn't Live Here Anymore* (1974), the protagonist was divorced or widowed and found romance in the process of finding herself. Other popular movies, such as *The Stepford Wives* (1975), used feminist catchphrases and offered harsh critiques of marriage and men's treatment of women. While they celebrated these new heroines, feminist critics and scholars feared these films still placed too much emphasis on romantic fulfillment — or represented a "battle of the sexes" that fueled antagonism toward men.[52]

Feminist critics also noted an acceleration of violence against women in film and an increasing eroticization of violence in media more broadly. Feminist film theorist E. Ann Kaplan argues that *Looking for Mr. Goodbar* followed the pattern of early 1970s films such as *Klute* (1971) that "showed women being raped and subjected to violence" and exposed men's "underlying hostility toward female sexuality."[53] In her 1974 book *From Reverence to Rape*, film critic Molly Haskell decried the prevalence in film of the "provocative, sex-obsessed bitch" who "is constantly fantasizing rape" — which she characterized as a "male chauvinist fantasy."[54] Some feminist groups also protested the mainstreaming of pornography through film: The year before *Goodbar* was released, activists disrupted screenings of *Snuff*, a film in which a woman is graphically murdered for the audience's titillation.[55]

These prominent themes of sexual self-discovery and sexual violence converged in popular films featuring single women. These movies borrowed conventions from the "women's films" of the mid- to late 1970s, as well as the earlier cycle of films featuring women's victimization.[56] However, their heroines also reflected common understandings of relationships in the seventies. They paired sexual forwardness with desperation and masochism and often alienated men with their aggressive and casual approach to sex.

These single heroines differed in one significant aspect from their counterparts in contemporaneous "women's films." While "women's films" and feminist novels of the 1970s tended to center on white, middle-class women, all three films that I analyze offer working-class, white ethnic, or Jewish heroines. This trend is partly the product of authorship. Jacqueline Susann and Gail Parent, who wrote the novels *Once Is Not Enough* and *Sheila Levine*, respectively, were Jewish. *Goodbar* seems a more strategic characterization, as both the novelist and filmmaker apparently transformed the middle-class Roseann Quinn into the working-class Theresa Dunn.[57] Regardless of cause, this characterization associates these groups with promiscuous sexuality and potentially provides the nonethnic white middle-class viewer a superior vantage point. (In a 1978 review, scholar Henry Giroux also criticized *Goodbar*'s portrayal of working-class *men* as "neurotic, explosive psychopaths, waging a war against the refined sensibilities of middle-class America.")[58]

The three films I analyze were significant for different reasons. The plain, pained heroine of *Sheila Levine* both appealed to and angered the single viewers she purported to represent. *Once Is Not Enough* garnered an Oscar nomination for its portrayal of an unstable promiscuous woman—a character even more brazen than she appeared in the Jacqueline Susann novel. *Goodbar*'s shocking ending sparked national dialogue about changing sexual roles and the risks inherent in casual sex. These memorable texts were not alone in associating single women's sexuality with self-destruction or antagonism toward men. The late 1970s play *Losing Time* portrayed a "brutal battle of the sexes" in which two female friends "insult, humiliate and terrorize" men during sex—and one woman is nearly killed when her male partner turns on her.[59] While Elizabeth McNeill's 1978 novel, *Nine and a Half Weeks*, explored the terrain of consensual sadomasochism, much like *Goodbar* it "pushed [women's sexuality] to an extreme that, for most women, exists only in fantasy" and offered a heroine desperate for sensation.[60] The mainstream novels and films that I explore addressed these fears and fantasies through a familiar figure: the single woman seeking ful-fillment in the city.

Suicidal Impulses and "Easy Lays": Sheila Levine's Survival

Gail Parent's novel *Sheila Levine Is Dead and Living in New York* features a self-destructive yet witty narrator who is desperate to marry and give up meaningless affairs. Although the novel is comical, it bears some serious intent. Parent claimed that as a former single woman, "getting married was my orientation to life." (Incidentally, she also wrote scripts for the self-deprecating and marriage-minded Rhoda on *The Mary Tyler Moore Show*.)[61] After the book became a best-seller in 1973, the story was adapted to film, and CBS commissioned Parent to write a pilot for a *Sheila Levine* sitcom.[62]

A depressed, unattractive woman who has had her fair share of lov-ers, Sheila prides herself on having overcome sexual "hang-ups" yet bemoans how promiscuity has devalued her dating relationships. She bitterly describes her college experiences: "Have you heard? Sheila Levine is an easy lay. All you have to do is call her. You don't have to buy her a drink or take her to parties or anything. You don't even have to be seen with her in public. Just call her and lay her."[63] Toward the beginning of the book, Sheila informs her overbearing mother about her plans to move to the city and reinvent herself. Her worried mother asks: "Do you really want to live in New York, where young, beautiful girls like you are murdered?"

"It's a fun neighborhood," Sheila insists.

"Getting murdered is fun?" her mother counters.[64]

Little does her mother know that Sheila herself poses the greatest risk to her own safety. Living single in New York is much harder than Sheila expected, having grown up watching cheery Doris Day films. "[Single women] didn't know that Hollywood had been deceiving [us] all these years," she admits.[65] Weary of looking for meaningful work and suitable dates, and plagued by her failure to find a husband, Sheila begins to plot her suicide in detail. This masochistic heroine's desire for release is matched only by her desire for sex. She alternates shopping for funeral plots with "deflowering" a male virgin and "fucking" a co-caine addict. The drug addict applauds her courage to kill herself—and is awed by her capacity for multiple orgasms. "You are truly a liberated woman," he says.[66] Although Sheila ultimately swallows an overdose of pills, she is saved by her mother's intervention and lives to date again.

However, critics complained that the character suffered a second death when the book was adapted to film in 1975. "Something disastrous happened to the heroine of Gail Parent's funny novel," the *New York Times* lamented. "[She] has lost her wit, her self-perceptions."[67] *Time* characterized actress Jeannie Berlin's portrayal of Sheila as "cow-eyed" and "clumsy."[68] The story, too, is more conventional, animated by Sheila's desire for romantic connection rather than suicide. However, shades of Sheila's masochism remain, and the revised story provides a less-than-subtle critique of sexual liberation as damaging to relationships. *New Yorker* reviewer Pauline Kael noted the film attracted young female viewers with its provocative themes, even as it angered them with its conventional happy ending: "There seems almost an anxiety to be liberated among young women now. Some of them in the audience may be so raw-nerved on [sex and relationship] issues, and so eager to see them treated on the screen, that they become indignant when they perceive that 'Sheila Levine' is no more than a sleazy con."[69]

Indeed, the film's bleak beginning offers little hint of a happy ending. The story opens with Sheila's parents driving her from Harrisburg to her New York apartment share. Her mother, a plump, aged woman carrying a soup tureen, reels in horror at the unkempt apartment, soiled bathroom, and menacing basement laundry room. "Welcome to the worst-run, dirtiest building in New York," pronounces Sheila's roommate, Kate (Rebecca Diana Smith), as she prances around half naked, preparing to leave on a date.[70] The contrast between the two women becomes apparent, according to one critic: "Her roommate is, as expected, a would-be actress who is as slovenly as Sheila is neat, as kooky as Sheila is straight."[71]

On her first night in New York, Sheila is invited by her roommate to a singles dance where danger and desire intertwine. As a rousing disco number plays, Sheila sits glumly in a corner, smoking a cigarette. "I killed somebody today," comes a slurred voice from the shadows. She turns cautiously to see an older man holding a cocktail. "You know what I did today? I performed an abortion," the doctor continues, declaring it was his first and his last.

"I was just thinking, what if the mother wants to . . ." Sheila begins, quietly.

"Screw the mother," he says. "You kidding? You realize how many brilliant people could have been victims of abortion? What if Einstein's mother didn't want him?"

Sheila volunteers, "We'd have no theory of relativity."

"You agree with me," he decides, impressed. Although the doctor, Sam (Roy Scheider), harshly criticizes the liberated woman who would opt for an abortion, he has no qualms about using a woman for casual sex. Identifying Sheila as a newcomer to the city, he invites her back to his apartment to "talk" and there bluntly asks, "You want to make it?"

Sheila hesitates, hinting at her inexperience. "This doesn't happen on a first date in Harrisburg," Sam surmises. He persuades Sheila to give in and is taken aback when she pledges her love for him afterward. When Sam clarifies they were merely "two people satisfying an urge, two people who want to get laid," she leaves angrily and abruptly.

Still, she is infatuated with Sam and saddened when he meets and falls for her roommate, Kate, a shrill-voiced, skinny, and sexually confident woman who is perpetually filmed in a state of undress. Lacking Sheila's skills for conversation, Kate captivates Sam by dancing provocatively to a disco number. Sam's gaze settles on Kate's lithe body, and the couple begin dating. Sheila, feeling outmaneuvered and pessimistic about her romantic prospects, moves home to Harrisburg until she decides to pursue Sam with new tactics.

"You're going to New York to chase after a man?" her mother asks, shocked. "Nice girls don't do such things. You have to have a little pride."

"I *am* a nice girl," Sheila insists, informing her mother of the loneliness that has defined her life. "I have to stop waiting and start doing."

Taking fashion tips from the likes of *Vogue,* she shows up at Sam's door looking more like a drag queen than a liberated woman. "She tries to lure him like the freakish Kate, since that's what he goes for," Kael observes.[72] In coiffed hair, heavy makeup, and unsteady heels, Sheila switches on music and gyrates seductively, but soon learns her performance is all for naught: Sam is engaged to marry the newly pregnant Kate.

Sheila flees to the tenement elevator, turning down a proposition

Far from Harrisburg: Sam (Roy Scheider) beds the traditional Sheila (Jeannie Berlin) at the beginning of Sheila Levine Is Dead and Living in New York. *Courtesy of Paramount Pictures/Photofest.*

from a lesbian en route. As she begins her descent to the first floor, she silently contemplates a graffiti scrawl on the elevator wall: "The Girls in this Joint are Easy Lays." Sheila is twice humiliated, first as an "easy lay," then by attempting to use sex as a form of control. Fortunately, in the tradition of the "woman's film," she rebounds emotionally and begins to establish an alternate identity in her new work role as a producer of children's records. She also develops a new look that is more glamorous than her original appearance but more natural than the liberated mask she wore earlier.

And we soon learn that Sheila is not the only character to have posed as sexually liberated to mask her inner insecurities. The sexualized Kate, who had earlier impressed Sheila by bragging about her acting career, trust fund, and frequent dates, is revealed to be a common prostitute and former teenage runaway. The child she is expecting is not Sam's—she plans to secure a secret abortion after they are married and tell him she had a miscarriage. "The only reason Sam wants to marry me is because he thinks I'm having his child," Kate pleads as Sheila responds with angry silence. "What can I do besides hustle? I need something to come home to." Kate weeps about her broken childhood, looking humbled and childlike in her pigtails and short dress.

The suave Sam, too, is revealed to be hiding behind noncommittal sex to assuage feelings of inadequacy. In an honest moment with Sheila, Sam shares a painful memory of being rebuffed by a childhood crush. "I knew I wasn't going to make that mistake again," he says, bowing his head in shame. "That's what bachelors are made of."

"You trust yourself and trust others," he tells Sheila. "I don't do that. I don't trust, commit, lay myself on the line." Kate, he explains, made for an initially "easy" relationship: "She just brings it all to you."

Yet sexual forwardness does not a relationship make. In the following scene, Sam and Kate call off the wedding, and Sam returns to see Sheila. He proposes marriage as Sheila sits open-mouthed—and as his earlier pained confession echoes in the background.

The film valorizes Sheila's openness and trustworthiness and suggests that a plain-looking woman with a good heart will ultimately triumph over the sexually forward, provocative, empty, and deceptive liberated woman. However, the film's ending failed to resonate with the same single women who had relished Gail Parent's novel. According to Kael, female viewers "booed" the ending because the premise that a less attractive, sexually restrained woman could earn a swinging bachelor's love did not resonate as "real."[73] As Kael described the film's contradictory messages, "Here comes 'Sheila Levine' to touch the sore spots and then fade out on a wish fulfillment."[74] Other viewers complained the sudden marriage proposal seemed to arrest Sheila's process of personal and career growth.[75] The *Los Angeles Times* located the problem in relationship dynamics: Because the movie set up Sam as "hopelessly insensitive" and Sheila as repeatedly humiliated, "the 'happy ending' has a distinctly sour taste." The *Times* identified Sheila as part of a larger problem facing Hollywood filmmakers in the mid-1970s: "No one knows how to create a strong, independent, liberated heroine who is also a romantic heroine."[76]

Conniving Women and Craven Men: *Once Is Not Enough*

The 1975 film *Once Is Not Enough*, based on a 1973 Jacqueline Susann novel of the same name, seems to illustrate the *Times'* premise by casting a soft, romantic character against a hardened, liberated one.[77] The film, which featured high emotion, hints of incest, and secret lesbian affairs between middle-aged wives, was largely panned by critics. The *New York Times* termed it "ludicrous, bad, terrible, horrendous," and *Time* called it "an accidentally entertaining piece of work . . . [treated] with both reverence for the source material and fearless vulgarity."[78] However, the fact that actress Brenda Vaccaro (formerly of *Midnight Cowboy*) both received an Oscar nomination and won a Golden Globe for her portrayal of a ruthlessly sexual, single professional woman suggests that her role was taken more seriously than the rest. Critics and costars praised Vaccaro's "wonderful, eccentric turn."[79]

The film stars Deborah Raffin as January, a twenty-year-old returning to her father's apartment in the city after treatment for a brain injury. As she enters the dating scene, January falls under the tutelage of the twenty-eight-year-old Linda (Brenda Vaccaro). January is excited to receive a phone call from Linda, whom she remembers as "the oldest, ugliest and smartest girl at school." She initially fails to recognize her friend, now a successful and attractive magazine editor. Linda explains she used her smarts to obtain extensive plastic surgery and "screwed every guy, literally and figuratively," on her way to the top. The streetwise Linda mocks January's virginal status, convinces her to move to an apartment in her building, and pledges to teach her a thing or two about dating.[80]

Linda, who brags about her position as the youngest editor at *Gloss* magazine, evokes comparisons to Helen Gurley Brown, who was in novelist Susann's social circle. Linda's character does hail Brown as one of her heroes in the novel, and her character's relentless commitment to self-improvement, career advancement, and sexual pleasure mark her as a quintessential "Cosmo Girl." Yet Linda's character—a woman's magazine editor with scant writing talent—was also rumored to be based on Gloria Steinem.[81] That Linda espouses "women's lib" in one sentence, and advises January to take aphrodisiacs in the next, suggests her sexually forward stance is inspired by feminism.

Linda's practice of "screwing every guy" in her quest for self-validation has a darker side. She tells January that she is apt to be "deliriously happy" one day and miserable the next, suggesting a dual personality. "Screwing" also serves as the balm for childhood scars that have not been healed by her plastic surgery and career success. "Even

With friends like these: January (Deborah Raffin), left, takes sex advice from Linda (Brenda Vaccaro), right, in Once Is Not Enough. *Courtesy of Paramount Pictures/Photofest.*

with my nose job and all, I still feel ugly," she admits to January. "That's why I screw around a lot. It makes me feel attractive."

Whether the average man finds Linda more attractive or threatening is up for question. The movie poster itself characterizes Linda as more fearsome than glamorous: With "silicon in her chest" and "ice water in her veins," Linda is a "high-fashion editor with low desires." When Linda joins January and her father at a restaurant, the group is accosted by Tom (David Jannsen), an embittered, middle-aged drunk who was once a colleague of January's father. The indiscriminating Linda sets her sights on the volatile man twice her age and asks him to walk them home. She hints to January that she may soon want to be alone with her date.

"Is there any man you don't go to bed with?" January asks, amazed.

"If there is, honey," Linda says crassly, "I haven't met him."

January takes her cue to leave, rejecting Tom's request that she stay. "I wouldn't feel safe [alone] with Linda," Tom begs. As Linda is in the next room, clearing off her cluttered bed for the expected tryst, Tom escapes out the window to January's apartment.

"Silicon tits and a computerized brain is not my idea of a sexy combination," he tells January. "I've had all the Lindas I need." Discovering she's been abandoned, Linda breaks plates and shouts curses out the window as January and Tom laugh conspiratorially.

Here *Once Is Not Enough* draws from popular dialogues that linked female aggression to male inadequacy. All those "Lindas" in Tom's past, it seems, have made him impotent. He laments to January that despite being a "barroom brawler" and novelist who writes about "raw, virile, violent sex," he has been unable to perform for years. Tom follows the path advocated by bachelors in the *New York Times*—he finds comfort in a younger woman who has not been ruined by women's liberation.[82] Over the course of a several-month affair, the meek, gentle, and virginal January becomes the cure for his impotence. (Actress Deborah Raffin bolstered January's comparatively innocent image. The actress reportedly refused to remove her clothes onscreen, or to even allow a body double to film a nude scene in her place. In interviews, Raffin explained she was merely a "modest and private person.")[83]

January's affair, however, is tainted by the suggestion that Tom is merely a surrogate for her emotionally unavailable father. And she is punished for her transgressions, losing her father in a plane crash and Tom to indifference in a single weekend. Noncommittal sex, for the appropriately feminine January, is ultimately unfulfilling.

Finding Tom in a bar, she urges him to return to her. "We had something special, didn't we?" she pleads.

"We did once," he grunts.

"Once is not enough," January concludes, ruefully.

After wandering the city streets bereft, January returns to her apartment building to find Linda—the very woman who had urged her to become sexually active—disheveled and distraught on her doorstep. "Where have you been?" Linda demands, seeming less concerned for the mourning January than for her own wretched evening. Linda, we learn, has just bedded her boss—and lost her job in the process. "First he laid me. Then he fired me. He said I was a great lay but a lousy editor," she shrieks. Her hair stringy, her manner shaky, Linda has not only lost her job at *Gloss*, but momentarily her poise and polish as well. Like the ruined Kate in *Sheila Levine*, she reverts to a childlike state.

In the film's final scenes, she is tucked into bed by January, comforting herself with the fact that she's still a "great lay" in her boss's estimation. "At least this way," She muses, "I can screw myself into another job."

This scene is doubly significant because it deviates from the novel. In Susann's novel, it is January who suffers a breakdown and apparently commits suicide. Although the novel's Linda is crass and engages in affairs with married men, she is more of a serial monogamist than the promiscuous woman that appears in the film. The filmmakers' choice to make Linda even more brazen and vulnerable than in the novel corresponds with negative perceptions of single women's sexuality. The humbling of Linda in the film's final scenes also adds a moral tone to an otherwise scandalous narrative, which incorporated not only casual affairs and impotence, but also incestuous impulses and lurid lesbian trysts.[84]

A Deadly Search for Sensation: *Goodbar*'s Theresa Dunn

The film adaptation of *Sheila Levine* tamed its protagonist's sexual and suicidal tendencies. *Once Is Not Enough* offered the aggressive Linda only as a secondary, cautionary tale in a larger narrative of love and loss. In contrast, *Looking for Mr. Goodbar* (1977) unflinchingly foregrounded a promiscuous protagonist who is killed in her quest for a sexual fix. Yet *Goodbar*'s Theresa Dunn (Diane Keaton) begs comparison to earlier single heroines: like Linda, she develops a dual personality and uses "screwing" to compensate for emotional wounds. And, like the novelized Sheila, Theresa is passionate in her pursuit of sex and self-destruction. However, Theresa's character is more developed and complex than these earlier representations, and *Goodbar*'s dark narrative evoked mixed responses from audiences. The controversy the film generated, and the fact it was received as a commentary on gender roles in the late 1970s, marks *Goodbar* as a particularly important film.[85]

The story, based on Judith Rossner's novel, dramatized one woman's psychological decline and murder, but it was also received as a harsh commentary on sexual politics more broadly. "She is not the mad Theresa, the police blotter Theresa, anymore," wrote one feminist reviewer of the film adaptation. "She is an object lesson, a nightmare about woman—woman adrift from the saving rules and structures that wise men have made for her protection."[86] While *Goodbar* does adhere to traditional film formulas that violently punish the wayward woman, another critic writing in the *Los Angeles Times* cautioned against reading the movie as "a simple anti-feminist parable." Rather, the reviewer argued, it addressed themes specific to the sexually liberated seventies: "Women who are no longer 'good girls' or 'bad girls' and who are without the protection that such categories offer are more exposed than ever; men, sexually insecure and without the titular power once conferred on their sex, are no longer in the driver's seat. The two sexes are locked in mortal combat, and [Director Richard] Brooks has captured both the numbness and the frenzied, murderous rage that lies just below the surface."[87]

Using Judith Rossner's 1975 novel as a template, director Richard Brooks endeavored to provide a broader commentary on a sexualized singles culture. "How do you do a movie about *today* and not make it about all woman-kind?" Brooks asked. While developing the script, he reportedly interviewed 600 single women about their response to the *Goodbar* novel, delving into their perspectives on sex in the process. He concluded that young women "were looking for 'sensation'—they wanted to feel something, strong emotions, briefly but strongly and (if possible) not to make a commitment."[88] In developing the setting and feel of the film, Brooks visited singles bars in cities as far-flung as Denver, Kansas City, and Chicago, ensuring that Theresa's story was tied no longer to a singular victim, nor the city she inhabited.[89]

Although the story ultimately connects female liberation to psychosis and violence, many viewers and critics were drawn to Theresa herself as a feminist heroine.[90] "Attractive, intelligent and vital," her journey corresponds with that taken by characters in late 1970s "women's films." When her domineering Catholic father accuses her of "whoring around" and attempts to limit her mobility, she asserts her independence and moves to the city. "I can't stay here and be myself," she yells, stressing the importance of "my place, my money, my rules."[91] Her autonomy extends to the workplace, where she is a dedicated and caring teacher of deaf children.

Theresa was also seen as groundbreaking for the amount of agency she possessed.[92] It is she who initiates her affairs, whether urging a professor to seduce her or approaching men at bars. Several elements of the film "compel viewers to see events almost entirely from Theresa's point

Courting danger: Theresa (Diane Keaton) frequents smoky singles bars in the deadly Looking for Mr. Goodbar. *Courtesy of Paramount Pictures/Photofest.*

of view," according to a *Village Voice* reviewer.[93] The camera lingers on Theresa's emotional responses: her pleasure during sex, her disbelief at having invited the first man home, her naive curiosity about cocaine. One young viewer remarked that she had rarely seen female desire portrayed so stridently by an American actress: "I loved her love of sex," she said.[94] The narrative also makes ample use of Theresa's flashbacks and fantasies to reflect her history of injury, her unstoppable lusts, and her premonitions of violence.

However, while some viewers read Theresa as a feminist heroine, the film text itself positions the feminist movement as merely a backdrop for her journey. The feminist context is first established in a television news report on the feminist movement that declares the seventies the "decade of the dames," united in their search for "sexual freedom." It is also reiterated in angry remarks from Theresa's father, who accuses her of joining the "women's holy crusade to burn the bra" and pursuing selfish freedom at the expense of her eternal soul. Theresa shows interest in the news broadcast and listens defiantly as her father rails against feminism. However, aside from her teaching vocation, Theresa lacks other political engagement, unlike the real-life Roseann Quinn, who was an active participant in the civil rights movement and advocate for women's rights.[95] As E. Ann Kaplan argued, "Clearly, to have had Theresa associate herself positively with the Women's Movement would have necessitated taking the movement seriously as offering alternatives for women."[96]

More dangerous than Theresa's political apathy, however, is that "she mistakes sexual freedom for women's liberation," as Brooks put it.[97] Her aggressive approach fails to satisfy her emotional needs and becomes a form of hostility and revenge toward men. In her first love affair, she is spurned by a married professor who claims, "I can't stand the company of a woman after I've fucked her." Theresa subsequently turns this noncommittal attitude on her dates, ordering one to leave after sex so she can prepare for work, and resisting another's attempts to possess and commit to her. "Don't love me," she tells him. "Just make love." That she pursues an "unbroken series of men whose most distinguishing trait is their sexism and propensity for psychotic violence" confirms single women's lament about the lack of worthy men.[98]

Theresa's story also supports the idea that promiscuous women suffer from poor psychological health. Like *Once*'s Linda Riggs, who feels unattractive and vulnerable beneath her plastic surgery and brash attitude, Theresa bears the emotional and physical scars of scoliosis, a congenital illness that immobilized her as a child. Although she lacks the telltale limp of the book's heroine, she shudders when her lovers try to touch the crooked scar on her back. As her promiscuity escalates, her mental health seems to decline: She turns to drugs for sensation, her work begins to slip, and her apartment becomes increasingly filthy. (Incidentally, the promiscuous characters in *Sheila Levine* and *Once Is Not Enough* also live in unkempt apartments, as if to illustrate the mess their lives have become.) Theresa's poor emotional health and combative attitude toward men hasten her violent end.

As in newspaper reports on Quinn's murder, Theresa's death is presented as the inevitable result of a long line of casual and risky encounters. The film eroticizes violence long before its murderous climax. Theresa's first pickup is Tony (Richard Gere), a volatile, working-class man she invites back to her apartment. Between sexual acts he dances wildly, brandishing a switchblade, and Theresa watches in frozen fascination as he wields the knife. Their relationship continues to blur the boundary between dangerous allure and deadly violence. In one scene their playful wrestling quickly becomes a fistfight. "Sex and violence are inextricably linked," director Brooks insisted. "There is more frustration and violence in the marriage bed than on the battlefields."[99] Accordingly, Theresa's murder stems not only from the dark risks she takes but also the seething sexual frustration on both sides. Her lovers are none too happy to be kept at arm's length. Angered by lack of access to Theresa, Tony breaks into her apartment and stalks her at work. The social worker who pursues Theresa throughout the film is stung by her refusal to commit and becomes sullen and controlling.

On the night of that fateful New Year's Eve, Theresa aims to escape from the clutches of these possessive men by walking to the neighborhood bar. Seeking protection from the former lover who has followed her there, she is drawn to a stranger with a luminous smile—a stranger established in a previous scene as a gay man and cross-dresser similarly seeking refuge from a cloying male partner. When he accompanies Theresa back to her apartment, their tryst is short-lived. He is unable to perform as commanded, she to find sexual release. He becomes agitated. "Goddamn women," he says, "all you gotta do is lay there. A guy's gotta do all the work." Theresa laughs and offers to call him a cab. He grabs her and brandishes a knife, ultimately stabbing and penetrating her simultaneously. Although she struggles, Theresa's final words express desire for release as well as sensation. "Do it," she says, and the film flickers out.

E. Ann Kaplan contends that *Goodbar*'s use of a gay cross-dresser as the killer protects heterosexual men from association with the final, most violent act.[100] Beth Bailey argues that the killer's homosexuality amplifies his characterization as "a man damaged by sexual liberation."[101] For seventies audiences, the gay killer seemed utterly emasculated, a "kept man attempting to prove his manhood with a knife," in the words of one reviewer.[102] However, the fact that the film closes with this violent encounter between a demanding woman and disempowered man corresponds with less deadly reports of relationship conflict in the 1970s.

Single women who saw *Goodbar* reportedly left the theater "looking shell shocked and dazed"—but often recognized themselves on the screen.[103] In an article that foregrounded conversations among single female moviegoers, *US* magazine noted that some took the film's brutal ending to heart: "Women who live sexually aggressive lives are courting danger," declared a twenty-six-year-old viewer from Delaware. "It scared me away from singles bars." Others were inspired by Theresa's sexual nature, regardless of the risks. "That was my life," said a forty-year-old Delaware viewer who claimed to have slept with 200 men she picked up at bars. "But I'm not fearful of something happening to me. . . . I guess I'm willing to take the risks to reach the highs."[104]

Other viewers related less to the details of Theresa's sex life than the symbolic importance of her character: "I admired Theresa Dunn's guts, her determination to get the most out of life," said a twenty-one-year-old viewer. "Theresa is a real feminist martyr. She was killed for what she believed in, and for doing what she wanted to do."[105] Significantly, this viewer not only recognized the film narrative as a violent response to feminism, but also respected Theresa as a feminist character.

While some seventies media celebrated the single woman's independence, these films foregrounded and stigmatized her aggressive sexuality. Similar to stereotypes that surfaced in sixties sex comedies, the promiscuous woman was thought to be compensating for inner neuroses or psychoses. However, these films followed melodramatic genre conventions and doled out consequences accordingly. Rather than providing the single woman a romantic cure, filmmakers often punished her by revoking her love and livelihood—and sometimes demanding her life.

These moral consequences were exaggerated versions of the punishments visited upon single, sexual heroines in early 1960s films. Characters were not necessarily punished merely for having sex, as the supposed "happy ending" of *Sheila Levine* reveals. Instead, their crime was pursuing sex as a form of manipulation or power, without romantic connection, and for being careless enough to invite strangers upstairs for sex. Although the fictional Theresa Dunn was an extreme case, her graphic murder conveyed chilling messages about the high cost of promiscuity and apparently convinced some women to stay away from singles bars. In the years before rape was adequately acknowledged and prosecuted, these movies suggested that women were to blame for the sexual brutalities they suffered.

These films conveyed a heightened fear of feminism, which animated many media representations of the seventies. In these particular stories, sexual liberation and women's liberation became conflated. Consider Brenda Vacarro's character in *Once Is Not Enough*, who was equal parts

Brown and Steinem and pursued sex with political gusto. These films, as well as some feminists, warned women against confusing sexual freedom with true liberation. Yet the movie narratives did not offer valid political alternatives, and they obscured the ways that feminism, as a multifaceted movement, was working to achieve equality both in and out of the bedroom. However, we must acknowledge that these films and novels may have served an inspirational function as well as a moralistic one. The popular press reported that women connected with Sheila's tirades and Theresa's lusts—that they desired representations that acknowledged their inner contradictions, their sexual drives and desires. Much like Theresa, they were "willing to take the risks to reach the highs."

As unmarried women developed greater professional and financial clout in the 1980s, popular movies continued to emphasize their desperate and predatory approach to sex. The early to mid-1980s signaled the development of what some authors have termed the "sexual counterrevolution": Women reported feeling weary of casual sex, and even former sex radicals advocated love and connection over one-night stands.[106] In films such as Fatal Attraction (1987), which featured Glenn Close as a corporate executive and murderous mistress, the single woman became the "other woman" who threatened the stability of marriage itself. The question posed by the Los Angeles Times in 1975 still resonated strongly: Why can't Hollywood create a heroine who is strong, liberated, independent . . . and romantic?[107]

Epilogue

As I write, the sixties "single girl" again graces the screen in the critically acclaimed series *Mad Men*. Set in the early 1960s, this cable drama positions single women as copywriters and clerical workers for a male-dominated advertising agency. *Mad Men* has been hailed by critics and scholars for being both feminist and historically accurate in its unflinching depiction of workplace sexism.[1] The storyline of Peggy (Elisabeth Moss) resembles earlier "single girl" narratives as Peggy assumes a new identity in the city, advances from secretary to copywriter, and pursues secret affairs. Her fiery colleague Joan (Christina Hendricks) wields her sexuality as a form of power in the workplace but is rarely recognized for her business acumen. Joan was reportedly modeled after Helen Gurley Brown, and her striking combination of sexiness and assertion seems straight out of Brown's best-seller.[2] Like many single women of their time, Joan and Peggy fight for recognition of their work, confront leering colleagues, and battle pernicious media stereotypes as they develop new marketing strategies to reach women. *Mad Men* directly references 1960s media texts—for example, the 1959 melodrama *The Best of Everything* surfaces in an early episode, and the film may have inspired *Mad Men*'s plotlines and set designs.[3] More than mere nostalgia, this series serves as a sobering reminder of the important role single women played in creating social change, and the discrimination they faced in their professional and personal lives prior to the rise of second-wave feminism.

Mad Men's agenda aligns with recent cultural histories that seek to offer more nuanced and accurate accounts of postwar women's lives. Scholars Joanne Meyerowitz, Ruth Rosen, Lauri Umansky, and many others have troubled easy assumptions about postwar domesticity by chronicling the lives of activists, workers, and cultural rebels who diverged from the dominant media image of the contented housewife.[4] Just as we have learned that many 1950s women were *Not June*

Cleaver—to name one such book—it is high time to reevaluate the image and importance of the "single girl." Historically, media have associated the 1960s–1970s young single woman with girlish femininity and a commercialized singles scene. As many of these singles embraced female beauty culture and eschewed feminism, they rarely are included in official histories of second-wave feminist activism. This book argues that single women, regardless of their feminist stance, were essential to processes of social and political change. As young single women dared to move away from their families, delay marriage, obtain birth control, and make their way in the workplace, they may have been following their individual desires. Yet they advanced the cause of women as they entered patriarchal professions, sought sexual pleasure on their own terms, and spoke out about sexual assault. In addition to consciousness-raising groups and protest marches, young women's life experiences helped spur changes in laws and societal attitudes. As Hilary Radner reminds us, "The terms of the current feminist debate were formulated not only by the groundbreaking work of activists . . . but also by a generation of women whose initial goal was to pay the rent."[5]

As I have argued throughout this book, formulaic and heavily regulated electronic media rarely represented single women's lives in all their diversity and complexity. Marketing concerns dictated what types of images appeared, and stringent censorship processes stripped films and programs of their more daring elements. Were it not for such script changes, Doris Day might have had a premarital affair in *Pillow Talk*—and *Police Woman*'s Pepper Anderson could have taken down a lady killer herself rather than diving and waiting for male rescue.[6] The dramatic changes that occurred between script and screen are significant, as they illustrate how marketing and moral concerns shaped media images of women. Furthermore, behind-the-scenes dialogues prove that scriptwriters frequently envisioned bold possibilities that were not realized in the final product. By censoring single-woman narratives, studios and networks attempted to appeal to youthful audiences without alienating or angering more traditional viewers and policymakers. This was a difficult balancing act.

Print media faced similar regulations as electronic media, and they caved to the demands of advertisers and readers. Yet, they often provided a forum for individual women to write openly about workplace discrimination, ruminate about sex and romance, and voice their frustrations with the series and films that purported to represent them. Indeed, one of my favorite parts of this research process was engaging with the plethora of print sources addressing young women—ranging from mimeographed activist newsletters to glossy magazines. Even magazines like *Cosmopolitan* and *Mademoiselle* treated young women as more than fashion plates. They offered career advice, addressed sexual assault, and provided tips for self-protection. They also directly engaged feminist ideas, including openly endorsing the Equal Rights Amendment. Media leaders like Helen Gurley Brown modeled both female ambition and career success in addition to shaping popular understandings of singleness.

As I have argued, popular media of the early 1960s repeatedly tried to put women like Brown in their place. Her book received hostile reviews, and the comedy film based on *Sex and the Single Girl* mocked her sexual authority. While Brown was a particularly polarizing figure, she was one of few prominent female authors who wrote media texts for single women. During these decades, men most often were the producers, directors, and authors of single-woman narratives, and male scriptwriters often adapted female-authored books like *Sex and the Single Girl* to the screen. The male voice of authority shaped many media narratives, whether it was a booming voiceover in *Peyton Place* that declared New York a "nightmare" for wayward Betty Anderson, or Mike's patronizing advice in the film adaptation of *The Best of Everything*. Male dominance was not unique to "single girl" representations. Industry reports documented the absence of women in media production more broadly, and certainly some men showed greater sensitivity to women and feminist issues than others.[7] But media veteran Marlo Thomas—who was initially the lone female producer of *That Girl* and later hired female scriptwriters—reminds us that a female perspective is essential to keep such a series relevant and realistic for women. Additionally, a team of female scriptwriters contributed to *The Mary Tyler Moore Show*'s enduring success.[8]

Production and authorship, of course, were only part of the picture. Perhaps because media and culture were changing so rapidly, media industries often misjudged which representations audiences would find appealing or off-putting. For example, the derivative program *Funny Face* was considered the hottest property of the 1971–1972 TV season, yet ultimately it was declared old-fashioned and failed to last beyond a year. *Mary Tyler Moore* initially received negative reviews for portraying Mary as "desperate" and Rhoda as a "man-crazy klutz," yet these quirky characters soon grew on audiences.[9] We also find evidence that single women responded to media texts in oppositional ways. For example, a preview audience questioned the moral implications of *Where the Boys Are*, responding more readily to scenes of youthful fun and rebellion than Melanie's downfall. Single viewers of the late 1970s also found pleasure in the sex-obsessed Theresa Dunn, despite her graphic murder in *Looking for Mr. Goodbar*.[10]

Throughout this study, we have often seen contradictions between producers' intent and viewer reception. Supposedly "relevant" heroines often seemed retrograde to feminist critics—and media often failed to accurately reflect single women's experiences. Of course, few media texts can claim to capture the complexities of women's lives or the nuances of diverse social movements like feminism. Thus, we repeatedly see heroines who are deeply conflicted, torn between new roles and traditional dictates, and trying to balance assertion and femininity. As I have argued, these conflicted stances made characters more marketable; for example, skimpy costumes eased superheroes' entrance into a programming genre and timeslot once closed to women. Mainstream film and television needed to reach a mass audience, so programs like *That Girl* effectively presented an image of the single woman that would appeal to new women and traditional parents alike. Genre conventions also shaped characters' internal and interpersonal conflicts. In a formula characteristic of situation comedy, for instance, *That Girl* exaggerated differences between Ann and her father for comedic value, then resolved them sweetly by episode's end, prioritizing family ties over individuality.

Feminist critics of the 1970s often seized upon these contradictions as an aspect of media that undermined feminism. For some viewers, Mary's reference to her boss as "Mr. Grant" belied her liberation, and Diana's wide-eyed infatuation with Steve Trevor minimized her superheroic strength. However, authors such as Susan Douglas and Wini Brienes have urged more productive engagements with media's inherent contradictions. As Douglas argues, viewers' frustration with the limitations of commercial media often spur them to feminist realizations and rebellions.[11] On another level, media viewers in this era were rarely unitary in their politics, sometimes expressing feminist and antifeminist sentiments in the same sentence. Conflicted characters may have spoken to that deeper ambivalence—and, at best, brought more nuance and humanity to fictional characters. Actress Lynda Carter, for example, claims she tried to bring warmth to Wonder Woman's interactions with children on the show, as she suspected the heroine might have longed to have children of her own.[12] Was her interpretation of the character a devaluation of Wonder Woman's singleness and power, or does Carter's idea bridge the divide between career and family, suggesting strong women can triumph in both realms? Much like these fictional characters, the single woman herself is a contradictory figure, bridging girlhood and adulthood, sometimes espousing feminist ideas and other times embracing tradition.

The cultural contradictions concerning sex were particularly frustrating for women of the postwar era, as historians have attested.[13] Throughout this study, single women are hemmed in by sexual dictates that mark them as dysfunctional if they refuse to yield to desire, but dangerous to the social order if they *do* have sex. The sexual revolution took place incrementally, and even during the 1970s, a time of heightened sexual content in media, characters were held to conservative standards. Thus, Mary Richards's overnight date and sexual past were vaguely defined to avoid alienating viewers. The Angels may have masqueraded as sex workers and nudists, but cohabitating with a committed boyfriend was out of the question for Farrah Fawcett's character.[14] When sex was explicitly and repeatedly shown on screen, as in the case of *Looking for Mr. Goodbar*, it served as fodder for gendered violence.

Media representations played an important role in political organizing. While the ERA might have been a tough sell, consumers readily rallied around feminist campaigns to diversify and improve images of women in media. And although emergent advertising campaigns and narratives often emphasized consumerism and reinforced innate sexual difference, single heroines did diversify existing genres and model new roles for women. Marlo Thomas claims that she became a feminist due to the large volume of viewer letters she received during the run of *That Girl*. In addition to the typical fan mail, many letter writers sought help with pressing issues like unwed pregnancy and domestic abuse, and they turned to this independent woman for advice.[15] In some cases, popular programs even gave single women scripts they could use to talk back to sexist ideas or advocate for change—as in Pepper's radio rant about female cops or Mary's reasoned demand for a raise.[16] As single women as a consumer group grew in size and visibility, they helped shape the acceptable perimeters for femininity and became representative of sweeping changes in women's work and family roles.

The single woman remains a central figure in media culture today. Interestingly, many recent narratives revive heroines from decades past. The retro sex comedy *Down with Love* spoofed Doris Day and Helen Gurley Brown in equal measure, pairing a headstrong female author with a manipulative playboy. *Charlie's Angels* once again commanded the screen in two feature films, and a short-lived TV series brought *The Bionic Woman* back to life. On a broader level, most contemporary media featuring young, unmarried working women engage themes markedly similar to those addressed in this book. While modern heroines may display higher career aspirations and sexual drives than their historical counterparts, they still often resist aligning with feminism, strategically use their sexuality as a means to power, and express deep ambivalence about remaining single. And a quick survey of scholarship on series such as *Sex and the City, Ugly Betty,* and *Mad Men* reveals that viewers and critics rarely agree on what constitutes an empowering narrative or a feminist character. Modern media and viewers, it seems, are still struggling to make sense of the "single girl."

Notes

Introduction. Screening the "Single Girl"

1. Hilary Radner, "Introduction," in *Swinging Single: Representing Sexuality in the 1960s*, ed. Hilary Radner and Moya Luckett (Minneapolis: University of Minnesota Press, 1999), 14–15.

2. "The Pleasures and Pain of the Single Life," *Time*, 15 September 1967, 26–27.

3. Susan Douglas, *Where the Girls Are: Growing up Female with the Mass Media* (New York: Times Books, 1994); Bonnie Dow, *Prime-Time Feminism: Television, Media Culture and the Women's Movement since 1970* (Philadelphia: University of Pennsylvania Press, 1996); Sherrie Inness, "'Strange Feverish Years': The 1970s and Women's Changing Roles," in *Disco Divas: Women and Popular Culture in the 1970s*, ed. Sherrie Inness (Philadelphia: University of Pennsylvania, 2003); Andrea Press, *Women Watching Television: Gender, Class, and Generation in the American Television Experience* (Philadelphia: University of Pennsylvania Press, 1991).

4. Douglas, *Where the Girls Are*; Dow, *Prime-Time Feminism*.

5. Estimated Median Age at First Marriage, by Sex: 1890 to the Present," U.S. Census Bureau, September 21, 2006, http://www.census.gov/population/socdemo/hh-fam/ms2.pdf.

6. Beth Bailey, *Sex in the Heartland* (Cambridge, Mass.: Harvard University Press, 1999), 77.

7. Susan Jacoby, "49 Million Singles Can't All Be Right," *New York Times*, 17 February 1974.

8. Beth Bailey, "She 'Can Bring Home the Bacon': Negotiating Gender in Seventies America," in *America in the Seventies*, ed. Beth Bailey and David Farber (Lawrence: University Press of Kansas, 2004), 107–128; Bruce J. Schulman, *The Seventies: The Great Shift in American Culture, Society, and Politics* (New York: Free Press, 2001); Dow, *Prime-Time Feminism*; Inness, "'Strange Feverish Years': The 1970s and Women's Changing Roles."

9. Douglas, *Where the Girls Are*, 61.

10. Ibid.; Leonard Leff and Jerold Simmons, *The Dame in the Kimono: Hollywood, Censorship and the Production Code*, 2nd ed. (Lexington: University Press of Kentucky, 2001); Wini Brienes, *Young, White and Miserable: Growing up Female in the Fifties* (Boston: Beacon Press, 1992).

11. Betty Friedan, "Television and the Feminine Mystique," in *TV Guide: The First 25 Years*, ed. J. S. Harris (New York: Simon & Schuster, 1978).

12. Dow, *Prime-Time Feminism;* Ella Taylor, *Prime Time Families: Television Culture in Postwar America* (Berkeley: University of California Press, 1989); Elana Levine, *Wallowing in Sex: The New Sexual Culture of 1970s American Television* (Durham, N.C.: Duke University Press, 2007); Julie D'Acci, "Nobody's Woman? *Honey West* and the New Sexuality," in *The Revolution Wasn't Televised: Sixties Television and Social Conflict*, ed. Lynn Spigel and Michael Curtin (New York: Routledge, 1997).

13. Dow, *Prime-Time Feminism;* Taylor, *Prime Time Families;* Kathrina Glitre, *Hollywood Romantic Comedy: States of the Union, 1934–65* (Manchester, UK: Manchester University Press, 2006), Levine, *Wallowing in Sex;* Julie D'Acci, *Defining Women: Television and the Case of Cagney and Lacey* (Chapel Hill: University of North Carolina Press, 1994).

14. Jane Feuer, Paul Kerr, and Tise Vahimagi, eds., *MTM 'Quality Television'* (London: BFI, 1984).

15. Dorothy Gilliam, "Too Few Men," *Washington Post (Potomac)*, 12 June 1966; Ruth Ross, "The Negro Girl Goes Job Hunting," *Cosmopolitan*, March 1967, 42–48; "A New Crop of Eligible Girls," *Ebony*, April 1970, 123.

16. Aniko Bodroghkozy, "'Is This What You Mean by Color TV?' Race, Gender and Conflicted Meanings in NBC's *Julia*," in *Private Screenings: Television and the Female Consumer*, ed. Lynn Spigel and Denise Mann (Minneapolis: University of Minnesota, 1992), 143–168.

17. Stephanie Dunn, "Foxy Brown on My Mind: The Racialized Gendered Politics of Representation," in *Disco Divas: Women and Popular Culture in the 1970s*, ed. Sherrie Inness (Philadelphia: University of Pennsylvania Press, 2003), 71–86.

18. Kimberly Springer, "Divas, Evil Black Bitches, and Bitter Black Women: African-American Women in Postfeminist and Post-Civil Rights Popular Culture," in *Feminist Television Criticism: A Reader*, 2nd Ed., ed. Charlotte Brunsdon and Lynn Spigel (Berkshire, UK: Open University Press, 2008), 72.

19. Gwendolyn Audrey Foster, *Performing Whiteness: Postmodern Re/Constructions in the Cinema* (Albany: State University of New York Press, 2003); Brienes, *Young, White and Miserable*.

20. Lee Israel, "Violence: How Does a Career Girl Cope?," *Cosmopolitan*, February 1968, 81–82.

21. Lacey Forsburgh, "Man Seen with Teacher on Slaying Night Is Sought," *New York Times*, 6 January 1973.

22. Douglas, *Where the Girls Are.*

23. Laurie Ouellette, "Inventing the Cosmo Girl: Class Identity and Girl-Style American Dreams," *Media, Culture and Society* 21, no. 3 (1999), 359–383.

24. "Theatrical Trailer," *The Best of Everything*, DVD, directed by Jean Negulesco (1959; Beverly Hills: Twentieth Century Fox, 2005).

25. Charlotte Pagni, "'Does She or Doesn't She?' Sexology and Female Sexuality in *Sex and the Single Girl*," *Spectator* 19, no. 2 (1999), 8–22.

26. Dow, *Prime-Time Feminism*; Taylor, *Prime Time Families: Television Culture in Postwar America.*

27. Dwight Whitney, "You've Come a Long Way, Baby," in *TV Guide: The First 25 Years*, ed. Jay S. Harris (New York: Simon & Schuster, 1978), 179.

28. Dow, *Prime-Time Feminism*, 60.

29. Rickie Solinger, *Wake Up Little Susie: Single Pregnancy and Race before Roe v. Wade* (New York: Routledge, 1992), 9.

30. Radner, "Introduction," 16.

Chapter 1. Challenging Convention: Single Women, Sex, and Censorship in Early 1960s Cinema

1. Helen Gurley Brown, *Sex and the Single Girl* (New York: Bernard Geis, 1962).

2. "What Price the Single Girl?" *Esquire*, October 1964, 109.

3. *Sex and the Single Girl*, DVD, directed by Richard Quine (1964; Burbank, CA: Warner Home Video, 2009).

4. Geoffrey Shurlock to Jack Warner, 4 March 1963, MPAA Production Code Administration Collection, Margaret Herrick Library, Academy of Motion Picture Arts and Sciences, Los Angeles.

5. Susan Douglas, *Where the Girls Are: Growing Up Female with the Mass Media* (New York: Times Books, 1994), 25.

6. Ibid.

7. Wini Brienes, *Young, White and Miserable: Growing up Female in the Fifties* (Boston: Beacon Press, 1992), 87.

8. Joanne Meyerowitz, "Beyond the Feminine Mystique: A Reassessment of Postwar Mass Culture, 1946–1958," in *Not June Cleaver: Women and Gender in Postwar America, 1945–1960*, ed. Joanne Meyerowitz (Philadelphia: Temple University Press, 1994), 250.

9. "Sex and the Single Girl," *Los Angeles Herald-Examiner*, 12 August 1962.

10. Moya Luckett, "Sensuous Women and Single Girls," in *Swinging*

Single: Representing Sexuality in the 1960s, ed. Hilary Radner and Moya Luckett (Minneapolis: University of Minnesota Press, 1999), 277.

11. Jennifer Scanlon, *Bad Girls Go Everywhere: The Life of Helen Gurley Brown* (New York: Oxford University Press, 2009), x–xi.

12. Larry Vershel, "Are Women People?" *Danbury (Conn.) News Times*, 2 August 1965.

13. Scanlon, *Bad Girls Go Everywhere*, 110–111.

14. Veshel, "Are Women People?"

15. Carol Grace, "Who's Manless?" *San Francisco Examiner*, 17 July 1962, 30.

16. Estelle Ries, *The Lonely Sex* (New York: Belmont Books, 1962), 13, located in Reevy Collection of Books on the History of Sexuality, Special Collections Library, Duke University, Durham, N.C.

17. Elaine Tyler May, *Homeward Bound: American Families in the Cold War Era* (New York: Basic Books, 1988), 98.

18. U.S. Census Bureau, Table MS-2, "Estimated Median Age at First Marriage, by Sex: 1890 to the Present," 21 September 2006, http://www.census.gov/population/www/socdemo/hh-fam.html.

19. Sam Blum, "A Defense of Women Who Refuse to Marry," *Redbook*, January 1969, 15.

20. Marion K. Sanders, "The Case of the Vanishing Spinster," *New York Times*, 22 September 1963, 216.

21. Eleanor Harris, "Women without Men," *Look*, 5 July 1960, 44.

22. Ruth Rosen, *The World Split Open: How the Modern Women's Movement Changed America* (New York: Viking, 2000), 19–20.

23. Ibid.

24. "A Good Man Is Hard to Find—So They Hire Women," *Time*, 4 November 1966.

25. Ibid.

26. Ibid.

27. Flora Davis, *Moving the Mountain: The Women's Movement in America since 1960* (New York: Simon & Schuster, 1991), 16–17.

28. Lerone Bennett Jr., "The Negro Woman," *Ebony*, September 1963, 88.

29. Ries, *The Lonely Sex*, 27.

30. Susan Cooper, "Gurley Talk from America," *London Sunday Times*, 12 May 1963.

31. Eve Merriam, "The Single-Minded Girl," *Nation*, 1 September 1962, 92–93.

32. Vershel, "Are Women People?"

33. Art Berman, "Helen's Book Was a Shock to Her Mother," *Los Angeles Times*, 24 June 1962, G2.

34. Rosen, *The World Split Open*, 21.

35. "Who Is That Cosmopolitan Girl?" *Advertising Report*, July 1965, located in Helen Gurley Brown Papers, Sophia Smith Collection, Smith College, Northampton, Mass.

36. Helen Gurley Brown, "A Proposal for Cosmopolitan," 1965, located in Helen Gurley Brown Papers, Sophia Smith Collection, box 37, folder 3.

37. "The Second Sexual Revolution," *Time*, 24 January 1964, 59.

38. Brown, *Sex and the Single Girl*, 4.

39. David Allyn, *Make Love, Not War* (Boston: Little, Brown & Co., 2000), 19–20.

40. Ibid.

41. Douglas, *Where the Girls Are*, 69–71.

42. Lillian Preston, *Sex Habits of Single Women* (New York: Universal Publishing, 1964), 13. Located in Reevy Collection of Books on the History of Sexuality, Special Collections Library, Duke University.

43. Gloria Steinem, "The Moral Disarmament of Betty Coed," *Esquire*, September 1962, 155–156.

44. Beth Bailey, *Sex in the Heartland* (Cambridge, Mass.: Harvard University Press, 1999), 117–118, 121.

45. Jennie Loitman Barron, "Too Much Sex on Campus," *Ladies' Home Journal*, January 1964, 48.

46. Steinem, "The Moral Disarmament of Betty Coed," 156.

47. "The Second Sexual Revolution," 57; Preston, *Sex Habits of Single Women*, 75.

48. Preston, *Sex Habits of Single Women*, 75.

49. Ibid.; Barron, "Too Much Sex on Campus," 48, 52; Steinem, "The Moral Disarmament of Betty Coed," 97.

50. Barron, "Too Much Sex on Campus," 48; Virgil G. Damon and Isabella Taves, "My Daughter Is in Trouble," *Look*, August 1962, 27; Preston, *Sex Habits of Single Women*, 53.

51. William Hanson Sprague, *Sex Behavior of the American Secretary* (New York: Chariot Books, 1960), located in Reevy Collection of Books on the History of Sexuality, Duke University.

52. Ibid.

53. Preston, *Sex Habits of Single Women*.

54. Steinem, "The Moral Disarmament of Betty Coed," 153; Preston, *Sex Habits of Single Women*, 57.

55. Benjamin Morse, *The Sexually Promiscuous Female* (Derby, Conn.: Monarch Books, 1963).

56. Douglas, *Where the Girls Are*, 65.

57. "Sexual Behavior of College Girls," *School and Society*, 3 April 1965, 208.

58. Gael Greene, *Sex and the College Girl* (New York: Dial Press, 1964), 19.

59. Preston, *Sex Habits of Single Women*, 34; Damon and Taves, "My Daughter Is in Trouble," 42.

60. Pearl S. Buck, "The Sexual Revolution," *Ladies' Home Journal*, September 1964, 45.

61. "The Second Sexual Revolution," 59.

62. Bailey, *Sex in the Heartland*, 77; Douglas, *Where the Girls Are*; "Sexual Behavior of College Girls," 208.

63. Sprague, *Sex Behavior of the American Secretary*, 71.

64. Preston, *Sex Habits of Single Women*.

65. Ferdinand Lundberg, *Modern Woman: The Lost Sex* (New York: Harper, 1947), 120, 268–269; Barbara Ehrenreich, Elizabeth Hess, and Gloria Jacobs, *Re-Making Love: The Feminization of Sex* (Garden City, N.Y.: Anchor Press, 1986), 45.

66. Abram Kardiner and Lionel Ovesey, *The Mark of Oppression: A Psychosocial Study of the American Negro* (New York: Norton, 1951), cited in Bennett, "The Negro Woman," 88.

67. Ehrenreich, Hess, and Jacobs, *Re-Making Love*, 51; Morse, *The Sexually Promiscuous Female*, 102.

68. Lundberg, *Modern Woman*, 120.

69. Ehrenreich, Hess, and Jacobs, *Re-Making Love*, 51; Morse, *The Sexually Promiscuous Female*, 102; Sprague, *Sex Behavior of the American Secretary*, 97; Preston, *Sex Habits of Single Women*, 65; Morse, *The Sexually Promiscuous Female*, 92–93.

70. Morse, *The Sexually Promiscuous Female*, 97.

71. Ibid.

72. Brienes, *Young, White and Miserable*, 30–31; Beth Bailey, *From Front Porch to Back Seat: Courtship in Twentieth-Century America* (Baltimore: Johns Hopkins University Press, 1988), 104–105.

73. Undated advertisement for Parker Pen Company, contained in the Helen Gurley Brown Papers, Sophia Smith Collection, box 21, folder 5.

74. "The Playboy Panel: The Womanization of America," *Playboy*, June 1962, 134.

75. Philip Wylie, "The Career Woman," *Playboy*, January 1963, 153, 156.

76. Bennett, "The Negro Woman," 88, 94.

77. Sprague, *Sex Behavior of the American Secretary*, 67.

78. Morse, *The Sexually Promiscuous Female*, 89.

79. Robert Kirsch, "'Sex and Single Girl' Falls Short of Its Promising Title," *Los Angeles Times*, 6 July 1962, 2.

80. Cooper, "Gurley Talk from America."

81. Jeanine Basinger, *A Woman's View: How Hollywood Spoke to Women, 1930–1960* (New York: Alfred A. Knopf, 1993).

82. Kathrina Glitre, *Hollywood Romantic Comedy: States of the Union, 1934–65* (Manchester, UK: Manchester University Press, 2006), 138.

83. Ibid., 35.

84. Ibid.

85. Suzanna Danuta Walters, *Material Girls: Making Sense of Feminist Cultural Theory* (Berkeley: University of California Press, 1995).

86. Douglas, *Where the Girls Are*, 73.

87. Ibid., 74.

88. Walters, *Material Girls*, 83.

89. Steinem, "The Moral Disarmament of Betty Coed," 97.

90. Leonard Leff and Jerold Simmons, *The Dame in the Kimono: Hollywood, Censorship and the Production Code*, 2nd ed. (Lexington: University Press of Kentucky, 2001), 185–203.

91. "The Code Changes," *Newsweek*, 24 December 1956, 61.

92. "Hollywood: Decoded," *Time*, 3 November 1958, 78.

93. Arthur Mayer, "How Much Can the Movies Say?" *Saturday Review*, 3 November 1962.

94. Frank Miller, *Censored Hollywood: Sex, Sin and Violence Onscreen* (Atlanta: Turner Publishing, 1994), 184.

95. Ibid., 166–167; Simmons, *The Dame in the Kimono*, 194–196.

96. Simmons, *The Dame in the Kimono*, 194–196.

97. Geoffrey Shurlock to Robert Vogel, 15 June 1960, contained in the MPAA Production Code Administration Collection, Margaret Herrick Library, Academy of Motion Picture Arts and Sciences, Los Angeles.

98. "Hollywood: Decoded," 78.

99. Geoffrey Shurlock to Jack Warner, March 4, 1963, MPAA Production Code Administration Files, Margaret Herrick Library, Los Angeles.

100. Charlotte Pagni, "'Does She or Doesn't She?' Sexology and Female Sexuality in *Sex and the Single Girl*," *Spectator* 19, no. 2 (1999): 8.

101. Brienes, *Young, White and Miserable*, 95.

102. Ibid., 87.

103. Gwendolyn Audrey Foster, *Performing Whiteness: Postmodern Re/Constructions in the Cinema* (Albany: State University of New York Press, 2003), 34.

104. Judith Roof, *All About Thelma and Eve: Sidekicks and Third Wheels* (Urbana: University of Illinois Press, 2002), 140.

105. Rosemary Tyler, "Single Women Need Sex, Money, Career," *Washington Afro-American*, 6 October 1962; Elizabeth Oliver, "Book Tells What Was Already Going On," *Afro Magazine*, 27 October 1962, Helen Gurley Brown Papers, Sophia Smith Collection, Smith College, Northampton, Mass., box 21, folder 5.

106. Radner, "Introduction," 6–9.

107. Joe Hyams, "Sex and the Single Girl," *Cosmopolitan* April 1964, 18.

108. Geoffrey Shurlock to Jack Warner, 3 October 1963, MPAA Production Code Administration Collection, Margaret Herrick Library, Los Angeles.

109. "The Second Sexual Revolution," 57; Steinem, "The Moral Disarmament of Betty Coed," 156.

110. "Helen Gurley Brown Is Not This Stupid," *Washington Post*, 26 December 1964, D6.

111. A. H. Weller, "Screen: Sex and the Single Girl," *New York Times*, 26 December 1964.

112. Thomas Thompson, "Non-Book Turns into a Fine Romp," *Life*, 8 January 1965.

113. Mayer, "How Much Can the Movies Say?" 119.

114. *Boys' Night Out*, VHS, directed by Michael Gordon (1962; Los Angeles: MGM Warner, 1994).

115. Film trailer, *Boys' Night Out*, VHS.

116. Brown, *Sex and the Single Girl*, 5.

117. George Christy, "Kim Novak: 'Why I'm Afraid of Marriage,'" *Ladies' Home Journal*, May 1962, 113.

118. Moira Walsh, "Boys' Night Out," *America*, 7 July 1962.

119. "Boys' Night Out," *Variety*, 1962, undated review, at http://www.variety.com.

120. J. A. Vizzard, "Memo for the Files," 10 October 1961, MPAA Production Code Administration Collection, Margaret Herrick Library, Los Angeles.

121. Marion Hargrove, "*Boys' Night Out* Treatment," 24 June 1961, 45,

MPAA Production Code Administration Collection, Margaret Herrick Library, Los Angeles.

122. "Step Outline," *Boys' Night Out*, 24 March 1961, Turner/MGM Script Collection, Margaret Herrick Library, Los Angeles.

123. Marion Hargrove, "*Boys' Night Out* Treatment," 24 June 1961, 23–24, 41–42, MPAA Production Code Administration Collection, Margaret Herrick Library, Los Angeles.

124. Pagni, "Does She or Doesn't She?" 17.

125. *Pillow Talk: 50th Anniversary Edition*, DVD, directed by Michael Gordon (1959; Universal City, CA: Universal Studios, 2009).

126. "At-a-Glance Synopsis," n.d., MPAA Production Code Administration Collection, Margaret Herrick Library, Los Angeles.

127. Pagni, "Does She or Doesn't She?" 18.

128. "Synopsis for *Sex and the Single Girl*," n.d., MPAA Production Code Administration Collection, Margaret Herrick Library, Los Angeles.

129. Geoffrey Shurlock to Jack Warner, 4 March 1963, MPAA Production Code Administration Collection, Margaret Herrick Library, Los Angeles.

130. "Speaking of Books . . . ," *Milwaukee Sentinel*, 25 January 1960, 5. "Fun in Florida," *Milwaukee Journal*, 17 January 1960, 4.

131. Glendon Swarthout, *Where the Boys Are* (New York: Random House, 1960), 39.

132. Geoffrey Shurlock to Robert Vogel, 15 June 1960, MPAA Production Code Administration Collection, Margaret Herrick Library, Los Angeles.

133. Douglas, *Where the Girls Are*, 79.

134. George Wells, "*Where the Boys Are* Outline," 18 August 1959, Turner/MGM Script Collection, Margaret Herrick Library, Los Angeles, file 501.

135. *Where the Boys Are*, DVD, directed by Henry Levin (1960; Burbank, CA: Turner Entertainment, 2004).

136. Geoffrey Shurlock to Robert Vogel, 15 June 1960, MPAA Production Code Administration Collection, Margaret Herrick Library, Los Angeles.

137. Bailey, *Sex in the Heartland*, 117–118.

138. Geoffrey Shurlock to Robert Vogel, 15 June 1960; George Wells, Script, 25 August 1959, folder 502, MPAA Production Code Administration Collection, Margaret Herrick Library, Los Angeles.

139. George Wells, "Revised Script," 10 November 1959, Turner/MGM Script Collection, Margaret Herrick Library, Los Angeles, file 502.

140. "Where the Boys Are," *Limelight*, 1 December 1960.

141. Swarthout, *Where the Boys Are*.

142. George Wells, *"Where the Boys Are* Outline," 18 August 1959.

143. *Where the Boys Are,* MGM Press Book, Turner/MGM Script Collection.

144. Barron, "Too Much Sex on Campus," 48; Damon and Taves, "My Daughter Is in Trouble," 27.

145. Douglas, *Where the Girls Are,* 80–81.

146. Ibid.

147. "Cinema: The New Comedies," *Time,* 20 January 1961.

148. "Good-Time Coed Cuties Cavort Gaily in Florida," *Spokesman-Review,* 1 February 1961, 5.

149. Bosley Crowther, "Collegiate Chase: 'Where the Boys Are' Opens at Music Hall," *New York Times,* 20 January 1961.

150. "Where the Boys Are," *America,* 4 February 1961; Justin Gilbert, "Where the Boys Are," *New York Mirror,* 20 January 1961.

151. "Where the Boys Are," *Variety,* 30 November 1960.

152. Howard Stricking, *Where the Boys Are,* first reports from preview at Picwood Theatre in West Los Angeles, 28 October 1960, George Wells Papers, American Heritage Center, University of Wyoming, Laramie, box 4.

153. Ibid.

154. Commentary by Rona Jaffe and Sylvia Stoddard, *The Best of Everything,* DVD, directed by Jean Negulesco (1959; Beverly Hills: Twentieth Century Fox, 2005).

155. Hal Boyle, "Young Novelist's First Might Be Best Seller," *Spencer Daily Reporter,* 14 August 1958.

156. B. C., "'Best' Girls Get Worst in Drive-in Film," *Sarasota Journal,* 7 December 1959, 9.

157. Ray Hoffman, "'Best of Everything' Falls Short of Goal," *Pittsburgh Press,* 18 October 1959, 17.

158. "The Best of Everything," *Variety,* 1959, undated review, at http://www.variety.com/review/VE1117789006.html?categoryid=31&cs=1.

159. *The Best of Everything,* DVD, directed by Jean Negulesco (1959; Beverly Hills: 20th Century Fox, 2005).

160. Wylie, "The Career Woman," 154.

161. Hoffman, "'Best of Everything' Falls Short of Goal," 17.

162. Harry Brand, "Synopsis," n.d., 4, located in Jean Negulesco Papers, Margaret Herrick Library, Los Angeles, box 6, folder 11.

163. Boyle, "Young Novelist's First Might Be Best Seller," 5.

164. Dorothy Kilgallen, "Joan to Tour," *Toledo Blade,* 30 September 1959;

Jean Sprain Wilson, "Joan Crawford—in Business World," *Miami News,* 6 December 1959, 15A.

165. Wylie, "The Career Woman," 153.

166. Commentary by Jaffe and Stoddard, *The Best of Everything,* DVD.

167. In the original synopsis, the warning is more pronounced: "[Farrow] warns her not to let her ambition prevent her from being a woman. Success is no substitute for marriage, a home and children." Harry Brand, "Synopsis," n.d., 5. Jean Negulesco Papers, Margaret Herrick Library, Los Angeles, box 6, folder 11.

168. Edith Sommer, "The Best of Everything," 26 May 1959, MPAA Production Code Administration Collection, Margaret Herrick Library, Los Angeles.

169. Ries, *The Lonely Sex,* 116.

170. Sommer, "The Best of Everything."

171. Commentary by Jaffe and Stoddard, *The Best of Everything,* DVD.

172. Swarthout, *Where the Boys Are.*

173. George Wells, "Outline," 25 August 1958, 6, Turner/MGM Script Collection, Margaret Herrick Library, Los Angeles, file 501.

174. "Synopsis of *The Best of Everything,*" n.d., MPAA Production Code Administration Collection, Margaret Herrick Library, Los Angeles.

175. *That Touch of Mink,* DVD, directed by Delbert Mann (1962; Santa Monica, CA: Artisan Entertainment, 2000).

176. Douglas, *Where the Girls Are,* 71.

177. Associated Press, "Doris Day Top $ Star," *Milwaukee Sentinel,* 29 December 1960.

178. Tamar Jeffers McDonald, "Performances of Desire and Inexperience: Doris Day's Fluctuating Filmic Virginity," in *Virgin Territory: Representing Sexual Inexperience in Film,* ed. Tamar Jeffers McDonald (Detroit: Wayne State University Press, 2010), 103–122.

179. Lawrence Lipskin, "That Touch of Mink," *Hollywood Reporter,* 9 May 1962.

180. Legion of Decency Report, 1 March 1962, *Where the Boys Are,* MPAA Production Code Administration Collection, Margaret Herrick Library, Los Angeles.

181. "At-a-Glance Synopsis," n.d., MPAA Production Code Administration Collection, Margaret Herrick Library, Los Angeles.

182. Ibid.

183. Geoffrey Shurlock to Kathryn McTaggart, 4 February 1959, MPAA Production Code Administration Collection, Margaret Herrick Library, Los Angeles.

184. Ibid.

185. "Pillow Talk," *Variety,* 12 August 1959.

Chapter 2. Leaving Home: Single Women's Perilous Journeys in Late 1960s Television and Film

1. "Good-Bye, Hello, Good-Bye," *That Girl: Season One,* DVD, directed by Bob Sweeney (1966; Los Angeles: Shout Factory, 2006).

2. *Valley of the Dolls: Special Edition,* DVD, directed by Mark Robson (1967; Beverly Hills: Twentieth Century Fox, 2006).

3. "The Pleasures and Pain of the Single Life," *Time,* 15 September 1967, 26–27. Also see Ragni Lantz, "The Pleasures and Problems of the Bachelor Girl," *Ebony,* August 1966.

4. U.S. Census Bureau, Table MS-2, "Estimated Median Age at First Marriage, by Sex: 1890 to the Present," 21 September 2006, http://www.census .gov/population/www/socdemo/hh-fam.html.

5. "What Educated Women Want," *Newsweek,* 13 June 1966, 68.

6. Ibid., 75.

7. Sam Blum, "A Defense of Women Who Refuse to Marry," *Redbook,* January 1968, 111–112; "The Singles," *Mademoiselle,* September 1968.

8. Amy Gross, "Young Lovers of the World—Unite! But Don't Get Married Yet," *Mademoiselle,* September 1969.

9. "The Singles," 121–123; Blum, "A Defense of Women Who Refuse to Marry," 111–112.

10. E. Waldman, "Changes in the Labor Force Activity of Women," *Monthly Labor Review,* June 1970, 10–11.

11. "A Good Man Is Hard to Find—So They Hire Women," *Time,* 4 November 1966

12. Jacqueline Jones, *Labor of Love, Labor of Sorrow: Black Women, Work and the Family from Slavery to the Present* (New York: Basic Books, 1985), 301–302; Waldman, "Changes in the Labor Force Activity of Women," 13.

13. U.S. Department of Labor, "Sex and Equal Employment Rights," *Monthly Labor Review* 1967, iii–iv.

14. Helen Gurley Brown, *Sex and the New Single Girl* (New York: Bernard Geis, 1970); Jack Olsen, *The Girls in the Office* (New York: Simon & Schuster, 1971).

15. Ruth Rosen, *The World Split Open: How the Modern Women's Movement Changed America* (New York: Viking, 2000), 51–52.

16. John D'Emilio and Estelle B. Freedman, *Intimate Matters: A History of Sexuality in America* (New York: Harper & Row, 1988), 305.

17. "The Pleasures and Pain of the Single Life," 26.

18. D'Emilio and Freedman, *Intimate Matters*, 306.

19. Beth Bailey, *Sex in the Heartland* (Cambridge, Mass.: Harvard University Press, 1999), 2–3.

20. Ibid., 2, 155.

21. Ibid.

22. Alice Shane, "Dear Cosmopolitan," *Cosmopolitan*, September 1965, 140; "Dear Cosmopolitan," *Cosmopolitan*, October 1965.

23. Shane, "Dear Cosmopolitan," 140.

24. Bailey, *Sex in the Heartland*, 202; David Allyn, *Make Love, Not War* (Boston: Little, Brown & Co., 2000), 98.

25. Allyn, *Make Love, Not War*, 99.

26. David Farber and Beth Bailey, eds., *The Columbia Guide to America in the 1960s* (New York: Columbia University Press, 2001); Blum, "A Defense of Women Who Refuse to Marry."

27. Beth Bailey, *From Front Porch to Back Seat: Courtship in Twentieth-Century America* (Baltimore: Johns Hopkins University Press, 1988), 142.

28. Farber and Bailey, *The Columbia Guide to America in the 1960s*.

29. A key example is Stanlee Miller Coy, *The Single Girl's Book: Making It in the Big City* (Englewood Cliffs, N.J.: Prentice-Hall, 1969).

30. Helen Gurley Brown, "A Proposal for *Cosmopolitan* Magazine," 1965. Contained in the Helen Gurley Brown Papers, Sophia Smith Collection, box 37, folder 3.

31. Olsen, *The Girls in the Office*.

32. Gael Greene, "For the Single Girl: A New Way of Life in California," *Ladies' Home Journal*, July 1966, 110.

33. Olsen, *The Girls in the Office*, 28.

34. "Where the Singles Are," *Newsweek*, 26 September 1966, 113.

35. Laurie Ouellette, "Inventing the Cosmo Girl: Class Identity and Girl-Style American Dreams," *Media, Culture and Society* 21, no. 3 (1999): 359–383.

36. Reprinted as "How to Have a Little Bit of Class," in Helen Gurley Brown, *The Cosmo Girl's Guide to the New Etiquette* (New York: Cosmopolitan Books, 1971), 35.

37. Dorothy Gilliam, "Too Few Men," *Washington Post Potomac*, 12 June 1966, 8–16.

38. Ibid.

39. John Howard, *Men Like That: A Southern Queer History* (Chicago: University of Chicago Press, 1999).; D'Emilio and Freedman, *Intimate Matters: A History of Sexuality in America*, 319.

40. Helen Gurley Brown, *Sex and the Single Girl* (New York: Bernard Geis, 1962); Coy, *The Single Girl's Book.*

41. "Male and Female: Dating Bars," *Time*, 17 February 1967, 47; "New Rules for the Singles Game," *Life*, 18 August 1967, 62–64.

42. "New Rules for the Singles Game," 61.

43. For a history of dating etiquette from the 1930s to the 1960s, see "The Etiquette of Masculinity and Femininity," in Bailey, *From Front Porch to Back Seat.*

44. "Male and Female: Dating Bars," 47.

45. "New Rules for the Singles Game," 62.

46. "Male and Female: Dating Bars," 47.

47. "New Rules for the Singles Game," 62.

48. "The Single Life: New York," *Mademoiselle*, September 1968, 193.

49. Nina McCain, "The Lonely Hours after Work Is Over," *New York World-Telegram and Sun*, n.d., 1965, press clipping, contained in the Helen Gurley Brown Papers, Sophia Smith Collection.

50. Olsen, *The Girls in the Office*, 19. This 1971 book was based on interviews conducted in the late 1960s.

51. Helen Gurley Brown, "Memo to the Art Department," 14 November 1967, Helen Gurley Brown Papers, Sophia Smith Collection, box 41, folder 8.

52. Brown, *The Cosmo Girl's Guide to the New Etiquette*, 229.

53. Ibid., 230.

54. "What Educated Women Want," 75.

55. Ibid., 68.

56. Greene, "For the Single Girl," 59, 112.

57. Ibid., 112, 159.

58. Ibid., 110, 159.

59. "Where the Singles Are," 113.

60. "Male and Female: Dating Bars," 47.

61. Ibid.; "New Rules for the Singles Game," 63.

62. Amy Gross, "An Opinion: On Spinster Kicks," *Mademoiselle*, September 1968, 36, 38.

63. David Newman and Robert Benton, "Man Talk: Desolation Row," *Mademoiselle*, June 1968, 52.

64. David Newman and Robert Benton, "Man Talk: The Desperate Hours," *Mademoiselle*, September 1968, 80.

65. Brown, *Sex and the New Single Girl*, 54.

66. John Krones, "Memo from a Bachelor: The Singles Scene," *Look*, 6 February 1968, 80.

67. Anne Barry, "My Long, Long Night in a Singles' Bar," *Cosmopolitan*, August 1969, 74.

68. Ibid.

69. Brown, *The Cosmo Girl's Guide to the New Etiquette*, 229–230.

70. Ibid., 233.

71. Olsen, *The Girls in the Office*, 202–203.

72. Jane Gerhard, *Desiring Revolution: Second-Wave Feminism and the Rewriting of American Sexual Thought, 1920 to 1982* (New York: Columbia University Press, 2001), 40–41.

73. Rosen, *The World Split Open*, 145.

74. Ibid., 146.

75. Ibid.

76. Ibid., 148–151.

77. Brown, *The Cosmo Girl's Guide to the New Etiquette*, 234.

78. Olsen, *The Girls in the Office*, 83.

79. Ibid.

80. Judith Viorst, "Avis and Gs-Zero," *Washington Post Potomac*, 12 June 1966, 8.

81. Gilliam, "Too Few Men."

82. Ibid.

83. Lantz, "The Pleasures and Problems of the Bachelor Girl," 102–104.

84. Gilliam, "Too Few Men," 10.

85. Olsen, *The Girls in the Office*.

86. Lee Israel, "Violence: How Does a Career Girl Cope?," *Cosmopolitan*, February 1968, 81–82.

87. Betty Israel, *Bachelor Girl: The Secret History of Single Women in the Twentieth Century* (New York: William Morrow, 2002), 228–231.

88. Julie D'Acci, "Nobody's Woman? *Honey West* and the New Sexuality," in *The Revolution Wasn't Televised: Sixties Television and Social Conflict*, ed. Lynn Spigel and Michael Curtin (New York: Routledge, 1997), 72–90.

89. Moya Luckett, "A Moral Crisis in Prime Time: Peyton Place and the

Rise of the Single Girl," in *Television, History and American Culture: Feminist Critical Essays*, ed. Mary Beth Haralovich and Lauren Rabinowitz (Durham, N.C.: Duke University Press, 1999), 75–97.

90. Vernon Scott, "Barbara Parkins Peps Peyton Place," *Herald-Tribune*, 1 March 1965, 30.

91. Richard Doan, "'Peyton Place' Expecting a Girl!," *Toledo Blade*, 18 January 1965.

92. *Peyton Place: Part Two*, DVD, directed by Walter Doniger and Ted Post (1965; Los Angeles: Shout Factory, 2007), episodes 36–37.

93. Memo from Robert Shaw, "Structure—Episode #41," 6 October 1964, Walter Doniger Papers, American Heritage Center, University of Wyoming, Laramie, box 109, folder 1.

94. *Peyton Place*, episode 40.

95. D'Acci, "Nobody's Woman?," 89.

96. Ibid., 87.

97. Leonard Leff and Jerold Simmons, *The Dame in the Kimono: Hollywood, Censorship and the Production Code*, 2nd ed. (Lexington: University Press of Kentucky, 2001).

98. Kevin Thomas, "Robson: Friendly Persuader," *Los Angeles Times*, 10 July 1967, C16.

99. Lenore Hershey, "What Women Think of the Movies," *McCall's*, May 1967, 28.

100. Thomas, "Robson," C16.

101. Bonnie Dow, *Prime-Time Feminism; Television, Media Culture and the Women's Movement since 1970* (Philadelphia: University of Pennsylvania Press, 1996). Susan Douglas, *Where the Girls Are: Growing Up Female with the Mass Media* (New York: Times Books, 1994); Barry Langford, *Film Genre: Hollywood and Beyond* (Edinburgh: Edinburgh University Press, 2006).

102. D'Acci, "Nobody's Woman?," 89; Farber and Bailey, *The Columbia Guide to America in the 1960s*, 400–401.

103. *That Girl*, ABC Pressbook, 1966–1967, Television Press Kit Collection, Special Collections Research Center, Syracuse University Library, Syracuse, N.Y., box 1.

104. Rocky Phillips, "Marlo Thomas: Danny's Girl," *Pittsburgh Press*, 4 September 1966, TV2.

105. *Marlo Thomas*, VHS, directed by Bob Waldman (New York: A&E Home Video, 2002).

106. "The Creation of That Girl: The Woman on Both Sides of the Camera," *That Girl: Season Three*, DVD directed by David Leaf (Los Angeles: Shout Factory, 2007).

107. Stephen Cole, *That Book About That Girl: The Unofficial Companion* (New York: Renaissance Books, 1999), 56–57.

108. *That Girl*, ABC Pressbook, 1966–1967; Cole, *That Book About That Girl*, 81.

109. "Good-Bye, Hello, Good-Bye."

110. "Original *That Girl* Pilot Episode," *That Girl: Season One*, DVD, directed by Jerry Paris (1966; Los Angeles: Shout Factory, 2006).

111. Dow, *Prime-Time Feminism*, 48, 80.

112. Ibid., 38–39.

113. Dick Kleiner, "Marlo Thomas Is No Daddy's Girl," *Milwaukee Journal*, 24 April 1966, 8. "What's in a Name?" *That Girl: Season One*, DVD, directed by Harry Falk (1966; Los Angeles: Shout Factory, 2006).

114. "What Are Your Intentions?" *That Girl: Season One*, DVD, directed by John Erman (1967; Los Angeles: Shout Factory, 2006).

115. "Rain, Snow and Rice," *That Girl: Season One*, DVD, directed by John Erman (1967; Los Angeles: Shout Factory, 2006).

116. "Marlo Thomas: That Girl Is Some Girl," *Look*, 17 October 1967, 124–125.

117. Ibid.

118. "Call of the Wild," *That Girl: Season Two*, DVD, directed by Hal Cooper (1968; Los Angeles: Shout Factory, 2006).

119. Milton Pascal, Ruth Brooks Flippen, and Danny Arnold, "Call of the Wild Final Draft," 27 November 1967, Danny Arnold Papers, American Heritage Center, box 6.

120. Ibid., 32.

121. Sean Cutler, Martin Donovan, and Danny Arnold, "Sock It to Me," 11, Danny Arnold Papers, American Heritage Center, box 8; "Sock It to Me," *That Girl: Season Three*, DVD, directed by James Sheldon (1968; Los Angeles: Shout Factory, 2007).

122. Milton Pascal, Danny Arnold, and Ruth Brooks Flippen, "There's Nothing to Be Afreud of but Freud Himself," 3 August 1967, 11–12, 18, Danny Arnold Papers, American Heritage Center, box 8; "There's Nothing to Be Afreud of but Freud Himself," *That Girl: Season Two*, DVD, directed by Hal Cooper (1967; Los Angeles: Shout Factory, 2006). Although the psychologist does label Ann as "aggressive," he also compliments her on her spirited, romantic personality.

123. "The Creation of That Girl: The Woman on Both Sides of the Camera," *That Girl: Season Three*, DVD (Los Angeles: Shout Factory, 2007).

124. Ibid.; "What Educated Women Want," 75.

125. *Marlo Thomas*; Cole, *That Book*, 65.

126. Ibid., 113; "The Defiant One," *That Girl: Season Three*, DVD, directed by Richard Kinon (1969; Los Angeles: Shout Factory, 2007).

127. Aniko Bodroghkozy, "'Is This What You Mean by Color TV?' Race, Gender and Conflicted Meanings in NBC's Julia," in *Private Screenings: Television and the Female Consumer*, ed. Lynn Spigel and Denise Mann (Minneapolis: University of Minnesota, 1992), 143–167.

128. *Gidget Grows Up*, directed by James Sheldon, 30 December 1969, ABC, viewed at the UCLA Film and Television Archive, University of California at Los Angeles; "Orientals Find Bias Is Down Sharply in U.S.," *New York Times*, 13 December 1970, A1.

129. Olsen, *The Girls in the Office*; John McGreevey, Step Outline, "Gidget Grows Up," 9 October 1968, 16, Harry Ackerman Papers, American Heritage Center, box 15, folder 1.

130. Gina Marchetti, *Romance and the "Yellow Peril": Race, Sex and Discursive Strategies in Hollywood Fiction* (Berkeley: University of California Press, 1993).

131. Israel, *Bachelor Girl*.

132. John D. Adams, "'Millie' Turns One 'Modern' Critic Purple," *Schenectady Gazette*, 26 September 1968, 39.

133. Kaspar Monahan, "Hilarious Hit 'Modern Millie' Opens at Nixon," *Pittsburgh Press*, 20 April 1967, 36.

134. Olsen, *The Girls in the Office*.

135. "Orientals Find Bias Is Down Sharply in U.S.," A1.

136. Israel, "Violence: How Does a Career Girl Cope?," 82. Sidney E. Zion, "Interracial Assaults; Studies Show That Most Violent Crimes by Negroes Are against Other Negroes," *New York Times*, 18 April 1967, 29.

137. Bosley Crowther, "Screen: 'Thoroughly Modern Millie,'" *New York Times*, 23 March 1967, at http://movies2.nytimes.com/gst/movies/movie.html?v_id=49603.

138. Monahan, "Hilarious Hit 'Modern Millie' Opens at Nixon," 36; "Millie Gets You," *Age*, 3 August 1967, 14.

139. *Thoroughly Modern Millie*, DVD, directed by George Roy Hill (1967; Universal City, CA: Universal Studios, 2003).

140. Brown, *The Cosmo Girl's Guide to the New Etiquette*; Olsen, *The Girls in the Office*.

141. "What Educated Women Want," 68.

142. Brown, "Memo to the Art Department," 14 November 1967, Helen Gurley Brown Papers, Sophia Smith Collection, Smith College, Northampton, Mass., box 41, folder 8.

143. "What Educated Women Want"; Olsen, *The Girls in the Office*; Kevin Thomas, "Miss Hayward: Tiger in 'Valley of the Dolls,'" *Los Angeles Times*, 5 June 1967.

144. "For Singles Only," *Variety*, 1 May 1968.

145. "*For Singles Only* Poster," Movieposter.com. http://www.movie poster.com/poster/MPW-12482/For_Singles_Only.html.

146. *For Singles Only*, directed by Arthur Dreifuss (Los Angeles: Columbia TriStar, 1968).

147. John Mahoney, "For Singles Only," *Hollywood Reporter*, 1 May 1968.

148. "For Singles Only," *Motion Picture Herald*, 8 May 1968.

149. Arthur Hoerl and Arthur Dreifuss, *For Singles Only* script, 6 September 1967, Hal Collins Papers, box 23, folder 4, Performing Arts Special Collections, Charles E. Young Research Library, University of California, Los Angeles.

150. Correspondence paired with Arthur Hoerl and Arthur Dreifuss, *For Singles Only* script, 6 September 1967, Hal Collins Papers, box 23, folder 4, UCLA Performing Arts Special Collections.

151. Ibid.

152. "For Singles Only," *Variety*, 1 May 1968.

153. Ibid.; Mahoney, "For Singles Only."

154. Greene, "For the Single Girl."

155. "The Last Resort," *Newsweek*, 15 January 1968, 53.

156. Mahoney, "For Singles Only."

157. "Jacqueline Susann and the Valley of the Dolls," documentary, *Valley of the Dolls: Special Edition*, DVD, directed by Mark Robson (1967; Beverly Hills: Twentieth Century Fox, 2006).

158. Commentary by Barbara Parkins, *Valley of the Dolls: Special Edition*, DVD, directed by Mark Robson (1967; Beverly Hills: Twentieth Century Fox, 2006).

159. Pressbook, *Valley of the Dolls*, 1967, Mark Robson Papers, UCLA Performing Arts Special Collections, box 25, folder 3.

160. Revised script, *Valley of the Dolls*, 27 February 1967, 103–104, Mark Robson Papers, UCLA Performing Arts Special Collections, box 33, folder 2.

161. Geoffrey Shurlock to Frank Ferguson, n.d., Mark Robson Papers, UCLA Performing Arts Special Collections, box 33, folder 2.

162. Advertisements contained in Mark Robson Papers, Performing Arts Special Collections, University of California, Los Angeles.

163. "The Movie Dames That Play the Dolls," *Look*, 5 September 1967, 53–56.

164. Ibid.

165. Jacqueline Susann, *Valley of the Dolls* (New York: Bernard Geis, 1966), 6–7.

166. Revised script, *Valley of the Dolls*, 27 February 1967, 6, Mark Robson Papers, UCLA Performing Arts Special Collections, box 33, folder 2.

167. Step Outline, *Valley of the Dolls*, n.d., 6, Mark Robson Papers, UCLA Performing Arts Special Collections, box 33, folder 2.

168. Susann, *Valley of the Dolls*, 215.

169. Judith Viorst, "Avis and Gs-Zero," *Washington Post (Potomac)*, June 12 1966, 8–16; Olsen, *The Girls in the Office*.

170. "Jacqueline Susann and the Valley of the Dolls."

171. Thomas, "Miss Hayward," D14.

172. Dorothy Kingsley, *Valley of the Dolls* screenplay, 6 January 1967, 130, Mark Robson Papers, UCLA Performing Arts Special Collections, box 33, folder 2.

173. *Marlo Thomas.*

Chapter 3. Living Liberated: Single Women in Early 1970s Sitcoms and Commercial Culture

1. Judith Adler Hennessee and Joan Nicholson, "NOW Says: TV Commercials Insult Women," *New York Times Magazine*, 28 May 1972, 12–13.

2. Betty Friedan, *The Feminine Mystique*, 20th anniv. ed. (New York: Laurel, 1983); Betty Friedan, "Television and the Feminine Mystique," in *TV Guide: The First 25 Years*, ed. Jay S. Harris (New York: Simon and Schuster, 1978), 93–98.

3. National Organization for Women (NOW), *Report on the Task Force of the Image of Women*, 1968, contained in the Women's Rights Collection, Sophia Smith Collection, Smith College; Susan Douglas, *Where the Girls Are: Growing up Female with the Mass Media* (New York: Times Books, 1994), 139.

4. Edith Efron, "Is Television Making a Mockery of the American Woman?" *TV Guide*, 8 August 1970, 7–9.

5. Cyclops, "Women on TV," *Newsweek*, 18 June 1973, 79; Judy Klemesrud, "TV's Women Are Dingbats," *New York Times*, 27 May 1973; Efron, "Is Television Making a Mockery of the American Woman?" 7–9; Caroline Bird, "What's Television Doing for 50.9% of Americans?" *TV Guide*, 27 February 1971, 5–8.

6. Hennessee and Nicholson, "NOW Says," 13.

7. Ibid.

8. Ruth Rosen, *The World Split Open: How the Modern Women's Movement Changed America* (New York: Viking, 2000), 297.

9. "Advertising: Liberating Women," *Time*, 15 June 1970, 93.

10. Cited in J. Patrick Kelly, Paul J. Solomon, and Marion Burke, "Male and Female Responses to Women's Roles in Advertising" (paper presented at the American Academy of Advertising, 1977), 27, contained in Rena Bartos Papers, John W. Hartman Center for Sales, Advertising and Marketing History, Duke University, Durham, N.C.

11. NOW, *Report on the Task Force of the Image of Women*.

12. Report contained in Atlanta Lesbian Feminist Alliance Archives and Periodicals Collection, Sallie Bingham Center for Women's History and Culture, Duke University, Durham, N.C.

13. Bird, "What's Television Doing for 50.9% of Americans?," 7.

14. Benita Roth, *Separate Roads to Feminism: Black, Chicana, and White Feminist Movements in America's Second Wave* (Cambridge, UK: Cambridge University Press, 2004), 188–189.

15. Renee Ferguson, "Women's Liberation Has a Different Meaning for Blacks," in *Black Women in White America: A Documentary History*, ed. Gerda Lerner (New York: Vintage Books, 1973), 587. This article originally appeared in the *Washington Post* on 3 October 1970.

16. Ibid.

17. Linda La Rue, "The Black Movement and Women's Liberation," in *Words of Fire: An Anthology of African-American Feminist Thought*, ed. Beverly Guy-Sheftall (New York: New Press, 1995), 164. This article originally appeared in the May 1970 issue of *Black Scholar*.

18. "NBFO Lists TV Complaints and Protests 'That's My Mama,'" *Media Report to Women*, 1 December 1974, 16.

19. Ibid.

20. "For Women: More Jobs, but Low Pay," *U.S. News and World Report*, 8 October 1973, 41–42.

21. Ibid.

22. La Frances Rodgers-Rose, "Some Demographic Characteristics of the Black Woman: 1940 to 1975," in *The Black Woman*, ed. La Frances Rodgers-Rose (Newbury Park, Calif.: Sage Publications, 1980), 34–35.

23. U.S. Bureau of the Census, *Current Population Reports: Number, Timing and Duration of Marriages and Divorces in the United States: June 1975* (Washington, D.C.: U.S. Government Printing Office, 1976), 6, 18.

24. U.S. Bureau of the Census, "The Social and Economic Status of the Black Population in the United States, 1973," in *Current Population Reports* (Washington, D.C.: U.S. Bureau of the Census, 1974), 90–91.

25. U.S. Bureau of the Census, *Current Population Reports*, 2, 8.

26. Helen Van Slyke, "The Sex Life of a Working Woman," *Harper's Bazaar*, August 1974, 52; Amy Gross, "Woman Loves Work," *Mademoiselle*, March 1973, 144.

27. Gross, "Woman Loves Work," 144.

28. Barbara Ajmone-Marsan, "I Don't Want to Live through a Man," *Redbook*, August 1969, 13.

29. Bonnie Dow, *Prime-Time Feminism: Television, Media Culture and the Women's Movement since 1970* (Philadelphia: University of Pennsylvania Press, 1996), 51.

30. F. B. Satterthwaite, "Segmenting the Women's Market by Women's Role, Women's Lib and Other Social Forces," 1973, University of California, San Francisco, Legacy Tobacco Documents Library, http://legacy.library.ucsf.edu/tid/xlx31e00.

31. Steve Craig, "Madison Avenue versus *The Feminine Mystique:* The Advertising Industry's Response to the Women's Movement," in *Disco Divas: Women and Popular Culture in the 1970s*, ed. Sherrie A. Inness (Philadelphia: University of Pennsylvania, 2003), 16–17.

32. Rena Bartos, "Untitled Presentation" (paper presented at the National Advertising Review Board Meeting, 30 October 1974), contained in Rena Bartos Papers, John W. Hartman Center for Sales, Advertising and Marketing History.

33. Franchellie Cadwell, "Advertising to Women: The Revolution That Did Not Happen," *Madison Avenue*, March 1973, 62.

34. Satterthwaite, "Segmenting the Women's Market," 7.

35. Ibid., 8.

36. Hal Weinstein, "How an Agency Builds a Brand—the Virginia Slims Story" (paper presented at the American Association of Advertising Agencies Eastern Annual Conference, New York, 28–29 October 1969), University of California, San Francisco, Legacy Tobacco Documents Library, http://legacy.library.ucsf.edu/tid/efc64e00.

37. Ibid.
38. Ibid.
39. Ibid.

40. "Merchant of Glamour," *Time*, 8 September 1975, 62.

41. Susan Faludi, *Backlash: The Undeclared War against American Women*, 2nd ed. (New York: Anchor Books, 1992), 204–205.

42. Ibid.

43. "Merchant of Glamour," 62.

44. Bill Abrams, "Why Revlon's Charlie Seems to Be Ready to Settle Down," *Wall Street Journal*, 23 December 1982, 9.

45. "Merchant of Glamour," 62; Rosen, *The World Split Open*, 163.

46. Abrams, "Why Revlon's Charlie Seems to Be Ready to Settle Down," 9.

47. Barbara Lippert, "New Romance in Ads—or Just the Same Old Story?" *Adweek*, 14 March 1983, 32.

48. David Hofstede and Jack Condon, *Charlie's Angels Casebook* (Beverly Hills: Pomegranate Press, 2000), 6.

49. For a contemporary reference to this common assumption, see Stuart Elliott, "A New Camel Brand Is Dressed to the Nines," *New York Times*, 15 February 2007.

50. "Is It the New Woman—or the New Market?" *NOW New York* 2, no. 8 (1969), contained in Atlanta Lesbian Feminist Alliance Archives and Periodicals Collection, Sallie Bingham Center.

51. Susan Sutheim, "The Subversion of Betty Crocker," in *The New Women: A Motive Anthology on Women's Liberation*, ed. Joanne Cooke, Charlotte Bunch-Weeks, and Robin Morgan (Greenwich, Conn.: Fawcett Publications, 1970), 84.

52. Barbara Ehrenreich and Deirdre English, *For Her Own Good: 150 Years of the Experts' Advice to Women* (Garden City, N.Y.: Anchor Press, 1978), 291.

53. From transcript of television program, "In Conversation," Helen Gurley Brown Papers, Sophia Smith Collection, box 102, folder 13.

54. Ellen Willis, "Whatever Happened to Women? Nothing—That's the Trouble," *Mademoiselle*, September 1969, 208.

55. Bird, "What's Television Doing for 50.9% of Americans?" 7.

56. Aniko Bodroghkozy, "'Is This What You Mean by Color TV?' Race, Gender and Conflicted Meanings in NBC's Julia," in *Private Screenings: Television and the Female Consumer*, ed. Lynn Spigel and Denise Mann (Minneapolis: University of Minnesota, 1992), 143–167; Diane Rosen, "TV and the Single Girl," *TV Guide*, 6 November 1971, 13–16.

57. Although the series *Funny Face* was billed as CBS's top new comedy hit in 1971, critics have speculated that Duncan's stardom was hindered by her illness and surgery that interrupted filming.

58. Jane Feuer, Paul Kerr, and Tise Vahimagi, eds., *MTM "Quality Television"* (London: BFI, 1984), 3.

59. Ibid.

60. Muriel Davidson, "An Exciting New Star Goes into Orbit," *Good Housekeeping*, November 1971, 228.

61. Dow, *Prime-Time Feminism*, xviii.

62. Ibid.; Elana Levine, *Wallowing in Sex: The New Sexual Culture of 1970s American Television* (Durham, N.C.: Duke University Press), 123–168.

63. Dow, *Prime-Time Feminism*, 36–37.

64. Ibid., 45.

65. Ella Taylor, *Prime Time Families: Television Culture in Postwar America* (Berkeley: University of California Press, 1989), 27.

66. Feuer, Kerr, and Vahimagi, *MTM "Quality Television."*

67. Dow, *Prime-Time Feminism*, 24–25.

68. Douglas, *Where the Girls Are*, 205.

69. Stephen Cole, *That Book About That Girl: The Unofficial Companion* (Los Angeles: Renaissance Books), 139–140; *Marlo Thomas*, VHS, directed by Bob Waldman (New York: A&E Home Video, 2002.)

70. "The Elevated Woman," *That Girl: Season Five*, DVD, directed by Roger Duchowny (1971; Los Angeles: Shout Factory, 2009).

71. Douglas, *Where the Girls Are*, 198.

72. Tracey Johnston, "Why 30 Million Are Mad about Mary," *New York Times Magazine*, 7 April 1974, 97.

73. Sally Bedell, *Up the Tube: Prime-Time TV and the Silverman Years* (New York: Viking Press, 1981), 66.

74. Horace Newcomb and Robert S. Alley, *The Producer's Medium: Conversations with Creators of American TV* (New York: Oxford University Press, 1983), 219.

75. Dow, *Prime-Time Feminism*, 29–30.

76. Ibid., 52.

77. Taylor, *Prime Time Families*, 47.

78. Ibid., 115.

79. "Love Is All Around," *The Mary Tyler Moore Show: The Complete First Season*, DVD, directed by Jay Sandrich (1970; Beverly Hills: Twentieth Century Fox, 2002).

80. Dow, *Prime-Time Feminism*, 31.

81. Douglas, *Where the Girls Are*, 206.

82. Quote by Darrell Hamamoto in Dow, *Prime-Time Feminism*, 31.

83. Ibid., 31–32.

84. "Why You Find the Next Eight Pages in the *Ladies' Home Journal*," *Ladies' Home Journal*, August 1970.

85. Dow, *Prime-Time Feminism*, 31.

86. "Sherri," *The Way We See It*, 26 August 1970.

87. "For Women: More Jobs, but Low Pay"; Klemesrud, "TV's Women Are Dingbats."

88. Arthur Turfa, "Mrs. Peel Strikes Out," *Penn State Daily Collegian*, 7 December 1973, 2.

89. "The Lady Comes Across," *Diana*, 10 September 1973, NBC, directed by Leonard Stern, viewed at the UCLA Film and Television Archive, University of California, Los Angeles.

90. "The Berkeley Club Caper," *Shirley's World: The Complete Series*, DVD, directed by Ralph Levy (1971; London, UK: Granada Ventures, 2009).

91. Georgina Hickey, "Barred from the Barroom: Second Wave Feminists and Public Accomodations in U.S. Cities," *Feminist Studies* 34, no. 3 (2008): 382.

92. John Goudas, "Karen Valentine Returns to TV as a Crusader," *Toledo Blade*, 26 January 1975, TV1, Lawrence Laurent, "Optimism Will Keep 'Karen' on the Air," *St. Petersburg Times*, 6 February 1975, 30D.

93. Barbara Holsopple, "Cute Government Fails in 'Karen,'" *Pittsburgh Press*, 31 January 1975, 33; Beth Slocum, "'Karen'—Good Idea Beaten to Death," *Milwaukee Journal Accent*, 30 January 1975, 8.

94. Dow, *Prime-Time Feminism*, 40.

95. Douglas, *Where the Girls Are*, 205.

96. Bird, "What's Television Doing for 50.9% of Americans?" 8.

97. "Love and Other Issues," *Karen*, NBC, 20 February 1975, directed by John Erman, viewed at the UCLA Film and Television Archive, University of California, Los Angeles; "Pilot," *The Sandy Duncan Show*, CBS, 11 December 1971, directed by Hal Cooper, viewed at the Paley Center for Media, New York.

98. Dow, *Prime-Time Feminism*, 38.

99. Taylor, *Prime Time Families*, 10–11.

100. Ibid., 2.

101. Melissa Frederick Morrison, "Mary Go Round: What Happened to TV's Independent Women?" *Bitch: Feminist Response to Pop Culture* (Winter 2006): 79.

102. Ibid.

103. "Pilot," *The Sandy Duncan Show.*

104. Nancy Vogel, "The Sandy Duncan Show," *Writer's Digest*, November 1972, 58–89.

105. "What Are Friends For?" *Karen*, NBC, 3 April 1975, directed by Jerry Paris, UCLA Film and Television Archive.

106. "Woman for All Seasons," *Newsweek*, 17 September 1973, 76.

107. Ibid.

108. Hennessee and Nicholson, "NOW Says," 13.

109. "Busch's Breakup," *Karen*, NBC, 13 March 1975, directed by John Erman, UCLA Film and Television Archive.

110. "Lou Dates Mary" and "Mary's Three Husbands," *The Mary Tyler Moore Show: The Complete Seventh Season*, DVD, directed by Jay Sandrich (1977; Beverly Hills: Twentieth Century Fox, 2010).

111. Robert Lewis Shayon, "Free Shirley!" *Saturday Review*, 23 October 1971, 26.

112. Dow, *Prime-Time Feminism*, 43.

113. "The Good-Time News," *The Mary Tyler Moore Show: The Complete Third Season*, DVD, directed by Hal Cooper (1972; Beverly Hills: Twentieth Century Fox, 2005).

114. Bill Davidson, "'The Mary Tyler Moore Show'—after Three Seasons," *TV Guide*, 19–25 May 1973.

115. Dow, *Primetime Feminism*.

116. "For Women: More Jobs, but Low Pay," 42.

117. "The Lady Comes Across," *Diana.*

118. Rosen, "TV and the Single Girl," 14.

119. Ibid. 14.

120. Whitney, "You've Come a Long Way, Baby," 179.

121. Johnston, "Why 30 Million Are Mad about Mary," 30.

122. Whitney, "You've Come a Long Way, Baby," 179.

123. Bedell, *Up the Tube*, 64.

124. Davidson, "'The Mary Tyler Moore Show'—after Three Seasons."

125. "Just around the Corner," *The Mary Tyler Moore Show: The Complete*

Third Season, DVD, directed by Jay Sandrich (1972; Beverly Hills: Twentieth Century Fox, 2005).

126. "Just Around the Corner," Second Draft, 9 March 1972, Steve Pritzker Papers, UCLA Performing Arts Special Collections, box 2, folder 6.

127. Davidson, "'The Mary Tyler Moore Show'—after Three Seasons."

128. "You've Got a Friend," *The Mary Tyler Moore Show: The Complete Third Season*, DVD, directed by Jerry Belson (1972; Beverly Hills: Twentieth Century Fox, 2005).

129. "You've Got a Friend," First Draft, 4 May 1972, Steve Pritzker Papers, UCLA Performing Arts Special Collections, box 2, folder 4.

130. Interview with Karen Valentine, "The Tonight Show," NBC, 23 January 1975, screened at the Paley Center for Media, New York.

131. "Whistle Blowing," *Karen*, NBC, 27 February 1975, directed by Hy Averback, UCLA Film and Television Archive.

132. "Hartford Revisited," *Karen*, NBC, 6 June 1975, directed by Gene Reynolds, UCLA Film and Television Archive; "Love and Other Issues."

133. "Hartford Revisited."

134. "Busch's Breakup."

135. "Remembrance of Things Past," *The Mary Tyler Moore Show: The Complete Third Season*, DVD, directed by Jay Sandrich (1973; Beverly Hills: Twentieth Century Fox, 2005).

136. Davidson, "'The Mary Tyler Moore Show'—after Three Seasons."

137. Ibid.

138. Ibid.

139. "Pilot," *Funny Face*.

140. Tom Donnelly, "New Format Sought for Sandy," *Tri-City Herald*, 5 January 1973, 8.

141. Ibid.; "A Crush on Sandy," *Funny Face*, 27 November 1971, directed by Richard Michaels, UCLA Film and Television Archive.

142. Shayon, "Free Shirley!" 26.

143. "You Can't Go Back," *Diana*, NBC, 12 November 1973, directed by Jay Sandrich, UCLA Film and Television Archive.

144. Ibid.

145. "For Singles, Life Isn't All 'Swinging,'" *U.S. News and World Report*, 8 December 1975, 67.

146. Dow, *Prime-Time Feminism*, 60.

147. Ibid.; "Pilot," *Fay*, NBC, 4 September 1975, screened at the Paley Center for Media, New York.

148. Dow, *Prime-Time Feminism*, 60.

149. Edith Efron, "Television after Dark," *TV Guide*, 25 October 1975, 32.

150. Ibid.

Chapter 4. Claiming Sexuality and Power: Working Women and Wonder Women in 1970s Action Series

1. "Nobody Here but Us Chickens," *That Girl: Season Four*, DVD, directed by Richard Kinon (1969; Los Angeles: Shout Factory, 2008).

2. *Get Christie Love*, DVD, directed by William Graham (1974; Edison, N.J.: Double D Distribution, 2005).

3. Edith Efron, "TV's Sex Crisis," *TV Guide*, 18 October 1975, 4–8; Elana Levine, *Wallowing in Sex: The New Sexual Culture of 1970s American Television* (Durham, N.C.: Duke University Press, 2007).

4. Levine, *Wallowing in Sex*, 4.

5. Sherrie Inness, "'Strange Feverish Years': The 1970s and Women's Changing Roles," in *Disco Divas: Women and Popular Culture in the 1970s*, ed. Sherrie Inness (Philadelphia: University of Pennsylvania Press, 2003), 5.

6. This term was in popular parlance by the late 1970s, as evidenced by its appearance in a 1979 report. "Window Dressing on the Set: An Update" (Washington, D.C.: U.S. Commission on Civil Rights, 1979).

7. Marjorie Rosen, "Farrah Fawcett-Majors Makes Me Want to Scream!" *Redbook*, September 1977, 106; "TV's Super Women," *Time*, 22 November 1976, 67–71.

8. Susan Douglas, *Where the Girls Are: Growing up Female with the Mass Media* (New York: Times Books, 1994), 212; Whitney Womack, "Reevaulating 'Jiggle TV': *Charlie's Angels* at Twenty-Five," in *Disco Divas: Women and Popular Culture in the 1970s*, ed. Sherrie Inness (Philadelphia: University of Pennsylvania Press, 2003), 151–171.

9. Levine, *Wallowing in Sex*, 154.

10. Ibid., 5.

11. Beth Bailey, "She 'Can Bring Home the Bacon': Negotiating Gender in Seventies America," in *America in the Seventies*, ed. Beth Bailey and David Farber (Lawrence: University Press of Kansas, 2004), 120.

12. Flora Davis, *Moving the Mountain: The Women's Movement in America since 1960* (New York: Simon & Schuster, 1991), 386.

13. Ibid.

14. Ibid., 391.

15. Phyllis Schlafly, "What 'Women's Lib' Really Means," *Phyllis Schlafly*

Report, December 1974, contained in the Southeast Women's Employment Coalition (SWEC) Records, Sallie Bingham Center for Women's History and Culture, Duke University, Durham, N.C.

16. Phyllis Schlafly, "What's Wrong with 'Equal Rights' for Women?" *Phyllis Schlafly Report*, February 1972, Southeast Women's Employment Coalition (SWEC) Records, Sallie Bingham Center for Women's History and Culture.

17. Davis, *Moving the Mountain*, 389.

18. Levine, *Wallowing in Sex*, 127.

19. "For Singles, Life Isn't All 'Swinging,'" *U.S. News & World Report*, 8 December 1975, 67.

20. As evidence of women's inferiority, McDaniel cited a 1976 study claiming the average woman had 60 percent of the strength of the average man, in "The Real World of the Working Woman" (Atlanta: Stop ERA, n.d.), brochure contained in Southeast Women's Employment Coalition (SWEC) Records, Sallie Bingham Center.

21. Ibid.

22. Frankie Muse Freeman, "The Equal Rights Amendment: What's in It for Black Women?" *Focus* (1973), Southeast Women's Employment Coalition (SWEC) Records, Sallie Bingham Center.

23. Schlafly, "What 'Women's Lib' Really Means."

24. Davis, *Moving the Mountain*, 398.

25. Michael Knight, "Hartford Police Curb Girl-Watchers," *New York Times*, 9 August 1973.

26. Ibid.

27. Ibid.

28. Gail Liberman, "Policemen Assigned to Restrain Oglers," 13 August 1973, press clipping from United Press International, contained in Southeast Women's Employment Coalition (SWEC) Records, Sallie Bingham Center.

29. Carrie N. Baker, "'He Said, She Said': Popular Representations of Sexual Harassment and Second-Wave Feminism," in *Disco Divas: Women and Popular Culture in the 1970s*, ed. Sherrie Inness (Philadelphia: University of Pennsylvania Press, 2003), 42.

30. Ibid., 48.

31. Ibid., 44.

32. Anne Taylor Fleming, "In Defense of Flirting," *Newsweek*, 26 April 1976, 17.

33. Amy Gross, "Verbal Sex: The World's Greatest Contact Sport," *Mademoiselle*, June 1977, 196–199.

34. Anne Fleming, "Flirting: How You Do It," *Redbook*, February 1977, 175–178.

35. Clark Whelton, "Instant Intimacy . . . and Safer Than Sex," *Mademoiselle*, June 1977, 78, 148.

36. John Mariani, "Flirting: How He Does It," *Redbook*, February 1977, 173–174.

37. Whelton, "Instant Intimacy . . . And Safer Than Sex," 78, 148.

38. Fleming, "Flirting," 175–178.

39. Baker, "He Said, She Said," 51.

40. Amanda D. Lotz, *Redesigning Women: Television after the Network Era* (Urbana: University of Illinois Press, 2006), 3.

41. Ibid., 32.

42. Levine, *Wallowing in Sex*, 129.

43. Jane Hall, "Discovering Ms. America," *TV Guide*, 18 December 1976, 26–30.

44. Bill Abrams, "Why Revlon's Charlie Seems to Be Ready to Settle Down," *Wall Street Journal*, 23 December 1982, 9.

45. Merrill Sheils, "State of the Movement," *Newsweek*, 28 November 1977.

46. "For Singles, Life Isn't All 'Swinging,'" 67.

47. Allyson Sherman Grossman, "The Labor Force Patterns of Single Women" (Washington: U.S. Department of Labor, Bureau of Statistics, 1980).

48. "For Singles, Life Isn't All 'Swinging,'" 67.

49. Ibid.

50. D. Atkin, "The Evolution of Television Series Addressing Single Women, 1966–1990," *Journal of Broadcasting and Electronic Media* 35, no. 4 (1991): 519.

51. Memo from Joe Goodson to Art Frankel, 13 June 1973; memo from David Goldsmith to Joseph Goodson, "Movie of the Week Project," 25 September 1973, contained in Douglas Cramer Papers, American Heritage Center.

52. Memo from Douglas Cramer to Bob Lovenheim, 9 August 1972, contained in the Douglas Cramer Papers, American Heritage Center, box 2, "Development Report" folder.

53. Bob Thomas, "Industry Braces for TV Violence Report," *Eugene Register-Guard*, 20 November 1971.

54. "Hunter," series proposal and memo from David Goldsmith to M. Scheff, 4 August 1972, contained in the Douglas Cramer Papers, American Heritage Center, box 2, "Development Report" folder.

55. Leonard Gross, "Why Can't a Woman Be More Like a Man?" *TV Guide*, 11 August 1973.

56. Douglas Cramer to Seymour Friedman, 24 February 1972, contained in the Douglas Cramer Papers, American Heritage Center, box 2, "Submissions" folder.

57. Gross, "Why Can't a Woman Be More Like a Man?" 8.

58. S. Harris, "TV Jibe: Television Lib," *TV Guide*, 23 September 1972.

59. "First Meeting: Woman's World," 1976, contained in the Ann Marcus Papers, American Heritage Center, box 26, scripts folder.

60. Gross, "Why Can't a Woman Be More Like a Man?" 6–11.

61. Levine, *Wallowing in Sex*, 128.

62. Robert L. Rose, "TV: Those Women in Blue," *Washington Post*, 1 September 1974.

63. Ibid.

64. Sue Cameron, "Police Drama: Women Are on the Case," *Ms.*, October 1974, 104, 108.

65. Commentary by Angie Dickinson, "The Gamble," *Police Woman: The Complete First Season*, DVD, directed by Richard Benedict (1974; Culver City, CA: Sony Pictures, 2006).

66. Julie D'Acci, *Defining Women: Television and the Case of Cagney and Lacey*, (Chapel Hill: University of North Carolina Press, 1994), 115–117.

67. Gerda Ray, "Police Forces," http://college.hmco.com/history/read erscomp/women/html/wh_029100_policeforces.htm.

68. Sheils, "State of the Movement," 59.

69. Ibid.

70. Rosen, "Farrah Fawcett-Majors Makes Me Want to Scream!" 106.

71. Jerry Buck, "Television Changing Women's Image," *Sarasota Herald-Tribune*, 22 September 1974, TV3.

72. Rose, "TV: Those Women in Blue," K7.

73. Cameron, "Police Drama," 108.

74. Rose, "TV: Those Women in Blue," K7.

75. Cameron, "Police Drama," 108.

76. Ibid., 104.

77. Ibid.

78. Peggy Crall, "Sexual Harrassment and Male Control of Women's Work" (New York: Working Women's Institute, 1981), 6, contained in the Southeast Women's Employment Coalition (SWEC) Records, Sallie Bingham Center.

79. Ibid.

80. Stephanie Dunn, "Foxy Brown on My Mind: The Racialized Gendered Politics of Representation," in *Disco Divas: Women and Popular Culture in the 1970s*, ed. Sherrie Inness (Philadelphia: University of Pennsylvania, 2003), 71.

81. "Window Dressing on the Set: Women and Minorities in Television" (Washington, D.C.: U.S. Commission on Civil Rights, 1977); Dunn, "Foxy Brown on My Mind," 73.

82. Mary Beltran notes that working-class Latinas in 1990s media often possess a street credibility that "presupposes their ability to fight, diminishing the need for such characters to prove their prowess through musculature." Mary Beltran, "Mas Macha: The New Latina Action Hero," in *Action and Adventure Cinema*, ed. Yvonne Tasker (London: Routledge, 2004), 186–200.

83. Although Sapphire historically has been positioned as the opponent of black men, Kimberly Springer's description of this archetype as innately violent, with a "fiery tongue," seems to apply to Christie Love. Kimberly Springer, "Waiting to Set It Off," in *Reel Knockouts: Violent Women in the Movies*, ed. Martha McCaughey and Neal King (Austin: University of Texas, 2001), 172–199.

84. Kimberly Springer, "Divas, Evil Black Bitches, and Bitter Black Women: African-American Women in Postfeminist and Post-Civil Rights Popular Culture," in *Feminist Television Criticism: A Reader*, 2nd ed., ed. Charlotte Brunsdon and Lynn Spigel (Berkshire, UK: Open University Press, 2008), 85.

85. Levine, *Wallowing in Sex*, 135.

86. Rose, "TV: Those Women in Blue." K7.

87. Cameron, "Police Drama," 104, 108.

88. "Fatal Image," *Get Christie Love*, 6 November 1974, directed by Richard Compton, viewed at the UCLA Film and Television Archive, University of California, Los Angeles.

89. Levine, *Wallowing in Sex*, 134; "Will the Real Teresa Graves Please Stand Up?" *Ebony*, December 1974, 67.

90. "Market for Murder," *Get Christie Love*, aired 11 September 1974, directed by Gene Nelson, viewed at the UCLA Film and Television Archive.

91. Levine, *Wallowing in Sex*, 135.

92. Cameron, "Police Drama," 108.

93. "Will the Real Teresa Graves Please Stand Up?" 66.

94. Rose, "TV: Those Women in Blue," K7.

95. "Fatal Image," *Get Christie Love*, aired 30 October 1974, directed by Ivan Dixon, UCLA Film and Television Archive.

96. "Highway to Murder," *Get Christie Love.*

97. Joel Dreyfuss, "Television Controversy: Covering the Black Experience," *Washington Post,* 1 September 1974.

98. Lawrence Laurent, "Network Television No Place for Even a Police Lady," *Citizen,* 20 August 1975, 66–67; Norman Mark, "Angie Dickinson: Everybody's Kid Sister," 17 August 1975, TV2.

99. "Angie Dickinson: Her Show 'Miracle,'" *Eugene Register Guard,* 19 October 1975, TV16; Mark, "Angie Dickinson," TV2.

100. Commentary by Angie Dickinson and Earl Holliman, "The End Game," *Police Woman: The Complete First Season,* DVD, directed by Alvin Ganzer (1974; Culver City, CA: Sony Pictures, 2006).

101. Ann Pincus, "Shape up, Bionic Woman!" *Newsweek,* 15 November 1976, 15.

102. Commentary by Angie Dickinson and Earl Holliman, "The End Game," *Police Woman: The Complete First Season,* DVD.

103. Cameron, "Police Drama," 104.

104. Pincus, "Shape up, Bionic Woman!" 15.

105. Mark, "Angie Dickinson," TV2.

106. Commentary by Angie Dickinson, "The Gamble," *Police Woman: The Complete First Season,* DVD, directed by Richard Benedict (1974; Culver City, CA: Sony Pictures, 2006).

107. "TV's Super Women," 69.

108. Mark, "Angie Dickinson," TV2.

109. Levine, *Wallowing in Sex,* 134.

110. Memo, Irving Elman, 29 March 1975, Irving Elman Papers, American Heritage Center, box 8, "Correspondence 1970–75" folder.

111. Irving Elman, "Death Pays All Debts," Story Outline, 11 June 1974, Irving Elman Papers, American Heritage Center, box 8. This episode became "Requiem for Bored Wives," *Police Woman: The Complete First Season,* DVD, directed by Alvin Ganzer (1974; Culver City, CA: Sony Pictures, 2006).

112. Irving Elman, "Death Pays All Debts," first draft, 8 July 1974, Irving Elman Papers, American Heritage Center, box 4, scripts folder.

113. Ibid.

114. Douglas, *Where the Girls Are,* 210.

115. Cameron, "Police Drama," 108.

116. Douglas, *Where the Girls Are,* 210.

117. Rosen, "Farrah Fawcett-Majors Makes Me Want to Scream!" 106.

118. Douglas, *Where the Girls Are,* 311.

119. Ibid.

120. Rosen, "Farrah Fawcett-Majors Makes Me Want to Scream!" 109.

121. Elman, "Death Pays All Debts," Story Outline, 11 June 1974, and "Final Draft," 16 September 1974, contained in Irving Elman Papers, American Heritage Center, box 8.

122. Correspondence on *Charlie's Angels* scripts reveals producers were concerned with minimizing "countable" incidents of violence and revised episodes accordingly. Contained in Ronald Austin Papers, American Heritage Center, boxes 1 and 3.

123. Judy Klemesrud, "Can Feminists Upstage Miss America?" *New York Times*, 8 September 1974, L58.

124. Ibid.

125. Marguerite Lamb, "Who Was Wonder Woman 1?" *Bostonia: The Alumni Quarterly of Boston University* (Fall 2001), http://www.bu.edu/bostonia/fall01/woman/.

126. Gloria Steinem, "I'm in Love with a Wonder Woman," n.d., unpublished script contained in the Gloria Steinem Papers, Sophia Smith Collection, box 107, folder 11; historical references indicate this script was written in the early 1970s.

127. Ibid.

128. Vernon Scott, "Blonde Beauty, Former Television Star Plans Television Special," *Nashua Telegraph*, 11 March 1974, 25.

129. *Wonder Woman*, ABC, 12 March 1974, directed by Vincent McEveety.

130. "Wonder Woman Comes to TV," *Ocala Star Banner*, 8 March 1974.

131. Scott, "Blonde Beauty, Former Television Star Plans Television Special," 13A.

132. "TV's Super Women," 70.

133. Levine, *Wallowing in Sex*, 139.

134. Douglas, *Where the Girls Are*, 217.

135. "Pilot: The New Original Wonder Woman," *Wonder Woman: The Complete Third Season*, DVD, directed by Leonard Horn (1975; Burbank, CA: Warner Brothers, 2004).

136. Douglas, *Where the Girls Are*, 217.

137. Levine, *Wallowing in Sex*, 143.

138. Pincus, "Shape up, Bionic Woman!" 15.

139. Levine, *Wallowing in Sex*, 139; commentary by Lynda Carter, "My Teenage Idol Is Missing," *Wonder Woman: The Complete Third Season*, DVD, directed by Seymour Robbie (1978; Burbank, CA: Warner Brothers, 2005).

140. "Beauty on Parade," *Wonder Woman: The Complete First Season,* DVD, directed by Richard Kinon (1976; Burbank, CA: Warner Brothers, 2004).

141. Carl Macek, "TV's Amazing Amazons Battle for the Ratings," *Mediascene* (January/February 1977). http://www.wonderland-site.com/html/mags/mags00003.htm.

142. "TV's Super Women."

143. Commentary by Lynda Carter, "My Teenage Idol Is Missing," *Wonder Woman: The Complete Third Season,* DVD, directed by Seymour Robbie (1978; Burbank, CA: Warner Brothers, 2005).

144. "The Return of Wonder Woman," *Wonder Woman: The Complete Second Season,* DVD, directed by Alan Crosland (1977; Burbank, CA: Warner Brothers, 2005).

145. Script for "Return of Wonder Woman," 4 July 1977, 17–18, contained in the Douglas Cramer Papers, American Heritage Center, box 60, folder 3.

146. Script for "Return of Wonder Woman," 22 June 1977, 17–18, Douglas Cramer Papers, American Heritage Center, box 60, folder 3.

147. Script for "Return of Wonder Woman," 4 July 1977, 57A, Douglas Cramer Papers, American Heritage Center, box 60, folder 3.

148. Script for "Return of Wonder Woman," 4 July 1977, 74, Douglas Cramer Papers, American Heritage Center, box 60, folder 3.

149. Douglas, *Where the Girls Are,* 218.

150. Vernon Scott, "Lindsay Wagner to Portray 'Bionic Woman' in New Show," *Sarasota Herald-Tribune,* 5 December 1975, 6B.

151. Tom Shales, "'Bionic Woman' a Step Ahead," *Pittsburgh Press,* 13 June 1976, 20.

152. Sherrie A. Inness, *Tough Girls: Warrior Women and Wonder Women in Popular Culture* (Philadelphia: University of Pennsylvania Press, 1999); Rosen, "Farrah Fawcett-Majors Makes Me Want to Scream!" 102.

153. "Welcome Home, Jaime," *The Bionic Woman,* directed by Alan Crosland, 11 January 1976, UCLA Film and Television Archive.

154. Scott, "Lindsay Wagner to Portray 'Bionic Woman' in New Show," 5B.

155. "TV's Super Women," 69.

156. Douglas, *Where the Girls Are,* 218.

157. Pincus, "Shape up, Bionic Woman!" 15.

158. Rosen, "Farrah Fawcett-Majors Makes Me Want to Scream!" 106.

159. "Angel of Mercy," *The Bionic Woman,* 28 January 1976, directed by Alan J. Levi, UCLA Film and Television Archive.

160. James D. Parriott, "Jaime's Shield: Part One," 18 June 1976, contained in Harve Bennett Papers, Performing Arts Special Collections, University of California, Los Angeles, box 6.

161. Douglas, *Where the Girls Are*, 218.

162. Parriott, "Jaime's Shield: Part One."

163. Tom Shales, "Farrah Fawcett-Majors: 'I Just Laugh,'" *Washington Post*, 5 January 1977, B1.

164. David Hofstede and Jack Condon, *Charlie's Angels Casebook* (Beverly Hills: Pomegranate Press, 2000), 34.

165. Inness, *Tough Girls*, 42.

166. *Douglas, Where the Girls Are*, 216.

167. Rosen, "Farrah Fawcett-Majors Makes Me Want to Scream!" 102.

168. "TV's Super Women."

169. Hofstede and Condon, *Charlie's Angels Casebook*, 5.

170. Levine, *Wallowing in Sex*, 150–151.

171. Womack, "Reevaulating 'Jiggle TV': *Charlie's Angels* at Twenty-Five"; Levine, *Wallowing in Sex*, 150.

172. "The Blue Angels," *Charlie's Angels: The Complete First Season*, DVD, directed by Georg Stanford Brown (1976; Culver City, CA: Sony Pictures, 2003).

173. "Angel Roles" memo, 17 March 1977, contained in Ronald Austin Papers, American Heritage Center, box 7, "Memos: Spelling and Goldberg" folder.

174. Ibid.; Megan Rosenfeld, "The 'Angel' Who Flew Charlie's Coop," *Washington Post*, 31 October 1979, B1; Womack, "Reevaulating 'Jiggle TV,'" 162.

175. Notes on "Sammy Davis Jr. Kidnap Plot," memo from Ron Austin to Ron Friedman and James D. Buchanan, 1 August 1977, Ronald Austin Papers, American Heritage Center, box 3.

176. Memo from Ron Austin to Carmella Ortiz, 18 December 1978, Ronald Austin Papers, American Heritage Center, box 1.

177. "Love Boat Angels," *Charlie's Angels: The Complete Fourth Season*, DVD, directed by Allen Baron (1979; Culver City, CA: Sony Pictures, 2009.)

178. Ivan Goff, "Angels in Paradise, Second Draft," 11 May 1977, Ronald Austin Papers, American Heritage Center, box 11.

179. "Angels in Paradise," *Charlie's Angels: The Complete Second Season*, DVD, directed by Charles S. Dubin (1977; Culver City, CA: Sony Pictures, 2004).

180. Ivan Goff, "Angels in Paradise, Second Draft," 11 May 1977, Ronald Austin Papers, American Heritage Center, box 11; Ronald McFarland, Shooting Script Review on "Angels in Paradise, Second Draft," 16 May 1977, Ronald Austin Papers, American Heritage Center, box 3.

181. Notes on "Sammy Davis Jr. Kidnap Plot," memo from Ron Austin to Ron Friedman and James D. Buchanan, 1 August 1977, Ronald Austin Papers, American Heritage Center, box 3.

182. McFarland, Shooting Script Review, 16 May 1977.

183. "Angels in Paradise Part II," *Charlie's Angels: The Complete Second Season*, DVD, directed by Charles S. Dubin (1977; Culver City, CA: Sony Pictures, 2004).

184. Levine, *Wallowing in Sex*, 150.

185. Memo from Aaron Spelling and Leonard Goldberg to Ron Austin and Jim Buchanan, "Angel on Fire," 26 May 1978, Ronald Austin Papers, American Heritage Center, box 1.

186. "Angel Come Home," *Charlie's Angels: The Complete Third Season*, DVD, directed by Paul Stanley (1978; Culver City, CA: Sony Pictures, 2006).

187. Notes on "Sammy Davis Jr. Kidnap Plot," memo from Ron Austin to Ron Friedman and James D. Buchanan, 1 August 1977, Ronald Austin Papers, American Heritage Center, box 3.

188. McFarland, Shooting Script Review.

189. "Angels in Paradise," *Charlie's Angels: The Complete Second Season*, DVD, directed by Charles S. Dubin (1977; Culver City, CA: Sony Pictures, 2004).

190. Carmella Ortiz, "Co-ed Angels, First Draft," 12 March 1979, 31, Ronald Austin Papers, American Heritage Center, box 1. This episode later became "Angels on Campus," *Charlie's Angels: The Complete Fourth Season*, DVD, directed by Don Chaffey (1979; Culver City, CA: Sony Pictures, 2009).

191. "TV's Super Women."

192. Ellen Farley and Jr. William Knoedelseder, "Rub-a-Dub-Dub," *Washington Post*, 19 February 1978, G1.

193. Ibid.

194. Ibid.

195. "New TV Season: Less Sex, Less Violence," *U.S. News and World Report*, 11 September 1978, 32.

196. "Window Dressing on the Set: An Update."

197. John Jacobs, "TV Accused of Perpetuating Stereotypes," *The Washington Post*, 16 August 1977, A1.

198. "Window Dressing on the Set: Women and Minorities in Television."

199. "Window Dressing on the Set: An Update."

200. Tom Shales, "Stereotypes in Videoland," *Washington Post*, 17 August 1977.

201. Ibid.

202. Aric Press, "Abusing Sex at the Office," *Newsweek*, 10 March 1980, 81.

203. Ibid.

204. Ibid.

205. Ibid.

206. Richard Corliss, "Television: The Bodies in Question," *Time*, 3 November 1980, 100.

207. D'Acci, *Defining Women*, 71.

208. Ibid., 47.

209. Aniko Bodroghkozy, "Where Have You Gone, Mary Richards? Feminism's Rise and Fall in Primetime Television," *Iris*, no. 49 (2004), 12.

210. D'Acci, *Defining Women*, 31–35.

211. Commentary by Angie Dickinson and Earl Holliman, "The End Game," *Police Woman: The Complete First Season*.

212. Douglas, *Where the Girls Are*, 214.

Chapter 5. Courting Danger: Single Women and Sexual Aggression in 1970s Film

1. Lacey Fosburgh, "Man Seen with Teacher on Slaying Night Is Sought," *New York Times*, 6 January 1973, 16; Lacey Fosburgh, *Closing Time: The True Story of the "Goodbar" Murder* (New York: Delacorte Press, 1977).

2. Judith Rossner, *Looking for Mr. Goodbar* (New York: Simon & Schuster, 1975); Gail Parent, *Sheila Levine Is Dead and Living in New York* (New York: G. P. Putnam's Sons, 1972).

3. Karen Durbin, "The Sexual Confusion," *Mademoiselle*, July 1972, 90.

4. Ibid.

5. Ibid.

6. "Has Something Gone Wrong between Them?" *Ebony*, August 1977.

7. Susan Jacoby, "49 Million Singles Can't All Be Right," *New York Times Magazine*, 17 February 1974, 41.

8. Amy Gross, "Woman Loves Work," *Mademoiselle*, March 1973, 144–145.

9. Ibid., 144.

10. Jane Gerhard, *Desiring Revolution: Second-Wave Feminism and the Rewriting of American Sexual Thought, 1920 to 1982* (New York: Columbia University Press, 2001), 107.

11. Ibid., 118.

12. Jean Seligmann, "The Hite Report," *Newsweek*, 18 October 1976, 85.

13. Barbara Ehrenreich, Elizabeth Hess, and Gloria Jacobs, *Re-Making Love: The Feminization of Sex* (Garden City, N.Y.: Anchor Press, 1986), 88.

14. Elizabeth Peer, "Sex and the Woman Writer," *Newsweek*, 5 May 1975, 70; Seligmann, "The Hite Report," 85.

15. Ruth Rosen, *The World Split Open: How the Modern Women's Movement Changed America* (New York: Viking, 2000), 157–159.

16. Beth Bailey, "She 'Can Bring Home the Bacon': Negotiating Gender in Seventies America," in *America in the Seventies*, ed. Beth Bailey and David Farber (Lawrence: University Press of Kansas, 2004), 116.

17. Jill Robinson, "I Hate Sex," *Vogue*, August 1977, 150.

18. Helen Singer Kaplan, "One Lover or Many?" *Harper's Bazaar*, March 1975, 79.

19. Anne Frisch and Diane Partie, "Why Do You Really Need a Man?" *Mademoiselle*, November 1975, 154.

20. Joyce Brothers, "Coping with Loneliness: Drugs, Alcohol and Anxiety," *Harper's Bazaar*, March 1975, 81–82, 112–113.

21. Gloria Emerson, "In a City of Crowds, So Many Lonely Women," *New York Times*, 28 January 1974.

22. Nan Robertson, "Single Women over 30: 'Where Are the Men Worthy of Us?'" *New York Times*, 14 July 1978.

23. Durbin, "The Sexual Confusion," 90.

24. Robertson, "Single Women over 30."

25. Karen Durbin, "The Intelligent Woman's Guide to Sex," *Mademoiselle*, April 1977, 34, 96.

26. Kaplan, "One Lover or Many?" 79.

27. Judy Klemesrud, "Bachelor's Life: Things Aren't Always Hunky-Dory in Paradise," *New York Times*, 3 May 1974.

28. Richard Kramer, "A Young Man Asks: Just What the Hell Does She Want from Me Anyway?" *Mademoiselle*, February 1976, 158.

29. Bailey, "She 'Can Bring Home the Bacon,'" 119.

30. Durbin, "The Sexual Confusion," 90.

31. "'You Can't Destroy This Movement,'" *U.S. News and World Report*, 8 December 1975, 71.

32. Kramer, "A Young Man Asks," 158.

33. Durbin, "The Sexual Confusion," 162.

34. Robertson, "Single Women over 30"; "Men Write to Challenge Single Women's Criticism," *New York Times*, 5 August 1978.

35. Mara Wolynski, "A Young Woman Says: The Thrill of the Cheap Thrill Has Faded," *Mademoiselle*, February 1976, 134; Kramer, "A Young Man Asks," 135.

36. Loudon Wainwright, "The Dying Girl That No One Helped," *Life*, 10 April 1964, 21.

37. "The Career-Girl Murders," *Cosmopolitan*, August 1967, 64.

38. Lee Israel, "Violence: How Does a Career Girl Cope?" *Cosmopolitan*, February 1968, 81–83.

39. Jack Olsen, *The Girls in the Office* (New York: Simon & Schuster, 1971),139–140.

40. Victims memorialized in the *New York Times* in the early 1970s included Patrice Leary, Carol Hoffmann, Roseann Quinn, and Brigitte Albrecht. Judy Klemesrud, "Single Women against a Dangerous City," *New York Times*, 12 January 1973.

41. Leslie Maitland, "For Singles, Scene Has Sordid Side," *New York Times*, 1 November 1974, 78.

42. Ibid., 41, 78.

43. Fosburgh, "Man Seen with Teacher on Slaying Night Is Sought," 16.

44. Fosburgh, *Closing Time.*

45. Gregg Kilday, "'Goodbar' Truth: Stranger Than Fiction?" *Los Angeles Times*, 20 November 1977, Calendar 39.

46. Grace Lichtenstein, "Slain Woman's Neighbors Express Both Horror and Detachment," *New York Times*, 25 October 1973.

47. According to Bruce Schulman, a victim in New York needed to "prove she was raped by force, that 'penetration' occurred, and that someone witnessed the rapist in the area of the attack." Given these stringent requirements, the vast majority of rape cases were thrown out of court. Bruce J. Schulman, *The Seventies: The Great Shift in American Culture, Society, and Politics* (New York: Free Press, 2001), 167.

48. Flora Davis, *Moving the Mountain: The Women's Movement in America since 1960* (New York: Simon & Schuster, 1991), 312.

49. Ibid.; Laura Lederer, ed., *Take Back the Night: Women on Pornography* (New York: William Morrow & Co., 1980), 24.

50. Gerhard, *Desiring Revolution*, 110.

51. Maitland, "For Singles, Scene Has Sordid Side," 78.

52. Janet Maslin, "The Independent Woman—from Hepburn to Clayburgh," *New York Times*, 2 November 1980, D17; Judy Klemesrud, "Feminists Recoil at a Film Designed to Relate to Them," *New York Times*, 26 February 1975, 29.

53. E. Ann Kaplan, "Forms of Phallic Domination in Contemporary Films: *Looking for Mr. Goodbar*," *Persistence of Vision*, no. 1 (1984): 48.

54. Molly Haskell, *From Reverence to Rape: The Treatment of Women in the Movies* (New York: Holt, Rinehart & Winston, 1974), 363.

55. Lederer, *Take Back the Night*.

56. Kaplan, "Forms of Phallic Domination in Contemporary Films," 48.

57. *New York Times* reporter Lacey Fosburgh described Quinn's hometown as a New Jersey suburb and Quinn's father as an accountant. The *Times* also framed 1970s crimes as stemming from white middle-class women mixing with "street people." Fosburgh, *Closing Time: The True Story of the "Goodbar" Murder*.

58. Henry A. Giroux, "Looking for Mr. Goodbar: Gender and the Politics of Pleasure," in *Breaking in to the Movies: Film and the Culture of Politics* (Malden, Mass.: Blackwell, 2002), 48. This article was originally published in the Summer 1978 issue of *Film Quarterly*.

59. Jack Kroll, "Brutal Battle of the Sexes," *Newsweek*, 8 October 1979, 107.

60. Peter Prescott, "The Far Side of Sex," 27 March 1978, 88.

61. Betsy Carter, "Alive and Funny," *Newsweek*, 23 August 1976, 61; "Sheila Levine Is Alive and Selling in Bookstores across the United States," *Publisher's Weekly*, 3 September 1973, 30–31.

62. Carter, "Alive and Funny," 61.

63. Parent, *Sheila Levine Is Dead and Living in New York*, 27.

64. Ibid., 43.

65. Ibid., 35.

66. Ibid., 180.

67. Vincent Canby, "Miss Berlin in 'Sheila Levine,'" *New York Times*, 17 May 1975.

68. "Jewish Princess," *Time*, 17 February 1975, 7.

69. Pauline Kael, "The Current Cinema: Don't Touch Me," *New Yorker*, 3 February 1975, 85.

70. *Sheila Levine Is Dead and Living in New York*, digital download, directed by Sidney J. Furie (1975; Los Angeles, CA: Paramount Pictures, 2007).

71. Hollis Alpert, "Seeing Things," *Saturday Review*, 22 February 1975, 49.

72. Kael, "The Current Cinema," 85.

73. Ibid., 84.

74. Ibid., 86.

75. Stephen Farber, "Hollywood and Love: Can't They Kiss and Make Up?" *Los Angeles Times*, 11 May 1975, Calendar 26.

76. Ibid.

77. Jacqueline Susann, *Once Is Not Enough* (New York: Morrow, 1973).

78. Vincent Canby, "If Once Is Not Enough, Then . . ." *New York Times*, 19 June 1975, 28; Jay Cocks, "Father Lusts Best," *Time*, 21 July 1975.

79. Earl Wilson, "Kirk Douglas Still Trying for an Oscar," *Milwaukee Sentinel* (1975): 52.

80. *Once Is Not Enough*, VHS, directed by Guy Green (1975; Los Angeles, CA: Paramount Home Video, 1994).

81. Abby Hirsch, "Novels and Stories, Kitsch and Quality," *New York Times*, 11 July 1976; Cocks, "Father Lusts Best."

82. "Men Write to Challenge Single Women's Criticism," 12.

83. Sandra Prsmens, "She Won't Strip for Kirk Douglas," *Miami News*, 2 June 1975, 3B.

84. Susann, *Once Is Not Enough*.

85. *Looking for Mr. Goodbar*, VHS, directed by Richard Brooks (1977; Los Angeles, CA: Paramount Home Video, 1997).

86. Jane Kramer, "The So-Called New Woman in Film," *Horizon*, May 1978, 32.

87. Charles Champlin, "Looking Again at Brooks' 'Mr. Goodbar,'" *Los Angeles Times*, 20 November 1977, Calendar 3.

88. "Background Notes," Pressbook, *Looking for Mr. Goodbar*, 1977, Margaret Herrick Library, Academy for Motion Picture Arts and Sciences, Los Angeles.

89. Ibid.

90. Ruthe Stein, Katherine Greenfield, and Terry Ryan, "How Single Women Feel About 'Goodbar,'" *US*, 13 December 1977; Kaplan, "Forms of Phallic Domination in Contemporary Films."

91. "'Mr. Goodbar' in Singles Snake Pit," *Los Angeles Times*, 19 October 1977.

92. Andrew Sarris, "Films in Focus: The Divine Diane," *Village Voice*, 17 October 1977; Stein, Greenfield, and Ryan, "How Single Women Feel About 'Goodbar,'" F1.

93. Sarris, "Films in Focus: The Divine Diane," 49.

94. Stein, Greenfield, and Ryan, "How Single Women Feel About 'Goodbar.'" F1.

95. Fosburgh, *Closing Time: The True Story of The "Goodbar" Murder.*

96. Kaplan, "Forms of Phallic Domination in Contemporary Films," 51.

97. Joyce Haber, "Brooks Betting," *Los Angeles Times*, 26 August 1975.

98. Giroux, "Looking for Mr. Goodbar," 42; Robertson, "Single Women over 30"; the Giroux essay was originally published in 1978.

99. Aljean Harmetz, "Will 'Mr. Goodbar' Make Voyeurs of Us All?" *New York Times*, 24 July 1977.

100. Kaplan, "Forms of Phallic Domination in Contemporary Films," 54.

101. Bailey, "She 'Can Bring Home the Bacon,'" 119.

102. Arthur Knight, "Looking for Mr. Goodbar," *Hollywood Reporter*, 14 October 1977.

103. Stein, Greenfield, and Ryan, "How Single Women Feel About 'Goodbar,'" F1.

104. Ibid.

105. Ibid.

106. Ehrenreich, Hess, and Jacobs, *Re-Making Love*, 77, 161.

107. Farber, "Hollywood and Love."

Epilogue

1. See Stephanie Coontz, "Why *Mad Men* Is TV's Most Feminist Show," *Washington Post*, 10 October 2010, http://www.washingtonpost.com/wp-dyn/content/article/2010/10/08/AR2010100802662.html?hpid=opinionsbox1& sid=ST2010101103521.

2. Alex Simon, "Christina Hendricks: The Hollywood Interview," *Hollywood Interview*, 2 November 2009, http://thehollywoodinterview.blogspot .com/2008/06/christina-hendricks-hollywood-interview.html.

3. Joe Meyers, "Rent It Now: 'The Best of Everything,'" *Connecticut News*, 17 January 2010.

4. Representative works include Avital Bloch and Lauri Umansky, *Impossible to Hold: Women and Culture in the 1960s* (New York: New York University Press, 2005); Joanne Meyerowitz, *Not June Cleaver: Women and Gender in Postwar America, 1945–1960* (Philadelphia: Temple University Press, 1994); Wini Brienes, *Young, White and Miserable: Growing Up Female in the Fifties* (Boston: Beacon Press, 1992); Hilary Radner and Moya Luckett, ed., *Swinging Single: Representing Sexuality in the 1960s* (Minneapolis: University of Minnesota Press, 1999); Ruth Rosen, *The World Split Open: How the Modern Women's Movement Changed America* (New York: Viking, 2000); Beth Bailey, *Sex in the Heartland* (Cambridge, Mass.: Harvard University Press, 1999).

5. Hilary Radner, "Introduction," in *Swinging Single: Representing Sexuality in the 1960s*, ed. Hilary Radner and Moya Luckett (Minneapolis: University of Minnesota Press, 1999), 10.

6. *Pillow Talk*, "At-a-Glance Synopsis," n.d., MPAA Production Code Administration Collection; Elman, "Death Pays All Debts," Story Outline, 11 June 1974, and "Final Draft," 16 September 1974, Irving Elman Papers, American Heritage Center, box 8.

7. U.S. Commission on Civil Rights, "Window Dressing on the Set: Women and Minorities in Television" (Washington, D.C.: U.S. Commission on Civil Rights, 1977).

8. "The Creation of That Girl: The Woman on Both Sides of the Camera," *That Girl: Season Three*, DVD, directed by David Leaf (Los Angeles: Shout Factory, 2007); Melissa Frederick Morrison, "Mary Go Round: What Happened to TV's Independent Women?," *Bitch: Feminist Response to Pop Culture*, Winter 2006, 77–79, 110.

9. Muriel Davidson, "An Exciting New Star Goes into Orbit," *Good Housekeeping*, November 1971, 228; "The Mary Tyler Moore Show," *TV Guide*, September 12–18, 1970.

10. Howard Stricking, *Where the Boys Are*, first reports from preview at Picwood Theatre in West Los Angeles, 28 October 1960, George Wells Papers, American Heritage Center, University of Wyoming, Laramie, box 4; Ruthe Stein, Katherine Greenfield, and Terry Ryan, "How Single Women Feel About 'Goodbar,'" *US*, 13 December 1977, F1.

11. Susan Douglas, *Where the Girls Are: Growing up Female with the Mass Media* (New York: Times Books, 1994); Brienes, *Young, White and Miserable*.

12. Commentary by Lynda Carter, "My Teenage Idol Is Missing," *Wonder Woman: The Complete Third Season*, DVD.

13. Douglas, *Where the Girls Are*; Brienes, *Young, White and Miserable*; Bailey, *Sex in the Heartland*; Rosen, *The World Split Open*.

14. "You've Got a Friend," First Draft, 4 May 1972, Steve Pritzker Papers, UCLA Performing Arts Special Collections, Los Angeles, box 2, folder 4; "Angel Roles" memo, 17 March 1977, Ronald Austin Papers, American Heritage Center, box 7, "Memos: Spelling and Goldberg" folder.

15. *Marlo Thomas*, VHS, directed by Bob Waldman (New York: A&E Home Video, 2002).

16. "Requiem for Bored Wives," *Police Woman*. "The Good-Time News," *The Mary Tyler Moore Show*.

Selected Bibliography

Abrams, Bill. "Why Revlon's Charlie Seems to Be Ready to Settle Down." *Wall Street Journal*, 23 December 1982, 9.

Ajmone-Marsan, Barbara. "I Don't Want to Live through a Man." *Redbook*, August 1969, 13, 21–22.

Allyn, David. *Make Love, Not War*. Boston: Little, Brown & Co., 2000.

Atkin, D. "The Evolution of Television Series Addressing Single Women, 1966–1990." *Journal of Broadcasting and Electronic Media* 35, no. 4 (1991): 517–523.

Bailey, Beth. *From Front Porch to Back Seat: Courtship in Twentieth-Century America*. Baltimore: Johns Hopkins University Press, 1988.

———. *Sex in the Heartland*. Cambridge, Mass.: Harvard University Press, 1999.

———. "She 'Can Bring Home the Bacon': Negotiating Gender in Seventies America." In *America in the Seventies*, edited by Beth Bailey and David Farber, 107–128. Lawrence: University Press of Kansas, 2004.

Baker, Carrie N. "'He Said, She Said': Popular Representations of Sexual Harassment and Second-Wave Feminism." In *Disco Divas: Women and Popular Culture in the 1970s*, edited by Sherrie Inness, 39–53. Philadelphia: University of Pennsylvania Press, 2003.

Barron, Jennie Loitman. "Too Much Sex on Campus." *Ladies' Home Journal*, January 1964, 48, 52.

Barry, Anne. "My Long, Long Night in a Singles' Bar." *Cosmopolitan*, August 1969, 72–75.

Basinger, Jeanine. *A Woman's View: How Hollywood Spoke to Women, 1930–1960*. New York: Alfred A. Knopf, 1993.

Bedell, Sally. *Up the Tube: Prime-Time TV and the Silverman Years*. New York: Viking Press, 1981.

Bennett, Lerone, Jr. "The Negro Woman." *Ebony*, September 1963, 86–90, 92–94.

Bird, Caroline. "What's Television Doing for 50.9% of Americans?" *TV Guide*, 27 February 1971, 5–8.

Blum, Sam. "A Defense of Women Who Refuse to Marry." *Redbook*, January 1969, 51, 110–117.

Bodroghkozy, Aniko. "'Is This What You Mean by Color TV?' Race, Gender and Conflicted Meanings in NBC's *Julia*." In *Private Screenings: Television and the Female Consumer*, edited by Lynn Spigel and Denise Mann, 143–168. Minneapolis: University of Minnesota, 1992.

Brienes, Wini. *Young, White and Miserable: Growing up Female in the Fifties.* Boston: Beacon Press, 1992.

Brown, Helen Gurley. *The Cosmo Girl's Guide to the New Etiquette.* New York: Cosmopolitan Books, 1971.

———. *Sex and the New Single Girl.* New York: Bernard Geis, 1970.

———. *Sex and the Single Girl.* New York: Bernard Geis, 1962.

Cameron, Sue. "Police Drama: Women Are on the Case." *Ms.*, October 1974, 104, 108.

Cole, Stephen. *That Book About That Girl: The Unofficial Companion.* New York: Renaissance Books, 1999.

Coy, Stanlee Miller. *The Single Girl's Book: Making It in the Big City.* Englewood Cliffs, N.J.: Prentice-Hall, 1969.

Craig, Steve. "Madison Avenue versus *the Feminine Mystique*: The Advertising Industry's Response to the Women's Movement." In *Disco Divas: Women and Popular Culture in the 1970s*, edited by Sherrie A. Inness, 13–23. Philadelphia: University of Pennsylvania Press, 2003.

D'Acci, Julie. *Defining Women: Television and the Case of Cagney and Lacey.* Chapel Hill: University of North Carolina Press, 1994.

———. "Nobody's Woman? *Honey West* and the New Sexuality." In *The Revolution Wasn't Televised: Sixties Television and Social Conflict*, edited by Lynn Spigel and Michael Curtin, 72–90. New York: Routledge, 1997.

Davis, Flora. *Moving the Mountain: The Women's Movement in America since 1960.* New York: Simon & Schuster, 1991.

D'Emilio, John, and Estelle B. Freedman. *Intimate Matters: A History of Sexuality in America.* New York: Harper & Row, 1988.

Douglas, Susan. *Where the Girls Are: Growing up Female with the Mass Media.* New York: Times Books, 1994.

Dow, Bonnie. *Prime-Time Feminism: Television, Media Culture and the Women's Movement since 1970.* Philadelphia: University of Pennsylvania Press, 1996.

Dreyfuss, Joel. "Television Controversy: Covering the Black Experience." *Washington Post*, 1 September 1974, K5.

Dunn, Stephanie. "Foxy Brown on My Mind: The Racialized Gendered Politics of Representation." In *Disco Divas: Women and Popular Culture in the 1970s*, edited by Sherrie A. Inness, 71–86. Philadelphia: University of Pennsylvania Press, 2003.

Durbin, Karen. "The Intelligent Woman's Guide to Sex." *Mademoiselle*, April 1977, 34, 96.

———. "The Sexual Confusion." *Mademoiselle*, July 1972, 90–91, 162.

Ebony. "Has Something Gone Wrong between Them?" August 1977, 160–162.

Efron, Edith. "Is Television Making a Mockery of the American Woman?" *TV Guide*, 8 August 1970, 7–9.

———. "Television after Dark." *TV Guide*, 25 October 1975, 26–32.

———. "TV's Sex Crisis." *TV Guide*, 18 October 1975, 4–8.

Ehrenreich, Barbara, Elizabeth Hess, and Gloria Jacobs. *Re-Making Love: The Feminization of Sex*. Garden City, N.Y.: Anchor Press, 1986.

Faludi, Susan. *Backlash: The Undeclared War against American Women*. 2nd ed. New York: Anchor Books, 1992.

Farber, David, and Beth Bailey, eds. *The Columbia Guide to America in the 1960s*. New York: Columbia University Press, 2001.

Ferguson, Renee. "Women's Liberation Has a Different Meaning for Blacks." In *Black Women in White America: A Documentary History*, edited by Gerda Lerner, 587–592. New York: Vintage Books, 1973.

Feuer, Jane, Paul Kerr, and Tise Vahimagi, eds. *MTM 'Quality Television'*. London: BFI, 1984.

Fosburgh, Lacey. *Closing Time: The True Story of the "Goodbar" Murder*. New York: Delacorte Press, 1977.

Foster, Gwendolyn Audrey. *Performing Whiteness: Postmodern Re/Constructions in the Cinema*. Albany: State University of New York Press, 2003.

Friedan, Betty. *The Feminine Mystique*. Twentieth Anniversary ed. New York: Laurel, 1983.

———. "Television and the Feminine Mystique." In *TV Guide: The First 25 Years*, edited by J. S. Harris, 93–98. New York: Simon & Schuster, 1978.

Gerhard, Jane. *Desiring Revolution: Second-Wave Feminism and the Rewriting of American Sexual Thought, 1920 to 1982*. New York: Columbia University Press, 2001.

Gilliam, Dorothy. "Too Few Men." *Washington Post Potomac*, 12 June 1966, 8–16.

Glitre, Kathrina. *Hollywood Romantic Comedy: States of the Union, 1934–65*. Manchester: Manchester University Press, 2006.

Greene, Gael. "For the Single Girl: A New Way of Life in California." *Ladies' Home Journal*, July 1966.

————. *Sex and the College Girl*. New York: Dial Press, 1964.

Gross, Amy. "Young Lovers of the World—Unite! But Don't Get Married Yet." *Mademoiselle*, September 1969.

Gross, Leonard. "Why Can't a Woman Be More Like a Man?" *TV Guide*, 11 August 1973, 6–11.

Grossman, Allyson Sherman. *The Labor Force Patterns of Single Women*. Washington: Department of Labor, Bureau of Statistics, 1980.

Harris, Eleanor. "Women without Men." *Look*, 5 July 1960, 43–46.

Haskell, Molly. *From Reverence to Rape: The Treatment of Women in the Movies*. New York: Holt, Rinehart & Winston, 1974.

Hennessee, Judith Adler, and Joan Nicholson. "NOW Says: TV Commercials Insult Women." *New York Times Magazine*, 28 May 1972, 12–13.

Hickey, Georgina. "Barred from the Barroom: Second Wave Feminists and Public Accomodations in U.S. Cities." *Feminist Studies* 34, no. 3 (2008): 382–408.

Hofstede, David, and Jack Condon. *Charlie's Angels Casebook*. Beverly Hills: Pomegranate Press, 2000.

Inness, Sherrie. "'Strange Feverish Years': The 1970s and Women's Changing Roles." In *Disco Divas: Women and Popular Culture in the 1970s*, edited by Sherrie Inness, 1–9. Philadelphia: University of Pennsylvania Press, 2003.

————. *Tough Girls: Warrior Women and Wonder Women in Popular Culture*. Philadelphia: University of Pennsylvania Press, 1999.

Israel, Betty. *Bachelor Girl: The Secret History of Single Women in the Twentieth Century*. New York: William Morrow, 2002.

Israel, Lee. "Violence: How Does a Career Girl Cope?" *Cosmopolitan*, February 1968, 81–82.

Jacoby, Susan. "49 Million Singles Can't All Be Right." *New York Times*, 17 February 1974.

Johnston, Tracey. "Why 30 Million Are Mad About Mary." *New York Times Magazine*, 7 April 1974, 30, 96–97.

Jones, Jacqueline. *Labor of Love, Labor of Sorrow: Black Women, Work and the Family from Slavery to the Present*. New York: Basic Books, 1985.

Kael, Pauline. "The Current Cinema: Don't Touch Me." *New Yorker*, 3 February 1975, 83–86.

Kaplan, E. Ann. "Forms of Phallic Domination in Contemporary Films: *Looking for Mr. Goodbar*." *Persistence of Vision*, no. 1 (1984): 47–55.

Kardiner, Abram, and Lionel Ovesey. *The Mark of Oppression: A Psychosocial Study of the American Negro*. New York: Norton, 1951.

Klemesrud, Judy. "Single Women against a Dangerous City." *New York Times*, 12 January 1973.

———. "TV's Women Are Dingbats." *New York Times*, 27 May 1973.

Kramer, Jane. "The So-Called New Woman in Film." *Horizon*, May 1978, 30–34.

Kramer, Richard. "A Young Man Asks: Just What the Hell Does She Want from Me Anyway?" *Mademoiselle*, February 1976, 56–58, 135.

Kroll, Jack. "Brutal Battle of the Sexes." *Newsweek*, 8 October 1979, 107.

Krones, John. "Memo from a Bachelor: The Singles Scene." *Look*, 6 February 1968, 80.

Lantz, Ragni. "The Pleasures and Problems of the Bachelor Girl." *Ebony*, August 1966, 102–104.

La Rue, Linda. "The Black Movement and Women's Liberation." In *Words of Fire: An Anthology of African-American Feminist Thought*, edited by Beverly Guy-Sheftall, 163–173. New York: New Press, 1995.

Lederer, Laura, ed. *Take Back the Night: Women on Pornography*. New York: William Morrow & Co., 1980.

Leff, Leonard, and Jerold Simmons. *The Dame in the Kimono: Hollywood, Censorship and the Production Code*. 2nd ed. Lexington: University Press of Kentucky, 2001.

Levine, Elana. *Wallowing in Sex: The New Sexual Culture of 1970s American Television*. Durham, N.C.: Duke University Press, 2007.

Lichtenstein, Grace. "Slain Woman's Neighbors Express Both Horror and Detachment." *New York Times*, 25 October 1973.

Life. "New Rules for the Singles Game." 18 August 1967.

Lotz, Amanda D. *Redesigning Women: Television after the Network Era*. Urbana: University of Illinois Press, 2006.

Luckett, Moya. "A Moral Crisis in Prime Time: *Peyton Place* and the Rise of the Single Girl." In *Television, History and American Culture: Feminist Critical Essays*, edited by Mary Beth Haralovich and Lauren Rabinowitz, 75–97. Durham, N.C.: Duke University Press, 1999.

———. "Sensuous Women and Single Girls: Reclaiming the Female Body on 1960s Television." In *Swinging Single: Representing Sexuality in the 1960s*, edited by Hilary Radner and Moya Luckett, 277–300. Minneapolis: University of Minnesota Press, 1999.

Lundberg, Ferdinand. *Modern Woman: The Lost Sex*. New York: Harper, 1947.

Maitland, Leslie. "For Singles, Scene Has Sordid Side." *New York Times*, 1 November 1974, 41, 78.

"Marlo Thomas: That Girl Is Some Girl." *Look*, 17 October 1967, 124–125.

May, Elaine Tyler. *Homeward Bound: American Families in the Cold War Era.* New York: Basic Books, 1988.

McDonald, Tamar Jeffers. "Performances of Desire and Inexperience: Doris Day's Fluctuating Filmic Virginity." In *Virgin Territory: Representing Sexual Inexperience in Film*, edited by Tamar Jeffers McDonald, 103–122. Detroit: Wayne State University Press, 2010.

Meyerowitz, Joanne. "Beyond the Feminine Mystique: A Reassessment of Postwar Mass Culture, 1946–1958." In *Not June Cleaver: Women and Gender in Postwar America, 1945–1960*, edited by Joanne Meyerowitz, 229–253. Philadelphia: Temple University Press, 1994.

Miller, Frank. *Censored Hollywood: Sex, Sin and Violence Onscreen.* Atlanta: Turner Publishing, 1994.

Morse, Benjamin. *The Sexually Promiscuous Female.* Derby, Conn.: Monarch Books, 1963.

Newcomb, Horace, and Robert S. Alley. *The Producer's Medium: Conversations with Creators of American TV.* New York: Oxford University Press, 1983.

Olsen, Jack. *The Girls in the Office.* New York: Simon & Schuster, 1971.

Ouellette, Laurie. "Inventing the Cosmo Girl: Class Identity and Girl-Style American Dreams." *Media, Culture and Society* 21, no. 3 (1999): 359–383.

Pagni, Charlotte. "'Does She or Doesn't She?' Sexology and Female Sexuality in *Sex and the Single Girl*." *Spectator* 19, no. 2 (1999): 8–25.

Parent, Gail. *Sheila Levine Is Dead and Living in New York.* New York: G. P. Putnam's Sons, 1972.

Pincus, Ann. "Shape up, Bionic Woman!" *Newsweek*, 15 November 1976, 15.

Playboy. "The Playboy Panel: The Womanization of America." June 1962.

Preston, Lillian. *Sex Habits of Single Women.* New York: Universal Publishing, 1964.

Radner, Hilary. "Introduction." In *Swinging Single: Representing Sexuality in the 1960s.* Minneapolis: University of Minnesota Press, 1999.

Ries, Estelle. *The Lonely Sex.* New York: Belmont Books, 1962.

Robertson, Nan. "Single Women over 30: 'Where Are the Men Worthy of Us?'" *New York Times*, 14 July 1978.

Roof, Judith. *All About Thelma and Eve: Sidekicks and Third Wheels.* Urbana: University of Illinois Press, 2002.

Rose, Robert L. "TV: Those Women in Blue." *Washington Post*, 1 September 1974.

Rosen, Diane. "TV and the Single Girl." *TV Guide*, 6 November 1971, 13–16.

Rosen, Marjorie. "Farrah Fawcett-Majors Makes Me Want to Scream!" *Redbook*, September 1977, 102–109.

Rosen, Ruth. *The World Split Open: How the Modern Women's Movement Changed America*. New York: Viking, 2000.

Rossner, Judith. *Looking for Mr. Goodbar*. New York: Simon & Schuster, 1975.

Roth, Benita. *Separate Roads to Feminism: Black, Chicana, and White Feminist Movements in America's Second Wave*. Cambridge, UK: Cambridge University Press, 2004.

Scanlon, Jennifer. *Bad Girls Go Everywhere: The Life of Helen Gurley Brown*. New York: Oxford University Press, 2009.

Schlafly, Phyllis. "What 'Women's Lib' Really Means." *Phyllis Schlafly Report*, December 1974.

———. "What's Wrong with 'Equal Rights' for Women?" *Phyllis Schlafly Report*, February 1972.

Schulman, Bruce J. *The Seventies: The Great Shift in American Culture, Society, and Politics*. New York: Free Press, 2001.

Solinger, Rickie. *Wake Up Little Susie: Single Pregnancy and Race before Roe v. Wade*. New York: Routledge, 1992.

Sprague, William Hanson. *Sex Behavior of the American Secretary*. New York: Chariot Books, 1960.

Springer, Kimberly. "Divas, Evil Black Bitches, and Bitter Black Women: African-American Women in Postfeminist and Post-Civil Rights Popular Culture." In *Feminist Television Criticism: A Reader*, edited by Charlotte Brunsdon and Lynn Spigel, 72–92. Berkshire, UK: Open University Press, 2008.

———. "Waiting to Set It Off." In *Reel Knockouts: Violent Women in the Movies*, edited by Martha McCaughey and Neal King, 172–199. Austin: University of Texas, 2001.

Stein, Ruthe, Katherine Greenfield, and Terry Ryan. "How Single Women Feel About 'Goodbar.'" *US*, 13 December 1977.

Steinem, Gloria. "The Moral Disarmament of Betty Coed." *Esquire*, September 1962.

Susann, Jacqueline. *Once Is Not Enough*. New York: Morrow, 1973.

———. *Valley of the Dolls*. New York: Bernard Geis, 1966.

Sutheim, Susan. "The Subversion of Betty Crocker." In *The New Women: A Motive Anthology on Women's Liberation*, edited by Joanne Cooke, Charlotte

Bunch-Weeks, and Robin Morgan, 83–94. Greenwich, Conn.: Fawcett Publications, 1970.

Swarthout, Glendon. *Where the Boys Are.* New York: Random House, 1960.

Taylor, Ella. *Prime Time Families: Television Culture in Postwar America.* Berkeley: University of California Press, 1989.

Time. "A Good Man Is Hard to Find—So They Hire Women." 4 November 1966.

———. "The Pleasures and Pain of the Single Life." 15 September 1967, 26–27.

———. "The Second Sexual Revolution." 24 January 1964, 54–59.

———. "TV's Super Women." 22 November 1976, 67–71.

U.S. Commission on Civil Rights. *Window Dressing on the Set: An Update.* Washington, D.C.: U.S. Commission on Civil Rights, 1979.

———. *Window Dressing on the Set: Women and Minorities in Television.* Washington, D.C.: U.S. Commission on Civil Rights, 1977.

U.S. Department of Labor. "Sex and Equal Employment Rights." *Monthly Labor Review* 1967, iii–iv.

U.S. News & World Report. "For Singles, Life Isn't All 'Swinging.'" 8 December 1975, 67.

———. "For Women: More Jobs, but Low Pay." 8 October 1973, 41–42.

———. "New TV Season: Less Sex, Less Violence." 11 September 1978, 32.

Van Slyke, Helen. "The Sex Life of a Working Woman." *Harper's Bazaar,* August 1974, 52–53, 124–125.

Vershel, Larry. "Are Women People?" *Danbury, Conn., News Times,* 2 August 1965.

Viorst, Judith. "Avis and Gs-Zero." *Washington Post Potomac,* June 12, 1966, 8–16.

Waldman, E. "Changes in the Labor Force Activity of Women." *Monthly Labor Review,* June 1970, 10–18.

Walters, Suzanna Danuta. *Material Girls: Making Sense of Feminist Cultural Theory.* Berkeley: University of California Press, 1995.

Washington Post. "Helen Gurley Brown Is Not This Stupid." 26 December 1964.

Weller, A. H. "Screen: Sex and the Single Girl." *New York Times,* 26 December 1964.

"What Educated Women Want." *Newsweek,* 13 June 1966, 68, 71–75.

Whitney, Dwight. "You've Come a Long Way, Baby." In *TV Guide: The First*

25 Years, edited by Jay S. Harris, 178–180. New York: Simon & Schuster, 1978.

"Why You Find the Next Eight Pages in the Ladies' Home Journal." *Ladies' Home Journal*, August 1970.

Willis, Ellen. "Whatever Happened to Women? Nothing—That's the Trouble." *Mademoiselle*, September 1969, 150, 206–208.

Womack, Whitney. "Reevaulating 'Jiggle TV': *Charlie's Angels* at Twenty-Five." In *Disco Divas: Women and Popular Culture in the 1970s*, edited by Sherrie Inness, 151–171. Philadelphia: University of Pennsylvania Press, 2003.

Wylie, Philip. "The Career Woman." *Playboy*, January 1963, 152–158.

Index

Index

Index